"This is a wise book that breaks with the dominant paradigms and rethinks public relations in interdisciplinary, philosophical, and humanistic terms, bringing a new definition to a field that has long been seeking to define itself. Brown is a thinker who has thought long and hard about the field and has enriched this book with his wide reading and long professional experience."
—Ray Hiebert, Editor, *Public Relations Review*, USA

"In PRe, Rob Brown reconceptualises public relations as a humanity, shifting the field from the quantitatively distinct to the distinctly human: ambiguous, historical, interdisciplinary, and vocal. An accomplished scholar, he mines his own extensive experiences in public relations, along with works from academics, practitioners, pioneers, and poets, to present a fascinating, timely, and thought-provoking work."
—Margot Opdycke Lamme, Associate Professor, University of Alabama, USA

"Robert Brown deftly flips long-held conventions about public relations as man-agement of organizational communication. From history, theory and ethics to crisis communication, Brown argues that the study of public relations should expand to include 'everyday experience of individuals' as much as sociology, anthropology, politics and more. Written with dexterity, this compelling book will get readers thinking about public relations in new and refreshing ways."
—Amiso M. George, Associate Professor of Strategic Communication, Texas Christian University, USA

"This book is the essence of convergence in Public Relations: the convergence of means, the convergence of perspectives and the convergence of disciplines that merge into one in this field. With this book, Robert Brown will become a classic not only for the content but also for the ability of making poetry from the academic literature."
—Enric Ordeix, Professor, Ramon Llull University, Barcelona, Catalonia-Spain

The Public Relations of Everything

The Public Relations of Everything takes the radical position that public relations (PR) is a profoundly different creature from the one portrayed by a generation of its scholars and teachers. Today, it is clearly no longer limited, if it ever has been, to the management of communication in and between organizations. Rather, it has become an activity engaged in by everyone, and for the most basic human reasons: as an act of self-creation, self-expression, and self-protection. The book challenges both popular dismissals and ill-informed repudiations of PR as well as academic and classroom misconceptions.

In the age of digitization and social media, everyone with a smartphone, Twitter or Facebook account, and the will and skill to use them, is in the media. The PR of everything – the ubiquitousness of public relations – takes a perspective that is less concerned with ideas of communication and information than with experience and drama, a way of looking at PR inside out, upside down, and from a micro rather than a macro level.

Based on a combination of the research of PR practice and critical-thinking analysis of theory, and founded in the author's extensive corporate experience, this book will be invaluable reading for scholars and practitioners alike in PR, communications, and social media.

Robert E. Brown, former speechwriter for two Fortune 500 companies, is professor of communications at Salem State University, instructor at Harvard University Extension School, a member of the editorial boards of *Public Relations Review* and *Public Relations Inquiry*, and a published poet.

Routledge New Directions in Public Relations and Communication Research

Edited by Kevin Moloney

Routledge New Directions in Public Relations and Communication Research is a new forum for the publication of books of original research in public relations (PR) and related types of communication. Its goal is to publish critical and challenging responses to continuities and fractures in contemporary PR thinking and practice and PR's essential yet contested role in market-orientated, capitalist, liberal democracies around the world. The series reflects the multiple and interdisciplinary forms PR takes in a post-Grunigian world, the expanding roles that it performs and the increasing number of countries in which it is practised.

The series will examine current trends and explore new thinking on the key questions that impact PR and communications, including the following:

- Is the evolution of persuasive communications in Central and Eastern Europe, China, Latin America, Japan, the Middle East and South East Asia developing new forms or following Western models?
- What has been the impact of postmodern sociologies, cultural studies and methodologies which are often critical of the traditional, conservative role of PR in capitalist political economies, and in patriarchy, gender and ethnic roles?
- What is the impact of digital social media on politics, individual privacy and PR practice? Is new technology changing the nature of content communicated or simply reaching bigger audiences faster? Is digital PR a cause or a consequence of political and cultural change?

Books in this series will be of interest to academics and researchers involved in these expanding fields of study as well as students undertaking advanced studies in this area.

Public Relations and Nation Building
Influencing Israel
Margalit Toledano and David McKie

Gender and Public Relations
Critical perspectives on voice, image and identity
Edited by Christine Daymon and Kristin Demetrious

The Public Relations of Everything

The ancient, modern and postmodern dramatic history of an idea

Robert E. Brown

Routledge
Taylor & Francis Group

LONDON AND NEW YORK

First published 2015 by Routledge

2 Park Square, Milton Park, Abingdon, Oxfordshire OX14 4RN
52 Vanderbilt Avenue, New York, NY 10017

Routledge is an imprint of the Taylor & Francis Group, an informa business

First issued in paperback 2019

British Library Cataloguing in Publication Data
A catalogue record for this book is available from the British Library

Library of Congress Cataloging-in-Publication Data

Brown, Robert E., 1945–
  The public relations of everything : the ancient, modern and postmodern
dramatic history of an idea / Robert E. Brown.
     pages cm — (Routledge new directions in public relations &
communication research)
  Includes bibliographical references and index.
 1. Public relations. I. Title.
  HM1221.B766 2014
  659.2—dc23
  2014021481

ISBN: 978-0-415-64045-9 (hbk)
ISBN: 978-0-367-86734-8 (pbk)

Typeset in Times New Roman
by Apex CoVantage, LLC

For Jane Brown, my mother, from whom I learned the performances of diplomacy.

For Richard Brown, my brother and mentor.

For Sam Brown, my father: 1897–1971

Contents

Acknowledgments

First and foremost, I salute my editor, Kevin Moloney, a scholar, a gentleman and an influential public relations (PR) thinker whose generosity and wise counsel I was most fortunate to have thrashing me about during throughout the composition of this book. Professor Moloney can be credited with helping me preserve the book's best parts and deleting at least some of the worst. The book's faults are entirely mine.

I also wish to thank my longtime peer-journal editor and dear friend, Ray Hiebert, the esteemed biographer, historian and editor, who thought enough of my ideas to begin publishing them in the *Public Relations Review.*

Many others deserve to be acknowledged, including colleagues and the like-minded PR "radical" Jacquie L'Etang; the international crisis communication scholars, Amiso George and Cornelius Pratt; the prolific and eminent Bob Heath; Burton Saint John who is among those few PR scholars who have caught a whiff of the spiritual in a notoriously profane and secular institution; and my dear friends, the PR authors and spouses, David McKie and Margaret Toledano.

Without a trace of irony, I also wish to acknowledge Jim Grunig, PR's paradigm shifter, without whose extraordinary, prodigious and influential scholarship I would have had no shore from which to push away in my "radical" skiff.

Books need to be produced to see the light of day, and I've been fortunate to have had the meticulous, caring and responsive attentions of editorial consultants Sinead Waldron and Jacqueline Curthoys.

I am greatly indebted to Alan Kravitz, a PR professional, who not only proofread the manuscript with consummate skill, but has proved a valued sounding board from the book's conceptual stages.

As the book grew, in significant ways, from my real-world PR experience, I could hardly have dared to write it had I not had many mentors, bosses and colleagues in the marketplace wrangle of the corporate communications world. I number among these souls Sharon Merrill, founder of Sharon Merrill Associates, Inc., who hired me as a thrice-a-week editorial consultant, instructor, rewrite man and occasional tennis partner; my longtime, dear friend, Maureen Wolff-Reid, the president of the Merrill investor relations agency; J. Gregory Payne Jr., my communications colleague for three decades, who gave me ample opportunity to try out my "radical" ideas on his students at Emerson College; Ted Hollingworth, a professor's professor and my longtime friend and mentor; the poet, scholar and gentleman Ray Comeau, retired dean of the Harvard University Extension School; Marshall Lumsden, who first showed me the ropes of feature writing at his social science magazine and then hired me to write for his editorial services department the Atlantic Richfield Company in its pioneering days of corporate social responsibility; and Walter Coyne who taught me not only how to write a speech but to see with clear and unprejudiced eyes the abiding values of democratic, corporate capitalism.

On the family side, I offer my gratitude to my grown son, Sasha, who from an early age patiently (and with a minimum of eye-rolling) introduced me to the complexities, efficiencies and, ultimately, to the insights of the emerging technologies of the digital–social era.

Finally, I bow in the general direction of my wife, Delia Cabe, whose support I treasure and whose succinct prose style I can only envy.

I imagine I ought to have taken to heart the wisdom offered me by Bill Rueckert, the director of my doctoral dissertation. The author or five books on Kenneth Burke, Bill said rather pointedly, "Don't write articles. Write books."

That was 44 years ago. I figured it was time I took his advice.

Preface

The fox knows many things, but the hedgehog knows one big thing.

Archilochus

Over the past generation, scholars of public relations (PR) have debated many things about the idea of PR. Many or even most of those arguments are really about whether PR is one thing or many things.

Two opposing schools of thought have arisen on this issue – from social scientists and humanists. (Organizational managers are categorical cognates of social scientists.) Like the fox in the Greek poet's aphorism, the humanists view PR as many things that can be investigated from many methodologies, primarily qualitative ones. This school approaches PR from the perspective of rhetoric, critical thinking, ethnography, philosophy, literary theory and history. Their assessments of public relations range from Heath's rhetorical defense of PR as cocreated meaning to the radical skepticism of L'Etang, Pieczka, McKie and others. For these foxes, as for me, PR's interdisciplinarity is not merely something to acknowledge, but something indicative, if not definitive.

Still, for more than a generation, it has not been the foxes who have dominated the discussion. It has been the hedgehogs. Led by James E. Grunig, David Dozier and others, they have known one big thing. The hedgehogs' big thing has shape-shifted from "symmetry" in the 1980s to "excellence" in the 1990s to "a willingness to change" in the twenty-first century. But the shape of the big thing is less important than the belief in its existence. The hedgehog brings a passion for mathematical precision and an Enlightenment belief in objectivity, science, engineering and technology. In the twenty-first century, there are new technology theorists like Brian Solis (2011) who would drive PR into the embrace of marketing, confounding PR's strenuous attempts to be distinctive.

Although the hedgehog's passion is impressive, it reminds me of something the poet John Keats complained of in a letter he wrote about a friend. The friend's unpleasant habit was, Keats wrote, an "irritable searching after fact & reason," which made the friend and people like him simply not "capable of being in uncertainties, Mysteries, doubts." Keats preferred the company of people who were content to acknowledge the reality of uncertainty and contingency, a sensibility he called *negative capability* (Bush, 1959, p. 261). What can be said of negative capability is that it's what the foxes have and the hedgehogs do not.

I came to PR scholarship from several directions, an appropriately eclectic background for a fox. (Critics of foxes have another name for us: *dilettantes*.) Before embarking on an academic career that has included communication theory, I was a PR practitioner with 20 years of service with Fortune 500 companies. During that stint I was a freelance writer and, later, a magazine editor. As for my academic training, it was in literature, my dissertation being the application of phenomenological theory to a very long poem. Whatever critical thinking I'm capable of is mostly the product of training in the humanities and the "close reading" of texts.

All that suggests that I bivouac with the foxes, which is true. Like many of them, I have approached public relations qualitatively from the margins, channeling many intellectual tributaries – history, literature, philosophy. Like my fellow foxes, I have a skeptical, critical-thinking sensibility.

Like my fellow foxes, I don't seek the hedgehog's universal theory of PR. I will be content to do what Kevin Moloney (2006), my editor, has done in the words of his book's title – to "rethink" PR – and to do so from multiple perspectives. My idea of PR is that it is something that opens out, rather than closes in. The hedgehogs have defined PR as communication management (Grunig) or negotiation (W. P Ehling). In the pages that follow, what I have sought is not another definition; there are already too many of those. PR needs to be understood as more than a container for managerial abstractions – objectives, strategies, and tactics – but as the lived, dramatic experience of human beings in the social world. The project of this book is to conceive of PR not as what must be *something* but what accrues *everything*. Such a hyperbolic description is, for me, a fair price to pay for the rewards of inclusivity.

The fox's vision opens the windows to the insights of dramaturgy, cultural anthropology and historiography. It even entertains the peculiar notion that there is a poetics of PR, and a place in PR for tragedy, comedy, irony, romance and satire. There is room for emotion and absurdity. Social media – which has altered the way PR is practiced and perceived – has revealed a vast, strange, new and rapidly changing communication space, a universe of everything. What matters in this space is not definition; what matters is navigation.

PR was once a matter of press releases, pitch letters and newspaper placements; it is now a matter of links, posts and videos. The gold standard is no longer targeting but sharing. The PR street no longer goes two ways; now it goes every which way. In the technological, globalized, interconnected, breathless world we have inherited and daily recreate, the only PR that makes sense is the PR of everything, everyone, and of every time, past present and future.

Breaking ranks: Why a public relations of *everything?*

What may be of service to the reader of this book is for the author to offer an explanation in advance for his argument and its flow from chapter to chapter.

The argument

The idea of a public relations of *everything* (PRe) diverges from much of PR's conventional thinking and its "dominant" theory. For starters, amid the inclusiveness of PRe and the forces of media convergence, PRe challenges PR's long-standing, strenuous insistence on being "distinctive." Other breaks with tradition flow in and out of the critique of the theory of symmetry. In PRe, PR is no longer boxed into the management of communication or the communication of organizations. In PRe, PR is rethought in sociological terms that open it to include the kind of everyday experience of individuals.

Simply put, the dominant theorists tailored a suit much too small for the realities of PR.

Explicit and implicit in framing public relations in this manner is the proposition that PR is not symmetrical. James Grunig, the founder and developer of symmetry theory, characteristically promotes his theory in his introductory essay to a Festschrift in his honor:

> We judge a theory to be good, therefore, if it makes sense of reality (in the case of a positive, or explanatory theory), or if it helps to improve reality (in the case of a normative theory).
>
> (Grunig, 2013, p. 2)

The fundamental problem with that proposition is that it fails to makes sense of the reality of PR which remains stubbornly resistant to depart from the energies of a marketplace instinctively, structurally and historically driven by competitive urges to triumph more than normative ideals. The argument that symmetry has influenced the practice of PR is, at most, problematic if that influence is adduced, as it generally has been, from promotional programs of cause branding and corporate social responsibility. But the realities of PR, when viewed through a lens not Vaselined for a softer, normative focus, are far more complex, indeterminate and, indeed, less didactic and more interesting.

That self-reporting practitioners express a preference for a kinder and gentler PR of symmetrical aspirations has been billed as a paradigm shift. But such a preference over rougher sorts of social Darwinian beliefs is hardly surprising.

Nor is the 5 percent of net income rule of thumb that the most ardently symmetrical companies report investing in corporate social responsibility (CSR) and cause-branding programs. There is, in the words of the economist David Vogel (2005), a "market for virtue."

The extension of the everyday enables the reconsideration of PR practice as enacted and theatrical. Such a rethinking channels a dramaturgical tradition that runs from microsociology and cultural anthropology to performance theory, with excursions into cultural and critical theory.

Another break with "dominant" PR theory is to advance an historiography of PR that rebuts its categorization as exclusively and definitively modern and fundamentally technological. This counterhistoriography draws on my own articles on Saint Paul and the Catholic Reformation popes as well as recent scholarship critiquing the conventional history of public relations and other scholarship associating PR more closely with religion, spirituality and aesthetics.

Where PR textbooks continue to frame crisis communication as a special application, in PRe, crisis is repositioned as central and fundamental. The bull market in crisis communication research and scholarship offers evidence for the growing recognition that crisis is no longer PR's Pluto but has become its overheated Mercury.

Another structural shift in PRe is the placement of the chapter on ethics not upfront but near the end of the book. Such a repositioning of ethics in the PR galaxy isn't meant to imply a cavalier disregard for ethics or truth but to face more squarely a truth more difficult to confess: that PR ethics is less a matter of truth and lies and more a matter of ambiguities. The rationale is to break with the tradition of PR texts and scholarly conversations that tend to be obsessed with the attempt to uncouple PR from the negativity of propaganda and, after the introduction of symmetry, even from persuasion.

Chapter by chapter

The first chapter in this volume identifies a big round number of ways – 20 in all – in which PR is viewed throughout the book. The big idea here is about expanding the idea of PR beyond where a generation of theory building has positioned it as the management of communication. But when PR is understood more broadly, or in other words, more deeply than what happens in and of and for organizations, a wider world opens. The surprising thing about such a new perspective is both its inclusiveness and its contradictions – the everyday with the extraordinary; the postmodern with the ancient; the public with the personal; the spoken with the silent.

Chapter Two is about crisis, which a generation ago had been viewed as peripheral to public relations. Today it is central. Amid the digital–social "revolution" and its behavioral consequences, expectations and new norms, crisis is the new normal and has generated sheaves of research, theory and scrambling. People, families, organizations, nations, economies and the very planet itself have entered what feels like a realm of impending apocalypse. Once crisis was Pluto; now it's Venus. Organizations are either attempting to battle a crisis, have just emerged from one, are closing in on one, or are seeking to prevent and prepare for one. It's a scenario similar to today's "flipped classroom" design in which students immerse themselves in video and readings the night before class so the ensuing discussion obviates the need for a professorial lecture the day of the class. In this way, public relations, too, has been flipped. Crisis is imminent – event immanent (as in "within"), not distant and without.

Chapter Three is about what crisis puts at perpetual risk: reputation (or "face"). This is a matter so fundamental – both to PR and to identity itself – that its importance hardly needs explaining. The way reputation is approached here is sociologically (or more precisely, microsociologically) in the vision of dramaturgists from the sociologist Erving Goffman to the anthropologist Victor Turner and the performance theorist Richard Schechner. Life – and the PR life – is here understood as theater, with its acting shallow and deep, involving its scenes, reactions, front-and back stages and improvisations. Reputation here becomes a matter of face, that is, making claims for it and saving it.

Chapter Four, which is about PR practitioners (or "actors"), continues the movement of the book's argument from crisis, risk, and the drama of reputation. When PR is understood as what its practitioners do, then it's important to observe, examine, interview and analyze the experience of practitioners. And what practitioners do can be understood theatrically – as acting, directing, producing, improvising. This chapter channels the dramaturgical and epistemological perspectives of a line running from Simmel and Durkheim to Goffman, Burke, cultural anthropologists and performance theorists. Such a way of seeing PR is a response to the call for a sociology and anthropology of PR voiced by PR critical-thinking scholars including Jacquie L'Etang.

Chapter Five, on history, challenges the conventional historiographical trope of PR textbooks, research and theory that PR is new, modern, American and the product of technology. On the contrary, unbundling PR history from such reductive frames is what reverses the "spin" on PR, as Lamme and Russell (2010) explained in their monograph. This chapter embraces, without the conventional tone of dismissal for premodern PR, the ancient, classical and continuing historiography of PR. It is a tradition that predates Aristotle's rhetoric and continues to the Reformation *Propagandio* to the legacy of religious, spiritual and aesthetic, mass and popular forms of PR. Within a few centuries of his martyrdom circa 50 AD the PR practices of Saint Paul had crystallized the opinion of the Roman Empire to Christianize. Were Paul to have traveled through the space–time continuum, he might well have had all two and a half billion Christians following him on Twitter; as it is, many thousands do follow the Pope. Further, this chapter critiques another modernist and conventional trope that PR has "evolved."

Chapter Six moves away from the conceptualization of public relations as functions, and rethinks public relations as four cultural-historical-expressive voices. These voices – prophetic, academic, aesthetic and artistic – are intended to make public relations less abstract and more audible. The chapter's organization is adapted from a schema by J.W. O'Malley that outlined the West's cultural and religious history from Biblical to Classical to Medieval to Renaissance times. The chapter departs from the common scholarly and textbook conception of public relations as composed of functions and whose history is exclusively and narrowly modern.

Chapter Seven, on persuasion, challenges the idea promoted by theory builders of the last generation that persuasion had to be dethroned as the foundation of PR on the grounds that it is "asymmetrical." But such a critique of symmetry is, at its source, the ancient argument that sought to equate rhetoric with sophistry. In the end, perhaps ironically, the attempt to dethrone persuasion and elevate in its place the "two-way symmetry" of "excellence and ethics" is a thesis that falls apart when the actualities and complexities of public relations practice are more closely observed. For a generation, the deepest division within the PR scholarly community has been this one: between the Grunigian symmetrists and the Heathean rhetoricians. By the end of the twentieth century, PR theory building was working to replace persuasion with other, seemingly more fair-minded and democratic models like negotiation. The advantage of these models was not their veracity but their palatability.

Chapter Eight, on politics, makes a case that what is political about PR cannot simply be siphoned off into the subdiscipline of public affairs. PR is not political in part but thoroughly – structurally, historically, continuingly. Its very nature is political – an argument that follows from the critiques of the dethroning of persuasion. PR practice and theory have attempted, without success, to have it both ways: a comprehensive "dominant" theory as well as a fractionated practice of subdisciplines like public affairs, corporate communications and crisis communication. However, a truly comprehensive theory of PR would manage to frame PR with an inclusiveness able to reintegrate these subdisciplines into the larger whole.

Chapter Nine, on the ambiguities of public relations ethics, begins by asking why PR is obsessed with ethics – the industry's perception of how others regard its ethics and its long and strenuous creation, promotion, and adumbration of ethical codes. Such a question flows naturally enough from the previous chapters on the critiques of PR history, the attempt to replace persuasion with "excellence" and the political nature of PR. In the end and the beginning, this obsession is perfectly reasonable because the obsession with ethics is about the explicit and implicit question of PR's legitimacy. For PR itself, as for its clients, what's central are the matters of crisis, threat, and reputation. There is no getting past these questions; they are the soil from which all PR theory has been grown. That PR is equivalent to propaganda is a persistent but mistaken critique. Unlike propagandists who traffic in the harshest sort of negativity, PR practitioners are so allergic to negativity that it has had the unintended consequence of weakening the very credibility that has been PR's calling card.

Chapter Ten reclaims, if not reclassifies, PR for the humanities. But in the spirit of the both – and inclusiveness of PRe, PRe's concept of the humanities embraces, not excludes, the disciplines of the social sciences. As much as any other image or symbol or concept, it is the idea of a poet – John Keats – that gets at the essence of a humanistic reclamation. It is what Keats called "negative capability" – the poet's capacity not to do something he found so distasteful in a friend. Not to be forever irritatingly reaching for fact and reason but to be content with the mystery, complexity, ambiguity, and contingency. The negative capability of the humanist is made of both critique and contentment.

References

Bush, D. (ed.). (1959). *John Keats: Selected poems and letters.* Cambridge, MA: Riverside Press.

Grunig, J. E. (2013). Furnishing the edifice: Ongoing research on public relations as a strategic management function. In K. Sriramesh, A. Zerfass & J.-N. Kim (Eds.), *Public relations and communication management: Current trends and topics.* New York, NY: Routledge.

Lamme, M. O. & Russell, K. (2010). Removing the spin: Toward a new theory of public relations history. *Journalism Communication Monographs,* 11(4), 280–362.

Moloney, K. (2006). *Rethinking Public Relations: PR, Propaganda and Democracy* (2nd ed.). New York, NY: Routledge.

Solis, B. (2011). *Rewire the way you work to succeed in the consumer revolution.* New York, NY: Wiley.

Vogel, D. (2005). *The market for virtue: The potential and limits of corporate social responsibility.* Washington, DC: Brookings Institution Press.

My aim is to try to isolate some of the basic frameworks of understanding available in our society for making sense our of events . . . I start with the fact that from an individual's particular point of view, while one thing may momentarily appear to be what is really going on, in fact what is actually happening is a plainly a joke, or a dream, or an accident, or a mistake, or a misunderstanding or a deception, or a theatrical performance.

Erving Goffman. Frame Analysis.

Part I

The theater of public relations

1 The principles of the public relations of everything

Authors are actors, books are theaters.

Wallace Stevens, *Adagia*

Almost everyone has an idea of what public relations (PR) is – and almost everyone is half right. But there's another half. This book seeks to explain it.

The conventional wisdom about PR by its scholars, textbook writers and practitioners isn't incorrect. But neither is it sufficient. The conventional wisdom about PR is that it exists as *something, somewhere* and *sometime.* The thesis of this book is that the conventional wisdom is misleading. Far from the narrow confines of its conventional conceptualizations, PR comprises not only some things but *everything, everyone, everywhere* and *every time.* For many scholars, PR is a matter of answers; for me it is a matter of questions. It is not about what's distinctive, as PR textbooks and PR trade organizations have said, but what's inclusive. It is as much a product of the imagination as the result of logic. In fact, PR in the twenty-first century is rapidly becoming less and less distinctive as it continues to converge with those strategies from which it was purported to be distinct, such as marketing, advertising and other rhetorically charged strategies.

What follows are principles of the public relations of everything (PRe). Here I omit the definite article, *the,* to insist that the 20 principles are not meant to be definitive so much as indicative. These principles are intended to suggest ways to understand public relations in what has been called a *postsymmetry age* (Brown, 2010). An author who can conceive of 20 principles can imagine 20 more. What's no less important than that number is the number-as-idea of multiplicity, multidisciplinary expansion and connection. It is an idea that challenges the old and ongoing attempt to define PR as *this* or *that,* rather than resist the idea that PR is both and more, growing outward rather than narrowing inward.

Principle 1: Public relations is ubiquitous, universal and timeless

Whatever it is, it must have
A stomach that can digest

> Rubber, coal, uranium, moon, poems.
> Like the shark, it contains a shoe.
> It must swim for miles through the desert
> Uttering cries that are almost human.
>   Louis Simpson (1963/2001);
>   "American Poetry"

The public relations of everything, or PRe, questions the conventional wisdom that PR is exclusively a phenomenon of modernity, or technology, any more than perception, opinion, reputation and identity were born from the nineteenth century like Athena from the forehead of Zeus. Like the shark in the Simpson poem, PR is omnivorous. But unlike the poem's title, the waters in which PR swims are not American but the oceans which touch the shores worldwide.

PR is new but it's old. The advent of the Internet, and in the last decade, web culture and social media tools, have made an extraordinary impact on history, culture, organizations, society, individuals, relationships and PR. Historiographically, PRe moves beyond the flawed notion of PR as exclusively and definitively modern.

PRe rejects PR's conventional wisdom theory of symmetry as a vestige of the mechanical age with its faith that the PR machine, if properly oiled with good will, can balance the needs of unequally powerful parties. That symmetry theory is posited as normative turns out to be a dodge, or a way of insisting that's how PR ought to be even if it isn't. By contrast, PRe prefers the *is* to the *ought*.

In its obsession with technology, PR has forgotten McLuhan's (1964) insight that technology is an extension of humanity. (He was, after all, not a professor of technology but of the transdisciplinary humanities.) Technologies, as well as opinion, influence, belief and awe, point to the individual's relationship with society (Brown, 2004; Gordon, 1997). PR is a social phenomenon, as are the typically cited rationales for PR practices: the creation, management and alteration of perception, opinion and reputation as they, in turn, affect the behavioral, economic and political situations of individuals, organizations and nations. But to posit humanity or PR as technology is the very meaning of "reductive" (Halpern, 2013).

PR has benefited from the insights of the social sciences. Yet despite the aspirations of PR to claim the status of a science, PRe regards PR as a humanity. (Chapter 10 makes this case in detail.) PRe understands PR in broadly inclusive, historical and personal terms. This is PR's ethos and its legacy, from Homer's poetry to Aristotle's rhetoric to Saint Paul's messianic persuasion to the Catholic Reformation *Propagandio,* and onward to modernity and the elegance of the algorithm.

PRe sees everything as human and everything as relational.

Principle 2: Public relations is experiential and contingent

The attention lavished by PR textbooks and scholars on planning, strategy, objectives, measurement and results misleads because it fails to account for the situation of PR. PR is no less bound than any other human and social institution by contingency. Indeed, management itself is an art, as the management theorist and ethnographer Henry Mintzberg (2005) concluded after observing managers in situ. Phenomenologically, PR is an art in the service of another art.

Everyday life is contingent, notwithstanding our effort to manage it. Or, as Kierkegaard said, our effort to distract ourselves from what we know. The Big Data we overlay upon that contingency produces statistical answers that are incapable of altering the foundation of our situation or that of organizations and their managers.

The experience *as* experience of people doing PR has not been an interest of the vast majority of PR scholars. Why has this been so? The project of the previous generation of PR scholarship has been to lift and separate PR from its taint of moral illegitimacy and intellectual unworthiness by building a collection of theories laid upon the putative foundation of science. Meanwhile, the practice of PR has thrived largely unaware of those theories.

In the phenomenology of Maurice Merleau-Ponty, lived, embodied experience is the source of meaning. But quite unlike the PR adage (or *enthymeme*) that perception is reality, which ignores or trivializes experience, Merleau-Ponty made embodied experience the basis of perception and consciousness, and the starting point for all philosophical explorations (Merleau-Ponty, 1945/2012). What's missing in much PR theory is the way in which Merleau-Ponty understood perception and experience. PR scholarship has too often been disembodied. In Merleau-Ponty's phenomenology, everyday perception has merged with the aesthetic, in eye of the Cezanne (Merleau-Ponty, 1948/1964).

PRe questions the trope of the rational manager who plans, organizes and controls, which is the classic definition of management. For PRe, the assumptions of rationality run aground in a world of radical contingency, and the notion of management as a science is rebutted by the lived experience of practitioners and their managers themselves. In PRe, the compelling trope is not functionalism or mechanism or balance; it is drama.

When framed conventionally, PR becomes just another mechanical operation in the organizational wheelworks. But even the voluminous and capacious definitions of the Public Relations Society of America (PRSA; see www.prsa.org) and the U.K. Chartered Institute of Public Relations' voluminous and capacious definitions of PR hardly object to the idea of PR as ubiquitous.

Principle 3: Public relations is a matter of places

> Life is a matter of people, not of places. But for me life is a matter of places, and that is the trouble.
>
> Wallace Stevens (1969, p. 158)

A PR truism is that the practice attracts "people persons." From a PRe perspective, places are people, too. The PR campaigns mounted by nations, cities, regions and other geographical entities is nothing new. The long-running *I Love New York* campaign with its substitution of a heart for the word *love* was ubiquitous on tee shirts, tabletop tents, buses, trains and taxis. In a world brought closer by cheaper, faster travel and globalized communication, place-branding campaigns are increasingly common.

Among the world's most popular tourist destinations, the architecturally compelling city of Barcelona has struggled with its branding strategy. Some Catalonians have worried that the reputation and brand of the city has been diminished with the rising profile of the city's soccer (or football) team's success. The stunning buildings of Gaudi have been trumped by a sports franchise.

Other cities, regions and nations, challenged by a variety of circumstances, have sought to personalize themselves by putting on a new or familiar face or removing a damaged one. Only recently has the nation of Colombia witnessed the perception of its brand change from a nation to avoid to a romantic destination.

Not that such changes happen overnight. Perceptions linger long on the collective retina of memory. Medical science may have innovated the face transplant; PR has discovered no such operational fixes.

Places have power, agency, glamour and influence. They are themselves actors who are preceded by a reputation that is hard to live up to. As the travel writer Colin Thubron (2012) wrote of a great city:

> Jerusalem has for so long incited fantasy that the geographical city may come as a shock. (p. 3)

What visitor to Paris has not wanted to see the Mona Lisa in the Louvre, the Champs Élysées, Monet's garden in Giverny, the cathedral of Notre Dame, Shakespeare & Company, the Bois de Boulogne, the Eiffel Tower? Places trail behind them a resonance and incite the thrill of expectation. They have PR mojo. They exude influence.

Principle 4: Public relations is dramatic

PR is largely what its practitioners do. But it is also what we do in what the sociologist Erving Goffman explored as self-presentation in everyday life (Goffman, 1959). What practitioners and the rest of us have in common is our acting. But it is a misconception of acting to conflate it with lying or to reject it on account of its most extreme emotional cost to the actor (Hochschild, 2003).

The necessity to act places crisis at or near the center of PR. (Chapter 2 elaborates.) To reconsider PR as a daily drama is a perspective that offers opportunity for insight into a social institution. Our everyday lives, like the lives of organizations, are less "managed" than intermittently conflictual and, at times, baffling.

Anyone familiar with the operations of PR agency and PR department practices will have little trouble recalling the anxious rhythm of expectation, rejection, skepticism, challenge, problem and crisis. Journalists ignore. Adversaries dismiss. Clients demand. Employees gossip. Voters rage. And this is very often the calling card for crisis communication, rebranding, corporate social responsibility, media relations and other PR practices. Corporate social responsibility has not revolutionized

PR; it has become PR's rationalized shibboleth. But there's a reality gap between Guth and Marsh's (2000) "value-driven" PR and the less inspirational asymmetries of PR practice.

Daily life replicates the conflict drama requires.

Life in pressured working environments is theater. Each conflict is a scene the actors must prepare for and then play face to face or in a conference room or supervisor's or employee's office. Each performance will be effective or inept. In our daily professional lives we may find ourselves in encounters that threaten our face, our job, our friendships, our solvency.

Anxious or confident, PR paid professionals and everyone else engages in a drama of expressiveness and face protection, of what is said or left unsaid, of gestures that are intended or unintended. When they must, individuals act to protect their faces, as well as the faces of the others, whether they are PR agency clients, organizational colleagues, spouses, siblings or Facebook friends. To understand PR in this broader social or interactional sense is to recognize it as a drama that is *ongoing* – a term which W. Timothy Coombs (2012, emphasis added) has used to define crisis communication. What is crisis communication but an ongoing effort in a world of contingency and threat? Crisis is what the anthropologist Victor Turner (1988) called a "social drama."

Principle 5: Public relations is conflictual

> Public relations is "a wrangle in the marketplace."
>
> R. L. Heath

What would drama be without conflict? Aristotle explained conflict's purpose in theatrical performance. Georg Simmel (1971) framed conflict as a challenging human and social phenomenon. From a micro or macro perspective, the life of the person and the organization is anything but smooth sailing. Things go wrong. Problems arise. Trends become issues, and issues crises. Credibility is questioned. The actor's gaffe undermines his reputation. To illuminate discredited credibility at its most extreme, Goffman (1961) produced a heartbreaking essay that humanizes the crisis of mental illness from the perspective of the involuntarily committed patient confounded by the apparent betrayal of trusted others.

Exponents of PR have advanced the idea that it is a win–win game, a conversation, a negotiation. But not necessarily or always. The conflictual world of PR is not separate from the violent world of the poet William Blake's "Songs of Innocence and Experience," and "The Marriage of Heaven and Hell." The experience of the world belies the fairy tale of symmetry (Brown, 2006). Blake knew that the lions rarely lie down with the lambs; usually they devour them.

The asymmetry of social reality is consistent with what the economist Joseph Schumpeter (1942) called the "creative destruction" wrought by the marketplace forces of capitalistic innovation. Leading the charge in the digital–social era are the lions of disruption – Facebook, Twitter, Amazon. Amid the heyday of newspapers, along comes the digital–social media revolution to make obsolescent the careers of innumerable journalists.

Like PR firms with clients caught in a scandal, drama thrives on conflict. The idea of "damage control," understood or not, is familiar to people both inside and outside the institutions of PR. Crisis and the attempt to manage it ought not to be considered a specialized area of PR, but of PR's most compelling selling propositions. When organizations are in crisis, it is not to the advertising or marketing department that they turn but to a crisis management team typically led by a PR professional with crisis communication experience.

Principle 6: Crisis has moved to the center of public relations

What follows from the conflictual and the *acted* nature of PR is the increasing centrality of crisis. Familiar now are the mini Internet social dramas that the crisis theorist Timothy Coombs called *paracrises* (or events that aren't crises but resemble them). While the marketing "function" of PR may well be its most common application and perception, what's especially compelling about PR is its familiarity with crisis.

Amid the dramaturgy of the face-threatened practitioner and the reputation-threatened organization, the PR of everything can be plotted along a continuum of crisis.

Crisis communication, as Coombs's (2012) title makes explicit, is "ongoing." The individual needs to be perpetually on guard against the social forces that threaten the claims it makes that constitute its face. Trouble comes quickly and unannounced. As organizations mine, monitor and respond to anonymous complaints on the Twittersphere, they seek to protect their brand and their reputation. As crisis has moved toward the center of PR, PR has become a matter of perpetual vigilance.

Principle 7: Public relations is ritualistic

Rituals do not adorn life so much as provide it with continuity, structure and meaning. The observer of PR is well aware of the ritualistic activities that participate in the PR nexus of drama, acting and crisis. As a humanity, PRe benefits from the contributions of anthropology without claiming to *be* anthropological. The cultural anthropologist Victor Turner (1988) constructed a theory of crisis that emerged from his observations of behavior he identified as *social drama*. Turner defined that term as a dramatic process resulting from conflict that develops into either a transformational and "harmonic" outcome or a "disharmonic," or unresolved, problematic and crisis situation. (p. 74).

The parallels with contemporary theories and practices of crisis PR are apparent. When crisis erupts, as it inevitably does for organizations and individuals, American media culture has its warring tribal groups, diviners and redressive rituals. The American television journalist Barbara Walters has made a career of performing a mediated ritual. She redresses the offense as a media priestess. Her role is to cast out the spirits of harsh public opinion over celebrities mired in scandals – sexual indiscretions, politically offense speech, abusive and bizarre behavior, clueless negligence. A probing question strikes a nerve. Celebrity tears flow. The ritual close-up visualizes and preserves the moment. The media dutifully report it through the news cycle. The evil is excised.

The list of breaching organizations is extensive. Like the single-name pop stars Beyoncé and Gaga, reputationally damaged organizations are instantly recognized because their organizational names are identified with their crises, long after the nature of the crisis is forgotten. Enron. Exxon. BP. Spoilt reputation is spliced into their reputations.

TV viewers tune in for the ritual shaming, tearful recognition and redemption. In Turner's terms, the redressive action moves the drama beyond the threshold of liminality and toward the reintegration of the offender.

Principle 8: Public relations is personal

For a generation, the theory-builders of PR have sought to quantify PR. For Grunig (1992), PR is, in essence, "communications management."

It is advertising that has been conventionally defined in the PR textbooks as impersonal – whereas PR's calling card was personal. But you wouldn't know that from reviewing the technocratic, bureaucratic, quantified impersonality of a systems and symmetry generation.

Unintended consequences have resulted from such a narrow and reductive perspective. What PRe seeks to identify are those consequences. What has been reduced comprises the insightful legacy of rhetorical, critical and historical methodologies. What has also been reduced is the sociological and psychological layered complexities of PR, as well as the actual inequalities of power and influence that systems-based symmetry's "normative" theory simply fails to account for.

For starters, an unintended consequence of "scientific" theory building has resulted in turning attention away from the lived, embodied experience of PR practitioners.

For PRSA, the trade organization that purports to speak for the U.S. PR industry, PR is framed in terms of what organizations and their managers do and say. Despite the conventional contrast of PR as "personal" compared with the impersonality of advertising, PR textbooks, scholars and teachers have grounded their understanding of PR in terms that lack the specificity of personality.

Such a conception of PR – modern, technological, unethical in nature – is well suited to the ambition of Bernays (1928) and others to raise the practice's profile and identify it as a science. But when PR is reimagined (if not exactly reconceptualized) as a fundamentally human drama, rather than the narrative of the emergence of dominating technologies, it must follow that PR belongs primarily to the humanities. Yet, such a humanistic classification goes against the grain of PR as it has been framed by a generation of scholars and practitioners as nothing more or less than the application of social science. For PRe, that PR is a science or can be truly understood and practiced scientifically is, at once, aspirational, misleading and problematic.

Principle 9: Public relations is social

If PR begins with the individual, is it a contradiction to observe the social nature of PR? Hardly. PR is a historically rooted social institution. It comes together at the junction of society and the self.

The PR industry is not a vast and random collection of atomistic individuals but a complex, multidisciplinary, multinational, transnational network of PR agencies and departments – single proprietorships, freelancers and boutiques, as well as global megafirms. It is thus a complexity that houses the individual and collective experience of people.

Each PR agency and department comprises teams or groups of individuals who are themselves networked within their agency or department, as well as within a panoply of professional and trade organizations. For Clay Shirkey (2008), a perceptive analyst of social media, "human beings are social creatures – not occasionally or by accident but always" (p. 14).

PRe is inclusive of the social and the human. L'Etang and Pieczka (2006) have argued that PR needs to be situated in the academy as an interdisciplinary study. Walking PR back from its scientific ambitions is consistent with understanding it in the inclusive sense of a humanity. To situate PR in this way is consistent with the principle of PRe: that PR is definitively inclusive rather than exclusive or even distinctive. The inter- (or multi-) disciplinary situation of PR permits PR to be understood as a humanity (as the final chapter of this book contends) while continuing to include the contributions of the social sciences. Such a situation for PR departs from the previous generations' strenuous and unpromising project to rebrand PR as a science while slipping into the intellectual sin of scientism.

PR, in its modern twentieth-century era of development, benefited both from the input of many disciplines – behavioral psychology, organizational theory and sociology to name just three. The PR theorist Jacquie L'Etang (2008) has called for just this sort of disciplinary expansion and resituating of PR from a theoretical and an academic perspective. However, PR's pollination by other disciplines is not the same as demonstrating that PR is a science. No single discipline owns or defines PR. The ability of PR to incorporate other disciplines is as much a hallmark of PR as its famous boundary-spanning nature.

Principle 10: Public relations is awesome

Recounting the life of Nero, Suetonius (1970) wrote:

> When he staged "The Fire," a Roman play by Africanius, the actors were allowed to keep the valuable furnishings they rescued from the burning house. Throughout the festival, all kinds of gifts were scattered to the people – 1,000 assorted birds daily, and quantities of food parcels; besides vouchers for corn, clothes, gold, silver, precious stones, pearls, paintings, slaves, transport animals, and even wild beasts – and finally for ships, blocks of City tenements, and farms. (p. 217)

Art forms have been an attribute of PR from the ancients to the postmoderns. In his essay about the World Trade Center Memorial, Martin Filler (2011) produced what sounds like a sense of awe:

> I wept, but about what precisely I cannot say. Much to my amazement, after having done everything possible to shut out the ubiquitous maudlin press coverage that engulfed the tenth anniversary of the 2001 terrorist attacks, I visited Michael Arad's National September 11 Memorial in New York City – which was dedicated exactly a decade after the disaster – to find that it impressed me at once as a sobering, disturbing, heartbreaking, and over-whelming masterpiece.
>
> The propulsive aural and visual excitement of the three-story-deep water-fall and its mysterious disappearance captures and holds your attention in a way most unusual for the static medium of conventional architecture. That distraction makes one's next perception all the more shocking, as you focus on the names of the victims, incised into the continuous tilted rim of bronze tablets that surround each pool.
>
> (p. 8)

In a previous publication I have proposed the idea of PR as the propagation of awe. Which is not to suggest that *all* PR is awe-inspiring. The PR agency account executives whose task it is to write compelling news releases about chicken potpie or Generic Software Program Release 2.3 are hardly trafficking in awe. But the models of PR as "communication management" and negotiation fail at the other end: they fail to account for the many electric moments of spectacle when we can catch a glimpse of the poetics of PR. That failure is a consequence of turning a blind eye to the influence of art, architecture and spectacle inherent in certain itera-tions of PR. To grasp this truth is to reject the view of Guy Debord's (2000) disgust at society corrupted by spectacle. The Gothic cathedral is spectacular without being a spectacle (Prina, 2011).

Principle 11: Public relations is ordinary

How can PR be both awesome and ordinary?

Introducing the Cupcake Terrorist. My colleague, Rebecca Hains, a feminist, media studies activist, and professor of advertising and media literacy, became famous for 15 Warholian minutes in the digital and social era. Or, rather, Hains didn't become famous; her cupcake did.

The Daily Kos, a politically liberal American website, posted an explanation on its page:

> A friend of mine was given two Wicked Good Cupcakes before a trip from Boston to Las Vegas. She carried them onto the plane (they come in glass jars to keep them fresh) and all that the Boston TSA checker said was that they looked delicious. She ate one on the flight out & decided to eat the other on the way home.

And that's when the security theatrical comedy began.

Checking into the Las Vegas airport, Hains had her other cupcake confiscated by a Transportation Security Administration (TSA) official on the grounds that it constituted a safety threat. Hains, a web-savvy former PR intern, responded in two strategic ways. She posted on her Facebook wall her comically and satirically framed outrage as a news story about the absurd behavior of what happens to be one of America's worst-reputed regulatory bureaucracies, the TSA:

> Dear TSA agents in Las Vegas: Thank you for keeping America safe by steal-ing my cupcake-in-a-jar from me. I'm sure the delicious-looking frosting indeed counts as a "liquid" which, like all liquids on airlines, presents a magi-cal but grave security threat to my fellow passengers and the entire flight crew. You are amazing. Bravo!!!
>
> (Rebecca Hains, 2011)

Trained in the kind of targeting peculiar to social media, Hains fired off an e-mail to boing.boing, a website whose editor features goofy and bizarre stories. She adopted a voice of ironically toned outrage.

The following day, this story appeared on boing.boing and went viral, aggregat-ing almost 10 million views:

TSA CONFISCATES CUPCAKES; CALLS FROSTING A 'GEL'

Meanwhile, the TSA launched a series of unfortunate rationales for the embarrass-ing cupcake incident, indicating, laughably, that the agency had nothing against cupcakes.

In the age of the social web, a certain alchemy has transformed the ordinary into the extraordinary. The PR world has room for real crises like environmental disas-ters and what Coombs (2012) called "paracrises" and, in a subsequent edition of his book, "social media crises." Whatever you call them, they've become frequent and common, which has changed crisis from a PR specialty to a PR commodity.

Or Cupcake Terrorism.

Principle 12: Objects have public relations

If the memes of cupcakes and sweatshirts crystallize public opinion, objects them-selves can be understood to "have" PR.

Few would dispute the influence of objects in drama, paintings, architecture, sculpture and poetry: Keats's Grecian Urn, Robert Frost's birch trees, Achilles' shield, Andy Warhol's serial Campbell Soup cans.

In *Stuff,* the ethnographic theorist Daniel Miller (2010) advanced what he called a "theory of *things*" (italics mine). Miller observed a "somewhat unexpected capacity of objects to fade in and out of focus and remain peripheral to our vision, and yet determinant of our behavior and identity" (p. 51). Objects – *things* – carry the weight of everyday experience, memory and emotion.

The American novelist Nathaniel Hawthorne offered what was nothing less than the revelation of the character of the heroine – the Colonial adulteress Hester Prynne:

> She took off the formal cap that confined her hair, and down it fell upon her shoulders, dark and rich, with at once a shadow and a light in its abundance, and imparting a charm of softness to her features.
>
> (Hawthorne, 1850/2009, p. 377)

It is not only Hester's gesture that compels us – it is her hair. Like the scarlet *A,* her hair has the influential and awesome agency of a thing – an object.

In the art historian Neil MacGregor's (2011) *A History of the World in 100 Objects,* the focus of what is compelling, famous and influential shifts from people to things. From 2 million BC to the present, and from the Mummy of Hornedjitef to the Ice Age and the figurine of lovers, the history of civilization is told through objects: an axe and a writing tablet of 2,000 years BC; a Sphinx, a chariot, a gold coin, a credit card; and finally, a solar-powered lamp.

For some, PR is a matter of people, but it is also a matter of things: the printing press, the camera, the automobile, the TV, the laptop, the iPhone. These, as McLuhan (1964) insisted, are but the extensions of the human nervous system. From another perspective, the objects themselves possess that compelling, dramatic power we associate with PR. No less than the world's greatest generals, politicians, dictators, scientists and artists, objects have not only influenced history; they've created it.

Principle 13: Public relations may be trivial or significant

If a cupcake, and to some extent its owner, can be said to have "gotten PR," can the speeches of Winston Churchill be said to occupy that same PR space?

Put another way, how can the glaring disparity between an ordinary, if sweet, little cupcake have the same PR attribute as the extraordinary gravitas of Churchill's memorable, quotable, stirring addresses to England as the nation prepared for the onslaught of Hitler's invasion of the island nation and the world itself?

Both the trivial and the significant have the capacity to disrupt. The activist goes ballistic and then viral. The statesman does the same.

But it is not the same space that the cupcake terrorist and the prime minister occupy. Rather, they are each points along a continuum of PR from extreme triviality to profound significance. Nor is such a disparity at all unfamiliar to PR practitioners. They are tasked with the positive, imaginative, persuasive framing of prime ministers and cupcakes alike. Sometimes in the same afternoon.

Q: When is a cupcake not only a cupcake?
A: *When it can melt down a huge and powerful organization like the TSA.*

We are living in an age of disruption brought about in large part by new technologies that both destroy and create whole industries. In the digital–social era, a confiscated cupcake has the capacity for more than viral publicity. It has the power to disrupt. It is quite apparent that the advent of the digital–social era has created a new elite class of communicators: the Kings and Queens of Disruption.

This is also the age of convergence. A generation ago, the critical culture theorist Susan Sontag (1966) announced the end of the boundary between "low" and "high" art. Highbrow was seen to consort with lowbrow. It would be hard to find a better example of such inclusive, post-elitist merging than in the realities of PR. The small, the large; the celebrity, the obscure; the brilliant, the foolish – all merge in the transformative inclusiveness of the PR of everything. All comers are welcome to be represented.

The result of this trivial–significant disruption has brought about the radical asymmetry of PR. Never before has there been such power in a cupcake.

Principle 14: Public relations is symbolic

It should strike no PR scholar as surprising to hear the old news that PR is symbolic. Nevertheless, it needs repeating so as to be included among the less familiar and traditionally recognized principles advanced in this chapter.

PR is a symbolic world. From Mead and Cooley and Blumer to Goffman, symbolic interactionism has influenced some insightful PR thinking, sometimes unwittingly.

But interactionism alone hasn't dominated PR thinking. Two warring schools of thought may be identified – symmetrists and rhetoricians. Both schools are in general agreement on at least one thing: that PR can produce social, economic and political benefits. A third faction – critical thinkers – appears to have allied itself with the second school – the rhetoricians.

Critical thinkers (the school with which I've been identified) approach PR with an ethical and epistemological skepticism at the overreach of systems-theory-based scientism. This camp embraces a broad, multidisciplinary, qualitative array of methodologies. At the farther end of the critical-thinking spectrum, another approach has been identified as *postmodern*, an approach that Heath (2006), in an essay, associated wittily and perhaps with some impatience as "fog."

In our data-driven age, it's not hard to understand how the symmetric model of PR, rooted in a scientific sensibility and argued with probabilistic methodologies and inferential statistics, could come to proliferate in the publications of research in the field (Brown, 2003). As an alternative to a mechanical model of PR, the schools of rhetoric and critical thinking, along with historical analysis and dramaturgy, offer alternative ways of thinking about PR.

PR and its scholarship are nothing if not fertile soil for ideas, approaches, theories, and movements. From that soil has come "action PR," which seeks ways to address the power inequities between dominant and marginalized cultures.

Today, it is accurate to say that PR scholarship and its practice is more a matter of diversity of approaches than dominance by any single approach. The case for pluralism has been persuasively argued by Elizabeth Toth (2009). However, unlike PRe, she offers no compelling objection to the conventions of symmetry theory.

Principle 15: Public relations is rhetorical

One could say that rhetoric's mother is poetry, its father history. PRe seeks to reawaken PR to its history, and thereby "removing the spin" in the conventional scholarly theory of PR history (Lamme & Miller, 2010).

PR did not begin in twentieth-century America. P.T. Barnum, that familiar straw man of PR, wasn't the first to practice PR because he orchestrated events that were photographed for newspaper readers. Barnum's real role has been to serve as a placeholder for the progressivist story PR scholars tell: that PR began in lies and contempt but has "evolved" towards truth, ethics and professionalism.

But the roots of PR are neither American nor modern. They're ancient, rhetorical, philosophical, messianic, aesthetic, social and political. Although Aristotle was far from the first rhetorician (nor was the rhetorically schooled practitioner, Saint Paul), Aristotle's *Ars Rhetorica* offers a classic model of the philosophy, strategies, style and ethics of PR.

Robert L. Heath (2009) accounted for PR in human, rhetorical and political terms:

> Rhetoric and public relations take their rationale from efforts humans make to influence one another, and to be influenced – [as] necessary to society.
>
> (p. 17)

Principle 16: Public relations is problematic

The ethical status of PR may be more intensively debated than any other its attributes. Unlike professions such as medicine, teaching, and law, PR requires a defense, if not a rationalization. Far more than those professions, PR thinking itself is, at the very least, problematic. And at the core of PR's problematics is the problem of its ethics.

That the ethical status of PR is problematic is an argument I advanced in considering a number of epistemological problems in PR (Brown, 2012). There is no shortage of popular and scholarly critics for whom PR is not problematically ethical – it is categorically unethical. Sisela Bok (1978) associated publicity as a source of lies: crisis lies, deceptive experimentation, governmental lies, lies to enemies, lies to protect confidentiality, lying to liars and paternalistic lies (p. 124). The argument that PR is more than publicity, although true, is an insufficient defense against Bok's critique.

How then should the ethics of PR be characterized? As lies? Kevin Moloney (2006) parsed PR as "weak propaganda," which is characteristic of his pragmatic approach to the complex and contentiously debated question closely associated with the ethical status of PR (p. 2). Although Moloney's index contains no references to *ethics,* it does include no less than 23 to *propaganda,* a term of opprobrium that has been applied to PR not only by its legion of critics but by the "pioneer" of PR, E. L. Bernays (1928) who titled a treatise on PR *Propaganda.* For Moloney, questions about propaganda, and by implication about the ethical status of PR, depend on the political and economic context. The "weak propaganda" of democratic societies is to be distinguished from the strong propaganda associated with totalitarian regimes.

Splitting the difference between the perspectives of Noam Chomsky's outright vilification of the ethics of PR, and its defenders who offer a persuasive defense of PR's association with liberal democracies and free markets, the ethical status of PR is anything but simple or apparent. Rather, from the perspective of PRe, the ethics of PR is ambiguous, as Chapter 9 in this book explains and elaborates.

Principle 17: Public relations is improvisational

Few influences have been more potent in shaping PR in the twentieth century than organizational management. For Grunig (1992), PR *is* management – the management of communication.

But from the perspective of PRe, PR, like management itself, is something more like an art. It is aspirationally managed but actually improvised. The management theorist Henry Mintzberg (2005) made a similar point about management – that it's not a science but an art. When Mintzberg observed managers managing, he noted that they responded to the rhythms of demand that occurred minute to minute during the day. They played their managerial role by ear. This is where Mintzberg's managers are in a creative space Merleau-Ponty could recognize: the manager as artist.

In my tenure as a middle manager at a U.S. Fortune 500 company, my anecdotal observations seemed to bear out Mintzberg's ethnography. As I sat in the office of the senior corporate vice president of corporate communications for W.R. Grace & Co., then one of the largest 100 companies on Fortune's list, I noticed that when his telephone rang (it was 1981, not 2014), he didn't hesitate to lift the receiver. Many of those calls were from the senior management of the company, including quite a few from J. Peter Grace Jr., CEO. Whatever had been on the corporate VP's to-do list were shuffled below the demands of the CEO. When the calls came from the *New York Times* or the *Washington Post* or *Business Week,* he performed the same routine. No matter how the manager had planned his day, he responded by doing what actors mean when they say that have to "be in the moment." Management abstracts time to offer the comforting illusion of control. But managers haven't that luxury.

Principle 18: Public relations is strategically ambiguous

In a world of contingency, and in a society embroiled in conflict that poses risk, the rational response of the organization and individual is strategic ambiguity, as the organizational theorist Eric Eisenberg (2007) has suggested. Perhaps the most common criticism of PR is the two-barreled charge that PR is "spin" and spin is anathema to PR textbooks, teachers and scholars, not to mention PR's critics from journalists to followers of Daniel Boorstin, Chomsky and like-minded others.

From a deontological perspective, that charge would surely be valid. But the implication that PR must be judged on deontological grounds is unpersuasive given the contingent, fragile, shifting structure of relationships and obligations that comprise the web of PR actors, organizations and their constituencies.

A more reasonable frame for PR is the nonabsolutist one proposed by Eisenberg (2007) who advocated "a shift in emphasis away from an overly Ideological adherence to clarity toward a more contingent, strategic orientation" (p. 5).

That such an orientation is problematic or even relativistic is a fair one, but perhaps no less fair than the critique of the futile attempt to impose a deontological absolutism on actors who must act in a world of contingency. The problematic nature of PR "thought" about contingency, among other things, was explored by me in an article I published in *Public Relations Inquiry* (Brown, 2012).

Principle 19: Public relations is a humanity

What PRe contends is to rethink the idea of PR as drama, art, poetry, conflict, improvisation, ritual, spectacle, trivia and awe. Donn Tilson (2011) saw PR as the merger of sacred and profane, a covenant between the individual and the object of desire, whether pope or pop star, Saint Teresa or sainted Princess Di. Although the conventional classification of PR regards it as an applied social science, and although the lion's share of the peer-journal publications are quantitative, PRe offers a stark contrast to this conventional framing. PRe proposes the idea of PR as a humanity. PRe advances the idea of approaching PR from the intellectual kingdoms of history, rhetoric, sociology and phenomenology. There is an unexplored poetics to PR that registers quite differently from what its severest, dismissive critics, and even many of its leading scholars and practitioners, imagine it to be.

To classify PR as a humanity is to situate it, not to define it.

Principle 20: Public relations is apophatic

The *apophatic* (or no-speaking) is that which can't be defined. Galloway (2013) made the intriguiging case that it is futile to define PR either by adducing an unwieldy number of existing definitions or by attempting to discover or craft one single succinct definition. Instead, he argued, PR should be regarded as apophatic, or beyond definition. Examples of apophatic framings exist in a variety of contexts. For example, God has been framed as apophatic: ubiquitous, immanent, transcendent. A *via negativa*.

Such a *via negativa* is curiously well suited to PRe. Although this chapter identifies 20 principles, this number in no way is intended to limit the number of principles but rather to indicate an attribute of multitiplicity.

Twenty principles represent an approach, not a definition.

References

Bernays, E. L. (1928). *Propaganda.* New York, NY: Horace Liveright.
Bok, S. (1978). *Lying: Moral choice in public and private life.* New York, NY: Vintage Books.
Brown, R. E. (2003). A matter of chance: The emergence of probability and the rise of public relations. *Public Relations Review, 29*(3), 385–399.

———. (2004). The propagation of awe: Public relations, art and belief in Reformation Europe. *Public Relations Review,* 30(3), 381–390.

———. (2006). The myth of symmetry: Public relations as cultural styles. *Public Relations Review,* 32(3), 206–212.

———. (2010). Symmetry and its critics: Antecedents, prospects, and implications for symmetry in a post-symmetry era. In R. L. Heath (Ed.), *Sage handbook of public relations* (Vol. 2, pp. 277–292). Thousand Oaks, CA: Sage.

———. (2012). Epistemological modesty: Critical reflections on public relations thought. *Public Relations Inquiry,* 1(1), 89–105.

Coombs, W. T. (2012). *Ongoing crisis communication: Planning, managing, and responding* (3rd ed.). Thousand Oaks, CA: Sage.

Debord, G. (2000). *Society of the spectacle.* Kalamazoo, MI: Black & Red.

Eisenberg, E. (2007). *Essays on communication, organization and identity.* Thousand Oaks, CA: Sage.

Filler, M. (2011). A masterpiece at ground zero. *New York Review of Books,* 58(16), pp. 8, 10.

Galloway, C. J. (2013) Deliver us from definitions: A fresh way of looking at public relations. *Public Relations Inquiry,* 2(2), 147–159.

Goffman, E. (1959). *The presentation of self in everyday life.* New York, NY: Anchor Books.

———. (1961). The moral career of the mental patient. In E. Goffman (1961). *Asylums: Essays on the social situation of mental patients and other inmates,* (pp. 125–169). New York: Vintage.

Gordon, W. T. (1997). *Marshall McLuhan: Escape into understanding. A biography.* New York, NY: Basic Books.

Grunig, J. E. (1992). (Ed.) *Excellence in public relations and communication management.* Hillsdale, NJ: Erlbaum.

Guth, D. W. & Marsh, C. (2000). *Public relations: A value-driven approach.* Boston: Allyn & Bacon.

Hains, Rebecca (2011). Personal communication with Salem State University colleague Rebecca Hains concerning Katrandjian, O. *Cupcake of mass destruction: TSA confiscates woman's frosted cupcake.* ABC TV News. abcnews.go.com/News.security-theatre

Halpern, S. (2013, November 7). Are we puppets in a wired world? *New York Review of Books.* Retrieved from www.nybooks.com/articles/archives/2013/nov/07/are-we-puppets-wired-world/

Hawthorne, N. (2009). *The scarlet letter.* North Charleston, SC: Booksurge.

Heath, R. L. (2006). Once more into the fog: Thoughts on public relations: Research directions. *Journal of Public Relations Research. 2006.*

———. (2009). The rhetorical tradition: Wrangle in the marketplace. In R. L. Heath & D. Waymer (Eds.), *Rhetorical and critical approaches to public relations* (Vol. 2, pp. 17–47). New York, NY: Routledge.

Hochschild, A. (2003). *The managed heart: Commercialization of human feeling.* Berkeley: University of California Press.

Lamme, M. O. & Miller, K. R. (2010). Removing the spin: Toward a new theory of public relations history. *Journalism Communication Monographs,* 11(4), 280–362.

L'Etang, J. (2008). *Public relations: Concepts, practice and critique.* London, England: Sage.

L'Etang, J. & Pieczka, M. (Eds.). (2006). *Public relations: Critical debates and contemporary practice.* Mahwah, NJ: Erlbaum.

MacGregor, N. (2011). *A history of the world in 100 objects.* New York, NY: Viking.

Merleau-Ponty, M. (1964). *Eye and mind.* In J. M. Edie & W. Cobb. (Eds.), *The primacy of perception* (pp. 159–60). Boston, MA: Northeastern University Press.

———. (2012). *The phenomenology of perception* (Trans. D. Landes). London, England: Routledge.

Miller, D. (2010). *Stuff.* Cambridge, England: Polity Press.

Mintzberg, H. (2005). *Managers not MBAs: A hard look at the soft practice of managers and management development.* San Francisco, CA: Berrett-Koehler.

Moloney, K. (2006). *Rethinking public relations: PR, propaganda and democracy* (2nd ed.). New York, NY: Routledge.

McLuhan, M. (1964). *Understanding media: The extensions of man.* New York, NY: McGraw-Hill.

Prina, F. (2011). *The story of gothic architecture.* Munich, Germany: Prestel.

Schumpter, J. (1942). *Capitalism, socialism and democracy.* New York and London: Harper & Brothers.

Shirkey, C. (2008). *Here comes everybody: The power of organizing without organizations.* New York, NY: Penguin.

Simmel, G. (1971). Conflict. In D. N. Levine (Ed.), *George Simmel on individuality and social forms* (pp. 70–95). Chicago: University of Chicago Press.

Simpson, L. (2001). *The owner of the house: New collected poems 1940–2001.* Rochester, NY: BOA Editions.

Solis, B. (2011). *Rewire the way you work to succeed in the consumer revolution.* New York, NY: Wiley.

Sontag, S. (1966). *Against interpretation.* New York: Farrar, Straus & Giroux.

Stevens, W. (1969). *Opus posthumous.* New York, NY: Alfred A. Knopf.

Suetonius. (1970). *The twelve Caesars.* B. Radice. & R. Baldick, Eds.; R. Graves. Trans. London, England: Penguin.

Thubron, C. (2012). Apocalypse city. Review of S.D. Montefiore *Jerusalem: The biography. New York Review of Books,* 59(1), 6, 8, 10.

Tilson, D. (2011) . *The promotion of devotion: Saints, celebrities and shrines.* Champaign, IL: Common Ground Press.

Toth, E. L. (2009). The case for pluralistic studies of public relations: Rhetorical, critical, and excellence perspectives. In R. L. Heath, E. L. Toth, & D. Waymer (Eds.), *Rhetorical and critical approaches to public relations* (2nd ed., pp. 48–60). New York, NY: Routledge.

Turner, V. (1988). *The anthropology of performance.* New York, NY: PAJ.

2   Crisis

Science does not permit us the illusion of certainty.

James Gates, theoretical physicist

If public relations (PR) can be understood in dramatic terms, there is no more emphatic example of it than crisis. In its attempt to manage crisis, PR is at its most theatrical. In a little more than a generation, crisis has moved from the periphery of PR as a special application to the center of PR. Today, in the digital–social era of instantaneous, globalized communication, everything either is a crisis, has been or is becoming one, or is an event that resembles one.

That crisis is inevitable reveals something that is not at all new: the contingency of the life of organizations and people.

PR is undergoing more than one kind of paradigm shift. The challenge of PR scholarship is to rethink PR outside the box of the management of organizational communication. As Lee Edwards (2012) noted in the journal *Public Relations Inquiry,* "the adherence to the organizational context reflects the influence of the functional paradigm even on researchers that have made a conscious effort to expand PR scholarship beyond what they see as a relatively limited area" (p. 13). She continued by proposing a new definition for PR based on "flow," not function.

Beyond organizational function lies the inclusivity and multidisciplinarity, which L'Etang (1996) argued represent the real situations of the PR discipline. Taken together, it is this multidisciplinary, extra-organizational, suprafunctional, ongoing crisis contingency that describes the space of the public relations of everything, or PRe; Coombs, 2012)

Several years ago I gave a talk on crisis communication called "Seven Ways of Looking at a Crisis" (Brown, 2010; I offer my apologies to Wallace Stevens, whose poem enumerated 13 ways of looking at a blackbird [Stevens, 1959]).

Although the types of crisis may not be infinite, they do appear to be numerous. Crises of all kinds are so frequently brought to our attention that they've lost much of their ability to shock when they seemed a rarer species. Crises – organizational, national, financial, personal – are everywhere on view in a communication era whose belief system is radical, universal, continuous, transparent. Crises are to be expected because they are both imminent and immanent – both about to happen and happening.

That crisis communication is a managerial discipline – framed managerially for planning, organizing and controlling – is one part aspiration, one part hubris and the rest paradox.

In one horrific week in October 2013, two teachers in two American states were murdered by two different students. *Black swan theory*, proposed by Nassim Taleb (2010), raises the stakes of these dystopic events by depicting the most deadly of crises as the very ones least likely to be anticipated by the smartest people in the room. The theory additionally states that it is the most improbable events, or crises, that result in most profound impact for bad or good – whether they are the hijacked planes that brought down New York's World Trade Center or the innovation of Google.

In the Darwinian sense of a nature red in tooth and claw, life was framed as a jungle where only the fittest survive. In our era of perpetual crisis, it's night in the jungle and the antagonists are blind.

How furious are the victims and stakeholders who demand not only answers but assurances in a crisis where there are few answers and no assurances? As the veteran crisis manager Lynn Kettleson (see www.kettlesoncommunications.com) has observed, in a crisis stakeholders and victims demand management's answers to three questions: What happened? Who's to blame? How will you assure us that it will never happen again? Rarely, if ever, can such assurances be reliably offered.

The command and control system of managerialism strategizes planning, organizing and controlling. But management also operates on the basis of belief, hope and denial. Coombs (2012) charted the "denial strategies" conventionally used by management when faced by a crisis management team's claims that a crisis exists (p. 155). For the failure of organizations to operate effectively before, during and after a crisis, Ian Mitroff (2003) blamed not only the faulty assumptions of managerial reasoning but management's lack of imagination. Management stumbles by attempting to resolve each new crisis with assumptions based on the previous crisis.

Probabilism

When the language of crisis management isn't a language of rational certainty, it's a language of statistical probabilism. From the paradigm shifts of the heliocentric universe to the inferential formulations of modernity, probabilism has been displacing other forms of evidence and authority that were not founded in statistics (Brown, 2003). Probablism is built into the epistemology of empiricism. It is a mathematics of assumption, formula and inference, not a language of reassurance. But crisis management is intended to provide reassurance. If only an organization would mine issues management, business records and other data, the risk of a crisis event could be ascertained and, if not prevented, then at least prepared for. But such reassurances do not and cannot go far enough because they ignore the weight of unknowability and what is all too conveniently dismissed as the antiquated concept of fate. Risk management is, in its application to crisis PR, a statistical language that frames a gamble as reassurance. But there could be no reassurance without certain exclusions. Natural disasters – the kind that Coombs (2012) called Category I (unpreventable Acts of God) – must be excluded from the risk-management language of probabilism. In *Cases in Public Relations Management*, Swann's (2010) framing of crisis management in terms of risk management joined a consensus of leading PR scholars that includes Heath. Swann cited organizational crises at Enron (fraud) Arthur Andersen (endorsement of fraud), Adelphia (conspiracy and fraud), Global Crossing (fraud), Nike (exploitation of foreign workers), McDonald's (sued by a woman scalded by overheated coffee), and Intel (missing the problem with its Pentium chip; p. 111).

Yet even discounting natural disasters as statistical outliers, there remains a questionable assumption: that human crises (ones caused intentionally or otherwise by one or more individuals in or external to an organization) are so unlike natural disasters that they can be discovered, prevented, contained, controlled. The ironist wonders whether we ourselves are not natural disasters.

Metaphor

Imagine for a moment that there exists a physics of PR. Imagine PR as a dynamic solar system with moving parts. In that imaginary space, picture the planet of crisis communication. A generation ago, the crisis planet was as remote as Pluto. But in a generation that has seen the Internet era and the rise of digital–social communication, the once-remote planet seems to have grown larger as it has approached us. Planet Crisis has been moving centripetally from the margins toward the center.

To extend this metaphor – and it is intended merely as a metaphor rather than a positivistic systems-based mechanistic symmetry theory – consider that asteroid, the press release. Although it continues to be visible to the naked eye, it has seemed to move at increasing speeds – as if by centrifugal force – away from the center of the PR galaxy toward the periphery.

What exactly is the centripetal force that has been pulling crisis communication toward the center of the galaxy of PR? Many would guess technology. Technology is one of those Usual Suspects used by many scholars to account for rise of PR. In that historiography, PR was Big Banged from the printing press, photography, telegraphy, broadcast, computing and the Internet. Symmetry theory narrows that narrative to the nineteenth-century American Midwest, when P.T. Barnum used newspaper photography to generate publicity for his circus and freak shows. That origin myth is the conventional historiography of PR, the basis for the theory that PR has "evolved" not only professionally but ethically.

These days, when PR agencies pitch their services to prospective clients, the pitch would need to address not only marketing objectives but risk management and crisis communication. *All you've worked so long and hard for can now be lost in an instant.* In the digital–social media era of instantaneity and viralism, this sort of apocalyptical rhetoric is quite compelling. What we know of the asymmetric principle of loss aversion – that we are far more unwilling to risk losing than we are compelled by the promise of winning – only underscores the persuasiveness of the crisis-based pitch. It is, after all, full of the anxiety, conflict and drama that engages organizations, nations and individuals – far more than the appeal of branding or even reputation. In the digital–social media era, branding and reputation converge into the black hole of crisis.

It must be said that using metaphors drawn *from* science ought not to pretend to frame PR *as* a science. Failure to distinguish the two leads to the misleading reification of PR's once-dominant theory of symmetry. To think metaphorically is an exercise in imagination, not the overreach of scientism. Practitioners are well aware that the tactics of PR have shifted in the metaphorical universe. For example, in the early twentieth century development of the PR industry, the press release occupied the center of the PR universe. Larry Weber, the CEO of several successful PR agencies, insists that, in the digital–social era, the press release is passé. One may imagine the press release as a comet disappearing into interstellar space or a star collapsing on itself. Weber (2009) ideas about PR refer to another way of looking at "everything" when he wrote, "The digitization of everything, especially 'the media,' has rendered long-standing ways of organizing, working, communicating, and competing obsolete" (p. ix).

If *crisis* was not indexed in Weber's book, it would seem to be because he framed every one of his anecdotes and case studies in the overall tumultuous crisis of digitization that has either undone or threatens to undo the reputations of his agencies' clients. In such a universe, crisis is understood; the mention of it is redundant or supererogatory. In Weber's vision, crisis hasn't moved from the periphery to the nucleus; it has become the universe itself. Where organizational crisis had, a generation ago, been perceived and experienced as a rare, atypical, devastating, game-changing event, in the early years of our century crisis communication is, in Coombs's apt term, "ongoing." Thirty years ago, crisis was a static thing, a painting; now it is a work of art that moves in space, like the mobiles of Alexander Calder. As a result, the price of effective PR is eternal vigilance.

Some of the credit for the increasing centralization of crisis communication within the PR scholarly community must go to a new generation of communication scholars who have sought to build a synthetic theory. Other drivers of the trend include history and culture, notably the apocalyptic tone of certain conversations concerning nuclear proliferation, ethnic and world wars, disease pandemics, extreme weather events and climate change. It can be fairly said that ours is an era defined by its crises. Although the 9/11 terrorist attacks occurred in New York and Washington, DC, the event has had global consequences. The financial meltdown of 2008 was not limited to America, nor was the exposé by the *Boston Globe* of the Catholic Church's sex abuse scandal limited to Boston. Arguably, these events not only altered history (more precisely, historiography), but compare with the first and second world wars of the twentieth century.

However, the centrality of crisis in PR can't be attributed to the scholars who recognized a theory-building opportunity when they saw one. What they saw was a trend in the life of organizations toward the need for a way to cope with events that were no longer few and far between but seeming to bear down on them faster and faster in an era of warp-speed communications. Digitization and a blurring succession of tech tools and innovations had blown open a widening space that was no less threatening for reputation than opportunistic for marketing.

In this historic scenario, not only doesn't the conventional wisdom about crisis communication feel secure ("tell the truth, tell it now, tell it all"); neither does the admirably constructed theory building of the past and present generation of PR scholars. Each of the crisis communication theories – largely rhetorical in nature – have expanded our understanding of organizational (if not personal) crisis (Barton, 1992; Benoit, 1994; Coombs, 2012; Hearit, 2005; Heath & O'Hair, 2010).

What these theories share, aside from assiduous description and analysis, is the assumption that crises are manageable at all. Not that such an assumption is entirely unreasonable. After all, what is the alternative to their assumption; that organizations must abandon any attempt to prevent, plan for, rehearse for, organize for, respond to and learn from potential reputation-damaging crises? Not at all. In recent years, there has been a marked boom in crisis communication scholarship, and much of it has been constructed on the foundation of rhetoric and perception rather than symmetry and excellence.

Blame

To err is human, to blame is also human. If crisis is central to PR, blame is central to crisis. In a crisis, in a world of risk and probability, victims and stakeholders want that unicorn of assurance: certainty. *What happened? Why (who's to blame?)? How can we be assured it will never happen again?*

We'll probe the assumptions behind the third question later in this chapter. As for the first question – *What happened?* – it's a question of fact. Facts are discoverable. The second question – *How?* – is less a matter of fact or *logos* and more one a matter of feeling or *pathos.* What the question of *how* is really asking is about causality and personality. We want to know *how* and *why,* but the victim or stakeholder is viscerally oriented to discover and punish the *who.* In this sense, these stakeholder and victim questions are about the quest for justice, if not revenge. Crisis is an Elizabethan tragedy – a revenge play.

Hardly a theory about crisis communication fails to identify blame as a fundamental feature. In his textbook on crisis communication, Coombs (2012) located the source of blame in attribution theory – the human tendency, especially when things go wrong, to attribute the mess to a cause (pp. 152–153). If that cause can be represented by a person or persons, so much the better.

A similar theoretical communication construct – sense-making theory – attempts to account for how people react, think, plan, and act to square the circle of complexity.

Both attribution and sense making point to the human need for answers. (It is at this human level that Mitroff [2003] turned to the Myers–Briggs personality quotients to organize the optimum crisis management team.)

The complexity of reality poses crises that threaten our ability to find our way through the dark wood. Dante turned to Beatrice to lead him from crisis to solution;

modern science and management turn to other epistemologies. Affixing blame (in Coombs's terms, "assigning crisis responsibility") may be natural but on closer inspection fails to provide a sufficient answer to the problems associated with complexity and irrationality (Coombs, 2012, p. 158).

Why should this be? For one thing, the rhetorical theoretical perspective of crisis communication – that crisis is perceptual – begs the unavoidable question of the imbalance between the irreducible complexity of crisis and the human need to assign crisis responsibility.

Theories of crisis communication that frame it rhetorically as "perception," as Coombs and others have done, advance our understanding of the nature of crises, if perhaps not so much about how to "manage" them. Coombs (2012) advanced a tripartite typology of crises: unpreventable/low or no assignment of blame; somewhat but not easily preventable/low assignment of blame; preventable/high level of blame.

Coombs's is what could safely be called a systematic and teachable typology, but it leaves out what can't be fitted into three categories. It doesn't provide adequate room for the irrational. From a scientific perspective, Eagleman (2011) believes that biology – our genetic programming – calls into question our assumptions of rationality and free will, and therefore, of the basis of blame. And what line of thinking has been more influential on contemporary economic theory than the one that questioned the economic trope of the rational actor who maximizes her benefits – and substitutes for her the irrational actor who is the protagonist of behavioral economics? In the case of crisis and economic action, it is not abnormal psychology we're speaking of, but the normality of irrationality.

Comedy

The attempt to understand crisis in particular, and PR in general, cannot be limited to the box of organizational communication. As it happens, crisis theory has been of interest to disciplines other than communications and management. Among these: cultural anthropology, ethnography, phenomenology, history, literary theory, sociology, performance and the arts and religion – that is, the humanities. The final chapter of this book elaborates the place of the humanities in PR and vice versa.

If PR were a literary genre, it would be a comedy. In the narrative of award-winning PR, all's well that ends well. Conflicts are resolved. Products grow in the awareness of consumers. Crises are prevented or resolved. PR brands itself as a problem-solving profession.

Crisis communication may be central to PR, but it approaches problems with a divergent sensibility. The world of crisis little resembles the world of branding, promotion and awareness raising that characterizes marketing PR. It's considerably darker, its sense of time far more compressed, its sense of danger imminent or even current and pervasive. Unlike the typical challenge of PR, which may be to raise awareness of a product or service, crisis communication begins with the rational paranoia of an "ongoing" preventative perspective and moves toward the confrontation of genuinely awful situations.

If the narrative genre of PR is comedy, the same can't be said for ongoing crisis communication. Things don't so much end well as decompress. The triumph of market penetration becomes the relief of survival.

When an enraged and deranged employee is fired and returns with an assault rifle to murder his boss along with other victims of circumstance, we are no longer in the land of marketing communication, much less the genre of comedy. Such murders do happen. The day after Christmas 2000, in the town of Wakefield, Massachusetts, a software engineer whose wages had been garnished brought several firearms into Edgewater Technology, his employer, and killed seven employees at random. He had no criminal record. To quote the early twentieth-century philosopher Miguel de Unamuno (2005), "There is something which, for want of a better name, we shall call the tragic sense of life" (p. 21). In December 2012, a young man entered an elementary school in Connecticut and used a rifle to kill 20 children and six of the adult staff before taking his own life. Events of this sort may be said to have become almost routine in the gun culture of America, but that does not make them predictable or preventable. They are tragic examples of Black Swans.

It is not a sense of life with which we associate PR or that PR would wish to cultivate. Tragedy – in which bad things happen and no one is to blame – is entirely alien to the communication comedy of crisis communication. However, tragedy is not infrequently at the core of crises, especially the virally visible variety of workplace violence, terrorist bombings, school shootings, disease pandemics, child molestation, sexual harassment and outright assaults, posttraumatic syndrome suicides, humongous petroleum spills and natural disasters.

Tragedy

These dark events, by no means exotic or rare, fly in the face of the resolution bias of the crisis communication comedy. What appears to be the curious case is this: that crisis communication is a comedy, but crisis itself is tragic. That extreme antinomy is one of those "tensions" and mysteries that appeal not to the sciences but to the humanities. It is not in the DNA of PR to be other than optimistic. But as Unamuno (1978) said, "It is not our ideas that make us optimists or pessimists, but our optimism or pessimism . . . that makes our ideas" (p. 5).

Yet pessimism, no matter its source, is very likely a dead end for PR. Poets and philosophers may have a tragic sense of life; PR practitioners can't afford one. Crisis communication consultants, plans, teams and research have helped fuel the growth of the PR industry. From the end of the 1980s to the present, the PR scholarship of crisis has been a growth industry. Theories of crisis were not on the radar screen – or, at least, not in the middle of the screen – of the major PR theorists such as Grunig (1992). Symmetry theory focused on reframing PR in two ways: as an ethically oriented profession and a practice whose strategies and results are amenable to valid and reliable statistical measurability. To the extent that crisis communication is a species of the PR genus, crisis communication would be approached with the proethical and quantitative methodology of symmetry. It is noteworthy that widely cited crisis communication theory is not symmetrically but rhetorically based, including Coombs's (2012) popularly cited situational crisis communication theory. This theoretic divergence might be interpreted to indicate at least two things: one, disagreement among theorists themselves or two, that crisis is itself sui generis rather than a species of PR.

Although crisis has never been far from politics, state diplomacy and matters of war and peace, crisis (and much less theories of crisis communication) was not central in early modern PR space. The exquisite attention paid to crises did not appear to be of particular concern to the fathers of modern twentieth-century PR. Although crises of all sorts occupied Bernays, Lee and other modern pioneers, they did not appear to perceive crises as distinctive from PR itself. Even near the end of the modern period, it is worth noting that Pavlik's (1987) summary of PR research has not a single indexed reference to *crisis*. Research interest picked up for organizational crisis communication in the 1990s, in the wake of the intense and continuous coverage and public awareness of the Exxon Valdez oil spill of 1989; research spiked in 2001 with a spate of corporate corruption crises led by the Enron scandal and subsequent bankruptcy.

What all the major crisis communication theory builders have in common is a rhetorical perspective, which Coombs (2012) captured in his definition: "A crisis is the perception of an unpredictable event that threatens important expectancies of stakeholders and can seriously impact an organization's performance and generate negative outcomes" (p. 2). In other words, crisis, not unlike beauty, is in the eye of the beholder.

In classrooms, textbooks and scholarly PR literature, crisis has been treated as a discrete, rather than continuous, phenomenon. The just-so stories of crisis abound in textbooks and classroom. They are the stars of crisis. In U.S.-focused texts and tellings, some of the suspects are political or international: for example, the Cuban missile crisis and Watergate (and other political or scandalous "gates" such as Monicagate, the cause of President Bill Clinton's impeachment).

Scandalous presidents notwithstanding, one of the tropes of crisis is that it has presented itself as a faceless, corrupt and giant corporation. Or if it does have a face, it is that of an octopus, the image that the nineteenth-century American muckraking journalists used for oil and railroad monopolies. In the early years of the twenty-first century, there was Enron, whose senior management's fraudulence, with which its accounting firm Arthur Anderson was complicitous, took down both companies. If the layman knows anything about crisis, the Exxon Valdez would be top of mind. It is a compelling story with a villain (the oil company with its drunken captain and incompetent CEO), its noble victims (natives of Alaska) and its visuals (oil-soaked birds).

We are beset with a panoply of risks that has wired crisis into everyday life. Not only is it "perceptual" (Coombs, 2012), it's actuarial. As Heath and others have shown (e.g., Heath & O'Hair, 2010), crisis communication can be framed as risk communication. Which makes the management of crisis something very much like insurance. Put another way, crisis PR is, like insurance, a bet, a roll of the dice. The more elegant term is *probabilism*. As evidence, persuasion and proof, probabilistic thinking began to replace Aristotelian syllogism and the weight of expert authority a half century ago with the tradition of the philosopher Blaise Pascal (Brown, 2003). To borrow the term favored by Scott Cutlip, "effective" crisis communication is unlikely, if not impossible, without the discipline of assessing the probability and impact of risk (Cutlip, et al., 2000).

Risk and crisis go hand in hand with the digital–social age. In the era of Wikileaks, society faces the asymmetry of individual privacy expectations and the snooping realities of government and technology companies alike. In the preface to his book about the digital transformation of PR, Larry Weber (2009) cautioned as follows:

> More and more people get their news and entertainment online; print news-papers, magazines, and the nightly TV news are dying a slow death. Now, thanks to the Web, anyone, anywhere, and at any time can be a publisher, producer of distributor of content. As a result of this uncontrolled explosion or information and opinion, reputation can be made or destroyed overnight with a few clicks of the mouse. It feels a lot like the Wild West and no one knows who the last man or woman standing will be.
>
> (p. xiii)

For Weber, the American PR entrepreneur who was one of the nation's first PR practitioners to recognize the profitable opportunities the web opened for PR, Satan isn't the web itself but its reputation-destroying power. Unlike the thorough-going resignation of Edwards's (1999) theology, which promised nothing, Weber does hold out the possibility of salvation if only the sinfully ignorant organization will open its abstract heart to the gospel of the web. Then, and only then, may the organization enter the gates of Heaven where it will join with the angelic brands like Zappo's, the maker and marketer of shoes; Travelocity; Dell; H&R Block; and others who have been saved. In the digital–social era, the ubiquity and destructive-ness of crisis has become a unique selling proposition for PR firms.

Although the tone of the foregoing analysis appears to be mocking, that is not my intention. The effects are the result of the odd, ironic, and even risible friction when displaying two sensibilities, separated by three centuries, side by side. The comparison is not intended to pass any test of historicity but to discover structural similarities between two very dissimilar modes of discourse. The new gospel of postmodern, digital PR shares with great awakening Protestant revivalism a great deal: a palpable sense of grave danger and its dire consequences, and the absolute belief that nothing less than the liberation from the errors of the past can save the ignorant from certain destruction.

Experience

At this point, I switch from third-person-scholarly to first-person narrator. It is a way of reconsidering a crisis case experientially from the inside rather than analyti-cally from the outside.

It was the summer of 1984. I had moved to Boston to take my first job in a PR agency, after having worked client-side for three large firms. In my first month as an account executive, I was summoned to a meeting with the firm's president, vice president and chief of media relations. It was worse than the proverbial fire to put out. It appeared to be a crisis.

It was a quarter of century before crisis would be defined by Coombs (2012), "synthesizing" lines of research by Barton, Benoit, Fearn-Banks, Hearit, Heath, Grunig and others, as "the perception of an unpredictable event that threatens important expectancies of stakeholders and can seriously impact an organization's performance and generate negative outcomes" (p. 2).

In the meeting, I was told that more than a dozen people in the New England states of Massachusetts, Connecticut and Rhode Island had become extremely ill in the past several weeks. All had at least two things in common. They had ingested milk, and the milk had been apparently been marketed by the agency's client, a supermarket chain.

But the facts regarding the supermarket's responsibility seemed – or could be made to seem – more speculative than factual. Local newspapers in the area of the supermarket's operations had no smoking-gun evidence that tied the outbreak of illness to the supermarket, although that seemed both likely and imminent. What I recall of the PR agency's (and my) role was twofold: to draft information materials in laymen's English and to be a "team player" supporting the best interests of the firm's supermarket client. It was a role that called for rhetoric, not prevarication. But at the same time, the agency's and my role was neither primarily neutral nor analytical. My sense of what the agency was doing was consistent with Heath et al.'s (1992) "wrangle in the market place" rather than Grunig's (1992) "symmetry–excellence (Grunig, 1992).

I recall the excitement of crisis communication. It was about critical issues of health and responsibility – indeed, of life and death. The supermarket milk crisis was no press-release job. It was secret agent stuff, everything on the Q.T. and hush-hush. There was a war room atmosphere, a kind of action movie pace and feel to the goings on. I imagine it felt a bit like a PR version of investigative journalism, the equivalent of the *Washington Post* tracing Watergate money all the way up the White House chain of command. It was, in a way, far more exciting than the usual run of no-news press release writing and pitching newsless stories to harried and wised-up newspaper reporters.

The goal of the supermarket client and its vendors, the agency and law firm, was, in part, to prevent the creation of a David versus Goliath story, a standard trope of the newsroom. I learned at that first meeting that the PR agency had been contacted by the supermarket's law firm. They would handle the legal matters, the potential liability, the legal negotiations. That was their expertise and their role. The PR firm was taking its orders from two bosses, the supermarket management and its law firm. As a result, crisis PR was performed with a cast of multiple team members who, as it turned out, hadn't always the same ideas, beliefs, agendas or priorities. I did not get the sense of the agency playing more than a supporting role.

The supermarket was a high-profile, ground-level consumer business. It has chosen the PR agency for the agency's reputation as a serious "business" PR firm, rather than as a "creative" or "boutique" firm. "Business" meant the "gray matter" of finance, commercial real estate, biotech, chemicals, oil, defense. These were the kinds of businesses that the PR agency attracted. It was the reason I was hired, having come from the oil, chemical and accounting-consulting industries. I had an ant's-eye perception of the supermarket crisis. Perhaps for that reason, my perspective was bottom-up and ambiguous. I was both within and without. The crisis team was created ad hoc. I perceived belonging to the crisis team as ambiguous, tenuous, and probationary.

The ant's-eye, experiential perspective not only foregrounds perception, it validates it. Standard PR role theory would describe the supermarket in terms of the components of a system comprising strategists, liaisons, managers, and technicians. But from a lived, phenomenological perspective, those roles can only analyze and explain but not really account for the practitioner's sense of what is really happening. What I learned of crisis PR is that is not so much systematic and scientific as provisional and improvisatory.

Continuum

If we imagine crisis as a continuum, the destruction of life on Earth by a nuclear war would be at one extreme. At the other, a pizza.

PR is not only vilified by its critics for being so powerful as to undermine reality (Boorstin, 1992) and truth (Herman & Chomsky, 2002). It is equally disdained for its banality. The social–digital web has spawned a species of crisis that some practitioners refer to as *paracrises* (incidents that haven't the scope and impact of a true crisis but do resemble one; Coombs, 2012, pp. 26–27). A Boston-based PR freelancer offers another term for these phenomena: *PR crises.* The term, however, is raises questions about the "reality" of paracrises, which certainly are experienced with some of the dread faced by individuals and organizations in crisis of a clearly serious nature and consequence.

Case in point: The spit-in-the-pizza paracrisis of Domino's. Domino's is a U.S. nationwide pizza chain that became better known for its low-cost product and almost recklessly fast delivery to homes and offices than for the high quality of its pies. (It has long since reformed that risky policy.) In 2009, a pair of nitwit employees in a North Carolina Domino's backroom created a paracrisis for the brand when one of the employees stuffed mozzarella cheese up his nose and covered a pie for delivery with his nasal mucous while his coworker provided the voiceover for a YouTube video the pair posted that drew a million views (Clifford, 2013).

In the drama of a crisis, *tempus fugit.* Although senior management tends to believe that it has more important things to do than bother handling an adolescent prank in one of its kitchens, the mess must be handled. Quickly. No temporizing.

Curtain up. Act I Scene 1: Employees post their spitting YouTube video, which goes viral. Scene 2: Same day: The nasty news comes to light in Domino's boardroom. Scene 3: The Internet savages the brand. Scene 4. Domino's executives hold off responding in the hopes that the incident will blow over. Scene 5: Days later. It doesn't. Domino's posts a YouTube video to contain damage to its brand. Scene 6: Some time later. The employees are arrested and charged with food-safety violations.

In a crisis, time flies. The speed of crisis time typically far outpaces the reaction of an organization or individual caught up in a crisis. What Domino's management gambled on was that time would provide them with the ability to be silent. It didn't. The problem of time in a crisis isn't about speed. It's about meaning.

One interesting difference between many paracrises and, say, a school shooting or massive Enron-like fraud is how management experiences them. When an angry employee of a Massachusetts technology company who'd been fired returned with firearms and killed seven employees, senior management was shaken, horrified, devastated, furious. Aside from experiencing some level of those emotions, Domino's suddenly embattled CEO may well have felt something that the CEO of Edgewater probably didn't: humiliation.

The crisis continuum stretches from murder to expectoration, from grief to embarrassment. The gulf is vast that separates spitting from killing.

In June 2011, U.S. soldiers returning from a war zone were charged $2,800 as a result of the excess baggage policy of Delta Airlines. Spitting mad, the men posted a YouTube video calling out Delta. It went viral, resulting in a paracrisis for Delta. Management reacted swiftly to tweak the policy (Terkel, 2011). The crisis was lightning in a bottle.

Like other kinds of PR practices, the PR associated with the attempt to manage a crisis can be plotted as a continuum from least to most impact. Although there is a substantial distance on that continuum between the unwanted breakdown of Twitter for a morning and, say, the horrific terrorist bombing attack in 2005 on the London Underground, *crisis* is commonly applied to these very different events, even though the inability to tweet is merely a temporary inconvenience, whereas the London attack, which killed more than 50 and injured hundreds, has had a continuing and profound impact on millions worldwide.

The PR trade website PR News categorized the London Underground bombing as A very different sort of crisis, one that involved Subway, the retail sandwich chain, resulted from a social media outcry over the company's unintentionally offensive attempt at a humorous advertising campaign. An anonymous consumer posted a scathing criticism of a Subway advertisement on a social media bulletin board and e-mailed the company:

> Just a comment on your latest ad campaign. I'm referring to the one in which a man is shown being hit in the groin at the end, for no reason, not that any would justify the physical harm. I wonder why you consider this funny. Your poor taste and insensitivity has just lost you another customer – after years of supporting you, no one in my family will eat at a Subway again. Fire the ad agency, clean up your act!
>
> (PR News, 2012, posted by Scott, an anomymous user, November 24, 2012. 7:05 a.m.)

The table of contents of PR News's *Top 100 PR Case Studies* (Barnes, 2012) listed "crisis communications" (with an *s*) as the second of 11 categories of PR practice, which, in the parlance of quantitative methodology, is one data point in the investigation of the possible emerging centrality of crisis communications in the PR practice. The first category in the table of contents is "branding/rebranding," a collection of 15 disparate cases that include the campaign of Kodak – the makers of the one-time industry-standard Brownie camera – to change its out-of-fashion face by rebranding itself in a way that twenty-first-century consumers of technology would find appealing.

This instance of corporate rebranding is strongly resonant with the sociologist Erving Goffman's insight into the challenge faced by persons who suffer the condition of stigma. The "central feature of the stigmatized individual's situation can now be stated [as one of] 'acceptance'" (Goffman, 1963, p. 13).

Anthropology

In PRe, performance is not only a guiding metaphor; it is a carefully detailed, anthropologically observed staging of ritualistic events.

Not only has crisis been imagined as social drama by social scientists; it has also been called a drama in PR textbooks (Newsom, et al., 2013, p. 315) and a socio-drama (Mickey, 1995). Crisis is theater par excellence. For the anthropologist Turner (1988, p. 74), the sociologist Goffman (1959, pp. 1–2) and the performance theorist Schechner (1988, pp. 266–280), the social and political worlds are dangerous environments that disrupt the self and society and place them at risk. Across those disciplines, two contentions are argued: one, that crisis is not a peripheral, exotic or rare event, but a central and definitive one – posing a dual threat to an individual's face as well as to a social system's stability; two, that crisis is central and imminent.

Crisis is crucial to a dramaturgical perspective, whether it is Goffman's (1959) everyday life, Turner's (1988) African village life, or Schechner's (1988) life in a literally theatrical performance. For Goffman, the continual threat to "face" created the need for disciplined acting in what he called "everyday life." For Turner, observing African village tribal life, the crisis threat to an elder man's honor – and to the integrity of the tribe itself – was remedied by entering into a liminal (or in-between) state, or a pilgrimage in which a series of rituals were performed, danced and enacted until the crisis was resolved or it wasn't (Turner, 1988, p. 2). For Schechner, the face-saving, ritualistic, improvisatory, coded performances were the format of the street theater and happenings of the post-Brechtian theater. The centrality of crisis is fundamental in the theoretical construct of performance – whether in everyday life, tribal societies or in film noir (Schechner, 1988, pp. 133–134).

As Turner defined them, social dramas are "units of aharmonic or disharmonic social process, arising in conflict situations" (Turner, 1988, p. 74). These social dramas are seen to have four phases of "public action" like a play in four acts: breach, crisis, redressive action and reintegration. Initially submerged, crisis starts in the first act with a breach that widens to a crisis in the second act. Turner identified "liminal characteristics" of a crisis, where the village lingers in the *limen*, or doorway or threshold of contingency. This phase leads either to resolution or dissolution, reconciliation or antagonism. In the third act, to bring about resolution, a public ritual is performed, such as an apology. The fourth and final act crystallizes as the reintegration of the village or its dissolution.

Turner's (1988) approach to what is really happening resonates with Goffman's (1959) microsociology and Schechner's (1988) performance theory, and the organizational crisis theories of Lawrence Barton (1992) and Timothy Coombs (2012).

Religion and spirituality

If crisis has migrated to the center of PR scholarship – as it has to the center of the global stage – finding solutions has become more urgent. The results can be understood in religious and spiritual terms. In this sense, we may regard time bearing down on our civilization not unlike the way time was viewed by primitive Christianity, as recorded in Paul's letters to the Romans, and John's famous apocalyptic gospel, as well as elsewhere in the New Testament. Perhaps no concepts in Christian theology are more central than redemption and salvation, typically addressed under the rubric of soteriology (Feldmeier, 2008).

A case has been made for St. Paul's messianic communication as an ancient example of a PR practitioner (Brown, 2003). Throughout the history of Western civilization, no unique selling proposition (often referred to as "USP") has been more influential than Paul's targeted promise of salvation and redemption, which he made through special events, lectures, one-on-ones, travel tours and his letters collected in the New Testament. To primitive Christendom's priority stakeholders and customer prospects, he tailored compelling messages: salvation, redemption and spiritual rebirth. Given first-century Christianity's eschatological message of the immanent end of the kingdom of Earth, time was most certainly of the essence.

The origin of corporate social responsibility (CSR) is not high ethics but the deep crisis; not the desire to do well by doing good but the desperation to avoid annihilation. That origin theory (Brown, 2008) is a minority opinion; corporate social responsibility is conventionally framed as proactive management founded on ethics and justified, in the cliché, as "doing well by doing good." Vogel (2005) advanced a different minority concept of CSR based on the economic idea that there is a marketplace for good deeds.

That reputations are ruined and individuals and other entities seek redemption is an established religious trope. The agony – literally, the struggle – transcends mere rebranding. This too is a feature of crisis communication. Disgraced politicians and actors have sought reputational redemption on television as the "new" Richard Nixon did by playing the piano before he won the presidency in 1968, and as the adulterous Bill Clinton did when he blew his saxophone on a talk show in the overture to his presidential victory in 1992. There's no business like show business, a lesson public figures have understood since bread and circuses.

Not only do organizations invest in avoiding bad reputations, but when the inevitable crisis sullies them, they find religion. Few themes are more central to Christian theology than salvation and redemption. For Van der Watt (2005), "The message of salvation does not only stand central to virtually all the books of the New Testament, but also forms a foundation for the self-definition and identity of early Christians" (p. 1).

Mediated reality: A hybrid case of crisis communication

In the historical imagination there is a plausible association between the sacred fervent wish for redemption and the profane strategies of crisis PR and rebranding. Such was the case for the Mexican city of Rosarito Beach (Brown, 2012).

Faced by the loss of 70 percent of its tourist income during the narcotics trade violence that besieged other Mexican cities, notably Juarez, the mayor of the once Hollywood-trendy beach city of Rosarito invested in a counteroffensive strategy that combined rebranding with crisis response tactics. Emerson College film students, led by their political communication professor, created a Rosarito film festival and other events designed to reframe the conversation by revisiting the city's legacy as a romantic getaway spot for millions of Southern Californians. A media relations specialist with ties to the city was hired to pitch upbeat news stories to the San Diego and Los Angeles press and rebut the massive negativity supported by the U.S. State Department website that warned against all travel to anywhere in Mexico. Media training polished the bilingual skills of the city's mayor, in effect the CEO of the city, who recognized the path to the city's reputational redemption. What is the root meaning of *redemption*, after all, but to "deem" or judge again? To reassess in the soft light of a cinema and the sun setting so prettily over the Pacific. Crisis PR as mise-en-scène.

Anthologized in a book about international crisis communication cases (Brown, 2012), Rosarito Beach was no textbook crisis communication narrative. It was, instead, a hybrid of crisis communication and conventional PR tactics of media relations, publicity and special events.

A Google search for *rebranding* (in August 2012) yielded 2,310,000 hits, with around twice that many for *branding*. Such magnitude defines immense popularity, if not exactly universality, although both branding and its redemptive cognate have their rightful place in the bible of Internet postmodernity, Wikipedia.

For organizations and individuals, crisis transcends the claims and solutions of commerce and rises to become a spiritual matter. For this reason, what is sought is a nothing less than redemption. Not only are corporations, nongovernmental organizations, nonprofits, nation states, organizations and individual of all kinds focusing these days on branding; they are also – it can be argued – seeking redemption through the salvific rebranding strategies of CSR. Adidas, the sports marketing manufacturer, continues to publish numerous reports on CSR annually. CSR strategies – philanthropy, cause marketing, sustainability – are enthroned currently as the royal road to marketplace redemption.

PR is an everything; crisis is an ongoing thing. What makes crisis especially interesting in the social–digital era is the way it exemplifies, comments on and diverges from PR. Amid the contingency, instantaneity, globalization, utopianism and dystopianism that characterize the welter of contemporary life, crisis communication continues to attract an increasing number of PR researchers and theorists – moving crisis ever closer to the center of the PR galaxy.

References

Barnes, C. (Ed.) (2012). *Top 100 case studies in PR* (Vol. 3). New York, NY: PR News Press.
Barton, L. (1992). *Crisis in organizations: Managing and communicating in the heat of chaos.* Cincinnati, OH: Southwestern.
Benoit, W. L. (1994). *Accounts, excuses and apologies: A theory of image restoration strategies.* Albany: State University of New York.
Boorstin, D. J. (1992). *The image: A guide to pseudo events in America.* New York: Vintage.
Brown, R. E. (2003). A matter of chance: The emergence of probability and the rise of public relations. *Public Relations Review, 29*(1), 385–399.
———. (2003). Saint Paul as a Public Relations Practitioner. *Public Relations Review, 29*(1), 1–12.
———. (2008). Sea change: Santa Barbara and the eruption of corporate social responsibility. *Public Relations Review, 34*(1), 1–8.
———. (2010) Seven ways of looking at a crisis. *Vital Speeches of the Day* (Journal), 76(6): 250–254.
———. (2012). Rosarito Beach: Mediated reality and the rebranding of a Mexican border city. In A.M. George & C.B. Pratt (Eds.), *Case studies in crisis communication: International perspectives on hits and misses* (pp. 419–36). New York, NY: Wiley.
Clifford, S. (2013, May 28). Video prank at Domino's taints brand. *New York Times.* Retrieved from www.nytimes.com/2009/04/16/business/media/16dominos.html?_r=0
Coombs, W. T. (2012). *Ongoing crisis communication.* Thousand Oaks, CA: Routledge.
Cutlip, S. M., Center, A. H., Broom, G. M. (2000). *Effective public relations.* Englewood Cliffs, NJ: Prentice-Hall.
Eagleman, D. (2011). *Incognito: The secret lives of the brain.* New York, NY: Pantheon.
Edwards, J. (1999). Sinners in the hands of an angry god. In W. H. Kimnach, R. H. Minkema & D. A. Sweeney (Eds.), *The Sermons of Jonathan Edwards* (pp. 49–68). New Haven, CT: Yale University Press.
Edwards, L. (2012). Defining the "object" of public relations research: A new starting point. *Public Relations Inquiry, 1*(1), 7–30.
Feldmeier, R. (2008). *The first letter of Peter.* Waco, TX: Baylor University Press.
Goffman, E. (1959). *The presentation of self in everyday life.* New York, NY: Anchor Doubleday.
———. (1963). *Stigma: Notes on the management of spoiled identity.* Englewood Cliffs, NJ: Prentice-Hall.
Grunig, J. E. (1992). *Excellence in public relations and communications management.* Mahway, NJ: Lawrence Erlbaum.
Hearit, K. M. (2005). *Crisis management by apology: Corporate response to allegations of wrongdoing.* New York, NY: Routledge.
Heath, R. L. (1992). A wrangle in the market place : Rhetorical perspectives of public relations. In E. L. Toth (Ed.), *Rhetorical and critical approaches to public relations* (pp. 17–36). Hillsdale, NJ: Lawrence Erlbaum.

Heath, R. L. & O'Hair, H. D. (Eds.). (2010). *Handbook of risk and crisis communication.* New York, NY: Routledge.

Herman, E. S. & Chomsky, N. (2002). *Manufacturing consent: The political economy of the mass media.* New York: Pantheon Books.

L'Etang, J. (1996). Public relations and rhetoric. In J. L'Etang and M. Pieczka (Eds.), *Critical perspectives in public relations*, pp. 106–123. London: International Thomson Business Press.

Mickey, T. (1995). *Sociodrama: An interpretive theory for the practice of public relations.* Lanham, MD: University Press of America.

Mitroff, I. (2003). *Crisis leadership: Planning for the unthinkable.* New York, NY: Wiley.

Newsom, D. Turk, J. & Kruckeberg, D. (2013). *This is PR: The realities of public relations.* Independence, KY: Cengage Learning.

Pavlik, J. V. (1987). *Public relations: What the research tells us.* Newbury Park, CA: Sage.

PR News. (2012). Post by Scott, an anomymous user. Nov. 24, 2012. 7:05 a.m. http://news.mensactivism.org/articles/03/11/23/195249.shtml

Schechner, R. (1988). *Performance theory.* New York, NY: Routledge.

Swann, P. (2010). *Cases in public relations management.* New York, NY: Routledge.

Taleb, N. (2010). *The black swan: The impact of the highly improbable.* New York: Random House

Terkel, A. (2011). Delta charges U.S. troops returning from Afghanistan $2,00 in Baggage Fees. *Huffington Post.* Retrieved from www.huffingtonpost.com/2011/06/08/delta-troops-afghanistan-baggage-fees_n_873027.html

Turner, V. (1988). *The anthropology of performance.* New York, NY: PAJ.

Unamuno, M de.(1978). *The tragic sense of life in men and nations.* Trans., A. Kerrigian. Princeton, NJ: Princeton University Press.

———. (2005). *The tragic sense of life.* New York, NY: Public Domain Books.

van der Watt, J. G. (2005). (Ed.). *Perspectives on the New Testament: Perspectives on soteriology.* (Supplements to Novum Testamentum.). Leiden, The Netherlands: Brill Academic Publishing.

Vogel, D. (2005). *The market for virtue: The potential and limits of corporate social responsibility.* Washington, DC: Brookings Institution Press.

Weber, L. (2009). *Sticks and stones: How digital reputations are created over time and lost in a click.* Hoboken, NJ: Wiley.

3　Face

Our bodies always participate in the everyday world, whatever our interest at the time, this participation implying a capacity to affect and be affected by the everyday world.

Erving Goffman (1974/1986, p. 5)

What exactly is *face?* And how can *face* help us understand (as Goffman might have put it) what really happens in public relations (PR)? Although PR is not sociology, sociological insights open fresh ways of understanding the dynamics of reputation and of the public relations of everything (PRe). Face and reputation contextualize each other.

In a post-symmetric era of PR, face provides a broader frame for reputation than Grunigian communication management. What happens on the stage of PR is about why and how the actors arrange their own faces and the faces of their clients and organizations.

Facework composes PR. It would not be an exaggeration to say that PR comprises the problematics of face. Few adages about PR are more common than "perception is reality." It is a saying that implies the starting point of PR practice – the recognition that reputation lies outside the practitioner's and the organization's locus of control. PR practitioners are engaged in a perceptually corrective effort. The Public Relations Society of America, the trade organization of PR, has followed the PR scholarship of the past generation's abandonment of PR as persuasion. The trade organization now frames PR as an adjustment of perception (really, of misperception) in the public interest. Missing from the PR industry's definition is the conflictual drama of face:

> Public relations is a strategic communication process that builds mutually beneficial relationships between organizations and their publics.
>
> (www.prsa.org)

Influenced by Goffman, as so many sociologists were, the social linguists Brown and Levinson (1987) conceptualized face as a quality that carries an emotional investment and can be lost, maintained or enhanced but is constantly in play.

Although people generally cooperate in supporting face claims, face is neverthe-less vulnerable (Brown, & Levinson, 1987, p. 86).

Brown and Levinson (1987) adopted the economic drama of investments in risky marketplace investments. Face concerns itself with commonly understood matters of dignity and respect, as well as honor and prestige. The bivalent, or two-faced, nature of face, as theorized by Brown and Levinson, is also present in Goff-man's persistently, vulnerably and dramatic concept of face. Maintaining it is well described by the poet Lawrence Ferlinghetti's (1968) snapshot of the poet as an acrobat "constantly risking absurdity/and death/whenever he performs." Looked at another way, PR's nucleus is composed largely of contingency, risk and crisis. For Brown and Levinson, as for Goffman, face carries within it the seeds of risk and crisis. It is something to be protected as well as projected.

Reputation, one of PR's most familiar themes, can be understood as the issues associated with face. If the center of PR is crisis, what's at stake is nothing less than face. In this sense, facework comprises the practices of PR as both claims and defenses.

From the crisis perspective that informs PRe, face is not merely static but typi-cally endangered. Face's conflictual nature is magnified because it is forever in play. Face is perpetually vulnerable, contingent, and situational, as well as percep-tual. It is something not entirely in one's possession, the very opposite of manage-ment. One is reminded of the philosopher Ortega Gasset's observation about animals in nature. When they are not sleeping, they are perpetually wary. Wariness is such a compelling feature of PR that it poses a serious challenge to the conven-tional idea of PR as that which can be managed. While PR concerns itself with such positive matters as recognition, endorsement and fame, the work of PR, like the management of face, is concerned with mistakes, failure, stigma, problems and crisis.

Two observations can be made about face as a way of talking about PR. First, that face's universality is consistent with the thinking about PR in the broad sense of everything, everyone and everywhere, which is Principle 1 in Chapter 1 in this book. Second, that the bivalent concept of face is consistent with the idea of PR as dramatic and thus conflictual.

To see the significance of face is to grasp the essence of PRe. Both the concepts of face and PRe suggest nothing less than the humanistic vision that the life of every individual must be considered a struggle, whether apparent or hidden. To a significant degree, PR is bound up with the attempt to avoid, prepare for, identify, respond to and otherwise manage crisis.

In the center of the PR galaxy, reputation finds itself locked in a dialogue with crisis. Opinion orbits around it and is attracted or repelled. Shakespeare's Iago, that villainous actor, was adamant on that point:

Good name in man and woman, dear my lord,
Is the immediate jewel of their souls.
Who steals my purse steals trash; 'tis something, nothing;
'Twas mine, 'tis his, and has been slave to thousands;

But he that filches from me my good name
Robs me of that which not enriches him,
And makes me poor indeed.
                    (Shakespeare, 1936, Act III
                              Scene 3, 155–161)

The metaphorical embodiment of name – of reputation – is face. Claims are made for it, demeanor is arranged on it, and as Iago says, nothing is more important than saving it.

In the close examination of face, PR may borrow profitably not only from the arts but from sociology. PR is, after all, a human and social institution. Creative and strategic energy swirls around the manifestations of face.

Goffman (1963), who explored face in the presentation of self in everyday life, expressed no interest in either PR or politics. But the theory of dramaturgy, which he innovated, offers PR scholarship ways of thinking about opinion, reputation, relationships, perception, and crisis. Goffman was skeptical that the discipline of communication was adequate to provide the granular answers he sought to the question of what really goes on in human encounters – face to face, in public, in such "total institutions" as prisons and mental hospitals. That microsociological perspective required something he regarded as less static, larger and more dynamic than anything communication or information alone could offer. What he chose instead was quasi-metaphorical: life as theater, humans as social actors challenged in a variety of scenes to make claims for and protect their face, while reading and responding to the faces of others.

What such dramaturgy has in common with PR is the centrality of risk, crisis, performance and reputation. In the social theater, the actor's face is endangered.

In the theaters of microsociology and PR, reputation is contingent, and everything moves toward or away from a crisis. The source of dramatic interest in this theater is about the interplay of reputation and crisis, a facial drama. The digital–social revolution has intensified the dramatic core of PR by underscoring both the asset value of reputation and its fragility. As the digital PR entrepreneur Larry Weber (2009) wrote, a digital reputation created over time can be lost in a click.

What makes dramaturgy especially relevant to PR is the way PR agencies and departments now rush to invest in resources to monitor and respond to the persistence of risk. Saving face is no longer a PR specialty. In the digital–social era, with its trolls and other masked vigilantes, PR has become a vigil. Among PR's characteristic differences from advertising and marketing is its pervasive sense of paranoia. (As the old joke goes, even paranoids have enemies.)

Terminology

Like Kenneth Burke, Goffman was a master builder of a highly developed, self-referential terminological universe (Burke, 1969). In Burke, dramatism, rhetoric of motives, rhetoric grammar; in Goffman, dramatic discipline, civil inattention, stigma. Where the object of Burke's focus was literature, social life occupied Goffman. In

Interaction Ritual, Goffman wrote, "The term face may be defined as the positive social value a person effectively claims for himself by the line others assume he has taken during a particular contact" (1967/2005, p. 5). To clarify his terms, Goffman took pains to note that "a line [is] a pattern of verbal and nonverbal acts by which [every person] expresses his view of the situation and through this his evaluation of the participants, especially himself" (p. 5), and further, that "face is an image of self delineated in terms of approved social attributes – albeit an image that others may share, as when a person makes a good showing for his profession or religion by making a good showing of himself." (p. 5).

Metaphor

Like an organization's connection with its brand, in dramaturgy the individual is "attached" to his face and *cathects* (emotionally encodes) his face with each encounter in a visible and invisible way. Encounter by encounter, the individual's face can either be "sustained," in which case he will have "few feelings" about the matter. Or if the individual actor's face is not sustained, then her "ordinary expectations are unfulfilled" and she will "feel bad" or "feel hurt." Alternatively, if "events establish a face for him that is better than he might have expected, he is likely to 'feel good' " (Goffman, 1967/2005, p. 6).

In the objectifying and abstracting mode of scientific discourse, dramaturgy wraps quotes around "feelings" in order to get an unobstructed view of the actor on the stage.

Because PR is a social institution whose members are not only organizations in the abstract but persons in the flesh, Goffman's descriptions of the strategies of face claims and defenses are suggestive of the dynamics of PR and its practitioners. He said, "Every person lives in a world of social encounters" (Goffman, 1967/2005, p. 5). Dramaturgy, like symmetry–excellence, is a system, but it's a far more highly articulated and lifelike system than the systems theory that underlies symmetry–excellence.

It's not that facework lacks emotion but that the quotes the sociologist wraps around good and bad "feelings" indicate that something more than emotion alone is happening when a person is in a social situation. That something comprises the social rules that govern the actual interaction and the metaphorical drama. These are the rules that, among the complexity and conflict, enable the existence of civil society.

Faceoff

Where sociology conceives of facework as the claims an individual makes to provide the perceptual legitimacy of his face, the facework of PR comprises the sum total of the work associated with branding and reputation. More broadly speaking, facework is the dramatic performances driving the creation of relationships and identity. PR terminology – *media relations, community relations, consumer relations* – directs our attention to the kind of investments practitioners make, value, defend, and protect. This could be called the policing function of PR. Sociologically speaking, identity is not a thing-in-itself or owned by a self. It is instead the product of interactive dramaturgy. It is a challenging and counterintuitive perspective that recalls nothing so much as the title of the Stevens (1959) poem, "The Good Man Has No Shape."

The pressing problem of PR is not its claim to present a scientific face but its strenuous efforts to save its face. Its reputation attacked on multiple fronts, it is unsurprising that modern PR has continued its battle to rebrand itself as an applied social science. Because persuasion is not consistent with science, symmetry theory has needed to dismiss persuasion as "asymmetric" and manipulative. Bernaysian persuasion could be disqualified, along with it much of the history of PR. The effort to rebrand PR as a science offers an explanation for Grunig's war against persuasion because persuasion is at cross-purposes with the bias-free, randomized epistemology of science (Grunig & Hunt, 1984).

Sociology

But whether scientific or merely "scientistic" (i.e., not truly scientific but posing as science), PR has always been social, relational, human, emotional and dramatic. It is the richness of those dimensions that may have moved Goffman to voice his skepticism that communication was a large enough frame to account for the dramatic nature of interaction. Following Goffman, the anthropologist Victor Turner (Turner & Bruner, 1986) observed the ritualistic interactions in African and South American villages as "social drama" (pp. 33–46).

A great deal has been researched and written about PR as applied communication or communication management, but precious little attention has been paid to PR as a drama, as a social institution or as a drama of everyday life. Yet few practitioners would deny that the effectiveness of what they do depends as much on dramatic action as it does on strategic planning.

Why risk going off the rails with radical reconsiderations of PR from outside the well-established frames of communication theory? Far from radical, PR abounds with scholarship from the margins. Much of PR's marginal scholarship has been of the critical and historical variety, such as Kruckeberg and Stark's (1988) "reconstructed theory" of PR as emerging from a historical tradition of community and cooperation.

This sort of thinking from the disciplinary margins inspired the organizers of the somewhat ironically named gathering of Radical PR scholars. In the summer of 2008, a conference of qualitatively oriented scholars of PR, organized by a group led by Jacquie L'Etang, was staged at Stirling University in Scotland. It brought together several dozen scholars whose publications have approached PR from a wide variety of postsymmetric, qualitative perspectives that L'Etang (2008) categorized broadly as "critical." The so-called radicals were selected from Europe, Australia, New Zealand, South America and the United States. They presented papers that approached PR outside the box of organizational communication theory and from the perspective of sociology, intellectual capital, ethnography, cultural theory, feminism, historiography, postcolonialism, postmodernism and rhetoric.

L'Etang (2008) observed in her critical-thinking PR textbook that PR "can be seen as a form of sociology, even though the sociology of PR is a term barely heard" (p. 5). The scholarly call to another discipline is certainly warranted. But perhaps it is not that PR is a form of sociology but that both can be seen to emerge from, and exist within, a larger and more inclusive idea of the humanities.

The besieged face of public relations

As PR practitioners doubtless know, PR is work. The titles of PR textbooks include such workaday terms as *practice, analysis, planning, tools, tactics, strategy, relationship development, management* and *results*. These heady, in-the-trenches descriptions of PR are at a far remove from the commonly held idea of PR as unearned publicity, spin and spectacle.

But what informs the work of PR? Unlike the muscular and repetitive work of certain kinds of manual labor, the work of PR is typically fraught with struggle. In the popular imagination, among a spectrum of journalists and academics, PR is perceived as illegitimate. In such critiques, PR is portrayed less as honest work than as a rigged game, lacking in seriousness, yet often about the manipulation of serious issues and/or important business.

In its own facial dynamics, PR struggles from two critiques: one that it is a master manipulator, the other (as a colleague of mine once characterized it) that it is set up to fail. Illogically enough, some individuals would appear to believe in both PR's power and its impotence.

Because it can be imagined as both impotent and powerful, PR continues to be an easy target. Boorstin's (1961/1987) dismissal of the ethical legitimacy of E. L. Bernays (1965; the "pioneer" of textbook PR and of PR itself as "pseudo-events") falls into the conventional historiography of PR as a modern American institution and therefore a pastiche of Wild West tall stories, hokum and manipulation. Boorstin portrayed PR as at once apparent, obvious and deceptive, an unsubtle collection of ruses that trick the gullible consumer who ought to know better (Boorstin, 1961/1987). Walter Lippmann's (1922) low opinion of the masses, which influenced Bernays, falls into a similar framing of PR.

Other critics of PR have represented PR as a vast, all-encompassing political and cultural conspiracy. Most well known for such dark views is Noam Chomsky, who has portrayed PR as an economic and political menace loosed on weaker nations by America. In a similarly harsh vein, Guy Debord mashed up PR, advertising, and hyperconsumerism as the quintessentially American creation of the dystopia he called "the society of the spectacle" (Debord, 2000).

These critiques of PR can be distinguished by whether they imagine PR to be visible and ridiculous, or hidden and tragic. In the latter perspectives – those of Chomsky and Debord – the unstated assumption about PR is that it is work – regrettable and egregious, but work, nonetheless (Herman & Chomsky, 2002). The former perspective – Boorstin's – is that PR doesn't rise to the level of work. In the literary critical terms that

Northrup Frye (1957) might have applied here, PR was classified by Boorstin as comedy, the genre of winter, where Chomsky and Debord would place it in Frye's generic category of tragedy, the genre of fall.

The dramaturgy of face

Goffman, from whose dramaturgical social ideas the theories of Brown and Levinson (1987) derive, was quite clear that for him, face is work. Goffman taxonomized the effort, skill, practice and rehearsal required by facework. The concept of face in Brown and Levinson's theory of politeness derived from Goffman's idea of life not only as theater but as struggle. Creative, imaginative, inventive, planned and improvisatory, facework is work the self does in such a persistent and effortful way as to constitute a definition of self in dramatic, theatrical terms. The self is an actor performing a role or roles in a constantly changing series of scenes with other actors in front of an audience on the stage. PR scholarship's concept of role is rather more narrowly framed as two circumscribed organizational functions – expert prescriber and technician (Dozier, 1992). The conceptualization is misleadingly static and circumscribed and fails to capture the provisional realities of role. Lattimore, et al., (2007) enlarged the frame when they defined *role* in PR in task terms as "the collection of daily activities that people do" (p. 52).

Another sociologist mining the theory of dramaturgy, Arlie Hochschild, rejected Goffman's idea of the self as blind to the investment in, and cost of, emotion. Investigating the interactions of flight attendants with passengers, and of debt collectors with debtors, Hochschild (1983/2003) found what she called the "commercialization of human feeling," the subtitle of her book. Hochschild diverged from Goffman, whose concept of the self, Hochschild contended, derived from Darwin's theory of emotions, which was not based on the observation of people in society but of the interaction of animals. In his tour-de-force and most famous work of microsociology, Goffman itemized what he called "the arts of impression management" (1959, pp. 208–237). *Impression management* has long been a term of art in PR, one that has a close parallel in sociology.

What the arts of impression management reveal is the primacy of threat and crisis inherent in the act of communication. One is reminded of the facetiously insightful title of former Intel CEO Andy Grove's (1996) professional memoir, *Only the Paranoid Survive*. In attempting to portray oneself, the individual – or to use the theatrical metaphor, *actor* – is severely challenged at virtually every turn to avoid any little gesture (gaffe) or verbal reference that could instantly degrade the performance.

The sword of contingency hangs over the head of the communicator in every imaginable situational array. The performer may spoil the self that he or she is attempting to present, whether face to face, in small groups or teams, large groups, public speeches, press conferences or in mass-mediated situations. As for the mass media, the notorious performance-discrediting example of U.S. presidential candidate Richard Nixon's makeup running down his cheeks under the hot lights of a televised debate with his opponent John F. Kennedy exemplifies the discrediting of a face in Goffman's sociological sense.

Not only are individuals prone to losing face with unmeant gestures in one-on-one interactions, but they also face the loss of their credibility in general.

Risk to face is a constant in the dramaturgic world. Goffman advanced a collection of do's and don'ts that reveal the enormous challenges to face credibility (Goffman, 1959, 1966, 1967/2005, 1971/2010, 1974/1986, 1979). Goffman's interest here was less in communication itself and more in the broader dimensions of theatrical performance. Not only is the actor responsible for the face credibility of his own body, the stage and backstage regions must also be carefully managed to avoid loss of face. In Goffman's inventively terministic universe, the actor must be careful to manage the *regions* of a performance (1959, pp. 106–139). Both the *front stage* and the *back stage* must be attended to, lest an unwanted observer see by accident or on purpose what was not meant for certain others to see. After or before the actor delivers an effective performance on the front stage – the account executive pitching business at a meeting with management – there is the risk that when the account executive returns to his office, or back stage, with the expectation of privacy, that the client (*intruder, outsider*) could breach the boundary and "catch those present flagrante delicto" in the act of firing a dart into a poster of the client. The account: down the drain.

Actors know their body is their instrument. Their performance may be ruined by "unmeant gestures, intrusions, and faux pas" (Goffman, 1974/1986, p. 210). Even more dramatically, perhaps, are *scenes* that obstreperously or violently spoil the actor's facework, or performance. (One mustn't cause a scene!) A personal example remains with me after more than 20 years. As a consultant to a PR firm in Boston, I witnessed a scene in which one of the 15-person agency's two vice presidents – a woman in her 20s – screwed up her courage, opened the door of her VP male counterpart and shut the door behind her; what followed was a good deal of shouting. I never learned was the argument was about, but it penetrated the office for a short few minutes. The staff could not help hearing a shouting match. The account executives, receptionist, intern and I – distracted by the half-heard verbal commotion in the other room – looked at and then away from the battle-ground office, and then at each other with varying degrees of incredulity and embarrassment, attempting without success to enact a face-saving performance of our own. It wasn't our own faces we were seeking to save; it was those of the combatants. This strategic act to appear unaware of an activity an actor understands he is not meant to see or hear is what Goffman called *civil inattention* (Goffman, 1971/2010, p. 83). At the same time, that "strip of experience" exemplifies how an audience engages in face-saving actions of its own. As that anecdote illustrates, the audience, too, is an integral part of the actors' performances, and like the actors engages in facework.

Branded faces

In the era of Facebook, when media is consumed on large and small screens, it should come as no surprise to learn that the importance of face can hardly be exaggerated. A 3-year study sponsored by the MacArthur Foundation looked at the web habits of young people. Researchers interviewed more than 800 young people and their parents and observed teenagers online for more than 5,000 hours, according to an article in the *New York Times.* Among the chief findings was that teenagers not only have a public image, but they are also "learning how to manage a public identity" (Lewin, 2008).

Dan Schawbel (2008), soon after his graduation from college, made a compelling case for reputation construction in the age of Facebook. Notwithstanding the debates about the differences between brand and reputation, the concerns associated with them are congruent, even if their tactics may vary. Personal branding is dramaturgy for the Facebook generation. It concerns itself with ways to build awareness, recognition, and reputation, although Schawbel did not concern himself much with risk, crisis and spoilage. The index to Schawbel's book *Me 2.0* has 10 references to *branding* and five to *public relations,* including a 10-page section devoted to "personal press releases," "personal press kits" and "maintaining good blogger relations" (2008, pp. 155–265).

What Schawbel (2008) never explicitly argued is what is implicit in his facial pragmatics: the trend toward convergence. Social media has resulted in the merger not only of brand and PR but of the public with the personal. That much is suggested by Schawbel's subhead, "Technology and the Brand YOU" (p. 16). The trend toward convergence – particularly with respect to new technologies – has spawned a considerable literature of its own (Brown, 2010). As for the convergence of person and brand, Schawbel argued that in the social media age they've become one and the same – at least for the pragmatics of Schawbel's job-hunting undergraduate demographic:

> As an individual, you must acknowledge that you are a brand.
>
> (Schawbel, 2008, p. 1)

Personal branding dictates new strategies and new ways of conceiving of the self as well as the media. When everyone is in the media, self-branding job seekers have the tools of publishing, packaging, dissemination and evaluation at their fingertips. Personal branding leverages multiple forms of convergence. The literature of PR has, until recently, taken a very different approach to conceptualization, steering clear of convergence, perhaps to make a face claim for PR. Traditionally, the industry has insisted on PR as a "distinctive" management function. But the disruptive, creative destruction and hierarchical flattening of the digital–social era has replaced PR's self-concept of distinctiveness with the all-inclusive dynamic of convergence. Voice and data, marketing, advertising, PR, personal branding, political campaigning – conducted simultaneously, evaluated instantly and algorithmically. The literature and the industry itself have devoted considerable energy over many decades to distinguish PR from its rivals, advertising, marketing and branding. Basic introductory courses in PR, as well as the textbooks that form their intellectual legitimacy, take pains to ensure that PR is recognized as something different from anything that could be conflated with it, such as word of mouth. Facebook and Twitter are defined down as "tools," subservient to the higher goals and sophisticated operations of PR. More typical of the textbook approach to facework is a statement like the following one about the relative merits of Facebook and face-to-face communication in the workplace:

Of course, every organization and every communications situation are differ-ent, but broadly speaking, in employee relations, face-to-face beats Facebook.
(Guth & Marsh, 2011)

The dramatic, face-claiming nature of personal, face-to-face communication recalls the roots of PR as speech, rhetoric and persuasion. Textbook authors quote the advice given by a recent inductee into the Public Relations Society of America's Atlanta chapter. Speaking to students at his induction, he offered a tip learned decades before from his own mentor: your highest priority should be to return all phone calls before any other work is done (Wilcox, et al., 2000).

Vulnerability

The instability of reputation and brand is one of the most frequent subjects of advice to persons and organizations, as well as nations. Loss of face – and thus reputation – is the angle of innumerable news stories in a U.S. election year. When, in a televised interview at the start of the summer 2012 Olympics in London, U.S. presidential candidate Mitt Romney cast doubt on the competency of Great Britain's preparations as a host, his aspersions made him the target of the ire of London's mayor, England's prime minister, and the butt of face-spoiling headlines like the one in the *New York Post* that read "MITT-WIT" (Daily Kos, 2012).

Such gaffes make news and damage face, reputation and, in the case of a politi-cal candidate, electability, the gold standard of candidacy. For Mr. Romney, that gaffe was very bad PR. Political campaigning in the endless campaign of U.S. elections is a minefield for a candidate's credibility. Competition is fierce among organizational rivals over such marketing matters as products and market penetra-tion. But the political environment raises the stakes. Campaign speech is PR on steroids, with fire and crossfire, accusation, allegation, hyperbole and distortion employed to create a crisis for candidates.

Among Goffman's itemization of impression-management arts, among the most essential for face management are dramaturgical discipline and dramatic circumspec-tion, or prudence. The following examples illustrate two kinds of face-management failure. The first is from *The Sweet Smell of Success,* a mid-twentieth-century novel about an emblematically sleazy publicity agent. In the scene, Sidney Falco, the anti-heroic publicity man, tries explaining to Susan, the younger sister of J. J. Hunsecker, the powerful and ruthless gossip columnist, the very worst thing that she could ever do to Hunsecker. What Susan wants is to persuade her brother to give his blessing to her plans to marry a man Hunsecker despises. Susan asks Falco's advice:

"So do tell me, Sidney. I'm only his sister."

I brushed it aside, shaking my head. "The worst thing you can ever do to J. J. is show him that he's wrong. If you want to win him over, you have to give him an out, you have to let him save face."
(Lehman, 1957/2007, p. 25)

Saving face

Face, like PR, is a two-way street, a "diatonic" aspect of PR that has been noted by many PR scholars, notably at mid-century by Goldman (1948). (Today, however, the streets are more like British roundabouts – they run every which way, not two ways.) Sociologically, facework amounts to a structural–functional consensus that involves self and other. A disciplined performer must take pains not to undermine the other's agreement to the performer's face claims. Face is not stable. It is perceptual, contingent and at perpetual risk. Face challenges PR with the task of saving it. What's at stake is more than a willingness to change, that symmetry-theory objective. What's at stake is the risk of losing face and, with it, reputation, brand and everything.

Symbolism

The communication adage that "context gives meaning" is a dramatic perspective. Whether in Burke's literary dramatism, Goffman's microsociology, scholar Richard Schechner's (1977/1988) performance studies, anthropologist Victor Turner's social drama (Turner & Bruner, 2001) or anthropologist Gregory Bateson's (2000) dramatics of play, dramaturgy seeks to understand "what is it that is happening here." It does this not by speculating on the causes of human behavior but on their context.

Goffman, who is credited (along with Burke) with the development of dramaturgical theory, created a highly descriptive terministic universe. His terms – *gestures, moves, contrivances, mystifications, facework, region management, dramaturgical discipline, civil inattention* – express a vision of a self wholly composed of face-claiming and face-protecting strategies. It is a self in all but perpetual motion, almost never at rest or at peace. Yet the sum total of these gestures and moves account for how society can exist in the first place.

That perspective has long seemed to me an interesting, if nontraditional, approach to what happens in PR. In Turner's African villages, Schechner's Balinese ritual theater, and Goffman's hospitals, asylums and face-to-face encounters, it is possible to see the drama of PR on the ground level. The diurnal drama of PR practice is itself a social drama of its actors' face claims, unmeant gestures, inopportune intrusions and faux pas, as well as their more obvious strips of creativity (one of Goffman's neologisms), blogger hits and new business pitches.

A keen observer of gestures, Bernays (1965) recalled an initial meeting with Washington Hill, an advertising industry mogul with an intimidating reputation as the holy terror of advertising. Bernays recalled that Hill wore a sombrero, which Bernays interpreted symbolically as a kingly crown (Bernays, 1965, p. 367). In Goffman's terms, Hill's sombrero-wearing behavior is a *sign* whose meaning Bernays assessed. As a kind of metonymy (or symbolic displacement), Hill strategically and theatrically chose to present his face, so to speak, as a sombrero. Bernays interpreted Hill's face claim as the behavior of a monarch. Indeed, the sombrero was more than a hat. It functioned as the face of the monarchial magnate.

Because Bernays was the nephew of Sigmund Freud, it is not surprising that symbolism would play a central role in his epistemology. The influence of Freud on the significance of symbolism was among the dominant ideas of the first half of the twentieth century. When the lips are silent, Freud said, the fingertips ooze symbolism (Freud & Rieff, 1963).

Dramaturgical discipline

Anyone who follows American political campaigns is likely to be familiar with the caution to candidates that they "stay on message." When a candidate, public figure, business executive or, in some cases, a private individual wanders "off script" and departs from agreed-on talking points, face management is at risk. Face, reputation and brand are perceptual. The impression manager's face is held hostage by the audience.

In Goffman's terminology, facework depends upon *dramaturgical discipline*. The disciplined actor is "someone who remembers his part and does not commit unmeant gestures or faux pas in performing it" (Goffman, 1959, p. 216). Following the explosion of a BP oil platform in the Gulf of Mexico, killing 11 of his employees and spilling millions of gallons of oil into the Gulf, company CEO Tony Hayward was notoriously, dramatically undisciplined with his tactless response to a reporter's question about the tragedy. Evidently forgetting the larger issues and focusing on his annoyance with the negative publicity, Hayward said, in a widely seen and replayed awkward interview moment, "I want my life back!"

Disruption

If a generation or two ago, business leaders were lionized for creating conglomerates, in the digital–social era the plaudits are going to the lords of disruption. In the spirit of Joseph Schumpeter's creative destruction, Facebook, Twitter, Google, Instagram and YouTube have made innovation a god of industry destruction. Down went one business and communication model after another – print newspapers, "sage-on-the-stage" teaching, face-to-face banking. These models have been quickly overrun by online media, massively open online courses (MOOCs), ATMs and smartphone apps. People whose livelihood had been based on those skills were also replaced by new, typically younger people with relevant skills.

Although much has changed, some things have remained the same. One of these things was described by Goffman as the skills of maintaining dramaturgic discipline. A politician, public affairs officer, CEO, lower level spokesperson or any individual in everyday life may discover how costly or fatal it is to commit a gaffe. Elections are lost, customers disappear, friendships sour off- and online, marriages fray and break. The "crucial test of one's ability as a performer" is the ability to keep in check not only one's message, but at a more biologically behavioral level, "one's face and voice" (Goffman, 1959, p. 217).

What hasn't changed in an era of disruptive innovation is the art of performance.

What's interesting about the management of face and voice is that it indicates a PR paradox. On the surface, the task of face and voice management is at once desirable, rational, objective, strategic and necessary for the maintenance of good reputation, brand maintenance and healthy relationships with internal and external constituencies.

There is no evidence that relationships in the practice of PR are any easier to nurture than relationships in other practices. The management of relationships is prone to the ruptures of Goffman's unmeant gestures and gaffes. Face management coexists uneasily with an array of undermining forces. These include the individual's conflicts and anxieties. Relationships are also undermined by subordinates, supervisors, competitors, anonymous commenters, gossipers, reporters, regulators, adversaries and enemies.

The actor must also be sufficiently disciplined to gracefully manage daily "supportive interchanges," and an individual who lacks this skill risks giving offense (Goffman, 1971/2010, p. 28). Thus, when a young PR intern passes by her account executive supervisor as they cross paths from cubicle to meeting room, the intern must make certain to express a greeting that obeys the organizational norms of such exchanges. Her greeting must demonstrate her command of verbal and nonverbal norms relative to her length of service and the existing nature of her relationship with her supervisor. The intern must also understand how her supervisor accurately perceives her, as opposed to guessing about how her supervisor perceives her. Failure to acknowledge her supervisor with a ritual "Hi," and possibly an accompanying gestural wave of her hand in passing, would risk giving offense and spoiling her face. In fact, her greeting should not be in any way inappropriate to the relational situation. She dare not descend to the inappropriate informality of a "Yo!" or a thumbs-up sign, unless informality is warranted by the relationship and the organizational culture.

The unequal status of intern and supervisor is an example of a common asymmetry in the workplace. The intern's supervisor, who occupies a higher status position than the intern, enjoys a broader palette of expressive choices. The supervisor may register approval by means of a broad smile or a nonleering, good-natured wink. But if the supervisor does not acknowledge the intern passing by (even unintentionally), the worried intern may perceive the meant or unmeant gesture as face spoiling. Trumbull (2004), an art historian, reviewed the history of the smile across the spectrum of its meanings from clarity to ambiguity.

Prudence

The management of face is "ongoing," to borrow Coombs's (2012) term for crisis communication. Facework, like crisis communication, is emotionally costly, as Hochschild (1983/2003) demonstrated in her observations of flight attendants, debt collectors and others who do what she called "emotional labor." Such labor must be performed with a seamless grace that conceals the performer's anxiety and distastefulness so that the labor may be considered an art. What informs that art is prudence, or *dramaturgical circumspection* in Goffman's terminology as early as

The Presentation of Self in Everyday Life (1959, p. 218). Regarding the members of a working team, the ethos needs to be the *dramaturgical loyalty* (p. 212) of each and every member:

> Prudence must be exercised. When there is little chance of being seen, opportunities for relaxation can be taken; when there is little chance of being put to the a test, the cold facts can be presented in a glowing light and the performers can play their part for all it is worth, investing it with full dignity.
>
> (Goffman, 1959, p. 218)

Silence

> Speech after long silence; it is right.
>
> William Butler Yeats

No comment is not only a poor choice for most sticky PR situations; it can be fatal for a PR job candidate.

The director of PR for a prominent communications agency in Boston told me that the interns I sent to her were doing very nicely, thank you – and could I please send a few more? But only ones that talk. Asked to explain, she cautioned, "I have no use for anyone who just sits there in a meeting and says nothing."

Which gives her something in common with King Lear. In Act I Scene 1, the King asks his daughters to tell him how much they love him. The duplicitous Regan and Goneril, seeking the King's favor of a large inheritance, are effusive. But when Lear asks Cordelia to speak, the good daughter, who truly loves her father, will not only refuse to hype, but like a J.D. Salinger child–saint character, takes refuge in the temple of silence:

> Nothing, my lord.
>
> Nothing will come of nothing.
>
> (Shakespeare, 1936, p. 1197)

Silence communicates – or it doesn't. The sociolinguist Adam Jaworski (1993) began his investigation of the linguistics of silence by posing a question: "Why do native speakers of the same language sometimes not understand each other in conversation?" (p. 2). Jaworski explicitly stated that miscommunication is what's central about silence. For both speaker and listener, silence is problematic and ambiguous. Whether silence's ambiguity is strategic is another matter. In framing organizational communication as "strategic ambiguity," Eisenberg (2007) implied a major role for what is left carefully unsaid.

If silence is ambiguous, it must follow that PR is, too. If so, that would account in a novel fashion for the problematic and controversial quality of PR.

The problematic nature of silence is common to other nonverbal as well as verbal communication. But just as PR spreads across everything, silence "cuts across different levels of linguistic usage" and cannot be confined to only one branch of linguistics" (Jaworski, 1993, p. 1). Silence is a communicative and theatrical laboratory. Its attributes – ambiguity, ambivalence, drama – resonate with the nature of PR itself. It was Ivy Lee, the innovator of the news release formatted for dialogue between PR practitioner and reporter, who counseled his corporate clients to avoid silence and speak up when asked to comment. The risk of silence outweighed that of speech.

Yet silence is wired into PR. Unlike the noise that advertising makes, PR is generally invisible. It speaks in undertones. It ventriloquizes. It uses third parties. It's indirect. There is, in PR's dramaturgical virtues – circumspection, discipline, prudence – the wisdom of understatement or no statement at all. These are the ancient and modern strategies of diplomacy. The diplomat's facework is guarded, muted and strategic. The diplomat's virtues are much of what Machiavelli, that Renaissance press secretary, counseled the Prince.

Who speaks and who remains silent is a crucial part of disciplined face management. In the hierarchical realm of a large public corporation, the organization's face is the CEO. This is particularly true when a crisis arises, or when reporters, bloggers and other stakeholders have reason to question the wisdom of a company decision. Examples abound. An acquisition is believed to be overpriced or unwisely made in the first place. A company's quarterly earnings fail to meet Wall Street's expectations. A member of the senior management team is rumored to be departing.

At the Atlantic Company, one of the largest oil companies in the United States (the senior executives preferred *earth resources company* to account for its acquisitions of copper and aluminum), a senior speechwriter found himself in the awkward position of being called by a reporter from the *Wall Street Journal* to explain the company's position on energy conservation. The reporter was on deadline and the CEO and the entire senior management team were unavailable for comment. Not wanting to disappoint the powerful *Journal,* the anxious staffer offered the reporter a quote, violating the protocol that reserved media commentary to senior staff. His anxiety was his recognition that by speaking to the media, he had failed in his duty to be dramatically disciplined.

In a cold panic, he realized that he had to act quickly or the company would be extremely unhappy to find him articulating company policy in the *Wall Street Journal*'s morning edition. Realizing the potentially disastrous consequences of losing face with his employers, the speechwriter telephoned the reporter and pleaded with him not to use his quote. The reporter took pity on him and found an alternative source.

Silence in PR, like silence in other contexts and environments, is situational and risky, as well as frequently purposive and strategic.

The regulation of the equities market prescribes silence in the public interest. Soon after a private corporation launches an initial public offering of stock, the company is required by the Securities and Exchange Commission to observe a "quiet period" during which it is not permitted to speak publicly in favor of the merits of the shares it has put out for sale.

The communication of a corporation's quarterly report during a period in which it underperformed Wall Street's expectations may employ the strategies of indirectness, extreme understatement, circumlocution, fogging verbosity or ambiguous truncation – or when senior management anticipates even worse results in future periods, flatly evasive. Even in the seemingly upbeat instance of an e-mail pitch – a marketing PR tactic now often favored over longer letters – brevity leverages silence.

The modus operandi of PR is quite the opposite of what is commonly supposed. While the man on the street, abetted by media references, imagines PR to be an obvious, unsubstantial, transparent grab for unmerited publicity, PR is largely a backstage phenomenon.

Advertising, unlike Cordelia, is rarely modest or silent. Unlike the patented invisibility of a media placement by a PR firm, an advertisement appears on the stage fully dressed (or in the sensual case of beer commercials, partially undressed). It isn't PR itself that reaches our notice, but the result of its staging and orchestration.

PR has the invisibility of the songwriter, not the charisma of the singer. In *The Fall of Advertising and the Rise of PR,* their paean to PR, Ries and Ries (2004) made a witty case for the credibility of PR by contrasting its definitive seriousness with advertising's self-indulgent and incredible silliness. Curiously, Boorstin (1992, p. 9), one of PR's most quoted and outraged critics, is apparently unaware of this fundamental quality of PR. What Boorstin has focused on is the most visible of PR strategies – the special event. Boorstin asserted that the very essence of PR is the creation of a kind of nonreality he identified as a *pseudo-event.*

The struggle of PR is to claim and protect a face that will be accepted as legitimate. It's a fascinating struggle in many ways, one full of ironies and contradictions. In the twentieth century, PR established itself as a recognizable industry of ascending importance. Now in the twenty-first century, its struggle for legitimacy is ascending as well.

References

Bateson, G. (2000). Steps to an ecology of mind: Collected essays in anthropology, psychiatry evolution and epistemology. Chicago, IL: University of Chicago Press.

Bernays, E. L. (1965). *Biography of an idea: Memoirs of public relations counsel Edward L. Bernays.* New York, NY: Simon & Schuster.

Boorstin, D. J. (1987). *The image: A guide to pseudo-events in America.* New York, NY: Vintage.

———. (1992). The image: A guide to pseudo- events in America. New York: Vintage.

Brown, R. E. (2010). The convergence of public relations and public diplomacy. *Vital Speeches of the Day,* 76(7), 297–301.

Brown, P. & Levinson, S. (1987). *Politeness: Some universals in language usage.* Cambridge, England: Cambridge University Press.

Burke, K. (1969). *A grammar of motives.* Berkeley, CA: University of California Press.

Coombs, T. (2012) *Ongoing crisis communication.* Thousand Oaks, CA: Sage.

Debord, G. (2000). *Society of the spectacle.* Trans. K. Knabb. London: Red & Black.

Dozier D. (1992). The organizational roles of communications and public relations practitioners. In J. E. Grunig (Ed.), *Excellence in public relations* (pp. 327–355). Mahwah, NJ: Erlbaum.

Eisbenberg, E. (2007). *Strategic ambiguities: Essays on communication, organization, and identity.* Thousand Oaks, CA: Sage.

Ferlinghetti, L. (1968). *A Coney Island of the mind.* New York, NY: New Directions.

Freud, Sigmund, and Philip Rieff. (1963). *Dora: An Analysis of a Case of Hysteria.* New York, N.Y: Collier.

Frye, N. (1957). *Anatomy of criticism: Four essays.* Princeton, NJ: Princeton University Press.

Goffman, E. (1959). *The presentation of self in everyday life.* New York, NY: Anchor Books.

————. (1963) *Behavior in public places.* New York: Glencoe: Free Press.

————. (1966). *Behavior in public places: Notes on the social organization of gatherings.* New York, NY: Free Press.

————. (1986). *Frame analysis: An essay on the organization of experience.* Boston, MA: Northeastern University Press.

————. (2005). *Interaction ritual: Essays in face-to-face behavior.* New Brunswick, NJ: Transaction.

————. (2010). *Relations in public: Microstudies of the public order.* New Brunswick, NJ: Transaction.

Goldman, E. F. (1948). *Two-way street: The emergence of the public relations counsel.* New York, NY: Bellman.

Grove, A. S. (1996). *Only the paranoid survive: How to exploit the points that challenge every company.* New York: Crown.

Grunig, J. E. & Hunt, T. (1984). *Managing public relations.* Mahwah, NJ: Lawrence Erlbaum.

Guth, D. W. & Marsh, C. (2011). *Public relations: A value-driven approach.* New York Pearson

Herman, E. S. & Chomsky, N. (2002). *Manufacturing consent: The political economy of the mass media.* New York: Pantheon,

Hochschild, A. (2003). *The managed heart: Commercialization of human feeling.* Berkeley: University of California Press.

jackspace. (2012). www.dailykos.com/story/2012/09/21/1135065/-Don-t-be-a-Mitt-Wit# retrieved July 25, 2012.

Jaworski, A. (1993). *The power of silence: Social and pragmatic perspectives.* Thousand Oaks, CA: Sage

Kruckeberg, D. & Stark, K. (1988). *Public relations and community: A reconstructed theory.* Westport, CT: Praeger.

Lattimore, D., Baskin, O., Heiman, S. T., Toth, E. L. & Van Leuven, J. K. (2007). *Public relations: The profession and the practice.* New York, NY: McGraw-Hill.

Lehman, E. (2007). *Sweet smell of success: The short fiction of Ernest Lehman.* Woodstock, NY: Overlook Press.

L'Etang, J. (2008). *Public relations: Concept, practice and critique.* Thousand Oaks, CA: Sage.

Lewin, T. (2008). Internet socializing is not a bad thing. *New York Times.* Retrieved from www.nytimes.com/2008/11/20us/20internet.html?_51&hp

Lippmann, W. (1922). *Public opinion.* New York: Harcourt-Brace.

Public Relations Society of America. (2014). Retrieved from www.prsa.org/aboutprsa/publicrelationsdefined/#.U9FA50ivwzU.

Ries, A. & Ries, L. (2004). *The fall of advertising and the rise of PR.* New York: HarperBusiness.

Schawbel, D. (2008). *Me 2.0: Build a powerful brand to achieve career success.* New York, NY: Kaplan.

Schechner, R. (1988). *Performance theory.* London, England: Routledge.

Shakespeare. W. (1936). *The complete works of Shakespeare* (G. L. Kittredge, Ed.). Boston, MA: Ginn & Company.

Stevens, W. (1959). *Poems.* (H. Stevens, Ed.). New York, NY: Vintage Books.

Trumbull, A. (2004). *A brief history of the smile.* New York, NY: Basic Books.

Turner, V. W. & Bruner, E. M. (Eds.) (1986: 2001). *The anthropology of experience.* Champaign, IL: University of Illinois Press.

Weber, L. (2009). *Sticks and stones: How digital business reputations are created over time and lost in a click.* New York, NY: Wiley.

Wilcox, D. L., Ault, P. A. Agee, W. K., & Cameron, G. T. (2001). *Essentials of public relations.* New York: Longman.

4 Actors

In everyday life we are all to some degree students of Stanislavsky.

Arlie Hochschild (1983, p. 194)

I am an actor.

Which is another way of saying that I am a public relations (PR) practitioner. Which is to reframe theatrically what the PR industry says about PR on its website: that PR is about adapting. So, too, is acting – from situation to situation, problem to problem, crisis to crisis, platform to platform. In the age of Big Data, algorithms and analytics, it's easy to forget that much of what PR practitioners do is improvise.

What I'm stipulating as acting is neither lying nor what is dismissed as "putting on an act." Acting, for practitioners, is expected to be a disciplined response their constituents, clients and coworkers in a variety of situations. In this sense, acting resonates with what the sociologist George Simmel (1950) called *sociation* (pp. 13–17) and twentieth-century sociologists called *structural functionalism*. The actor must summon the requisite energy and focus it strategically, often with particular attention to diplomacy (Simmel, 1950). None of this may be regarded as "authentic" or even sincere. But the practitioner's professional responsibility is to perform what constituents would be likely to regard as sincerity and authenticity. Such "seeming to be" is no less professionally essential for the practitioner than for the professional actors in the theater or on a movie set. As for sincerity, it would be difficult to find a more cynical view than De la Rochefoucauld's (1959) withering penetration of the self-serving performances of seventeenth-century French court aristocrats. But their Baroque vanities might well be matched by the so-called humble brags posted on Facebook in what has come to be called *self-branding*. These thinly veiled boasts follow a predictable format along the lines of "Oh, I am so weary of reporters hounding me for yet another interview!" Tight bodices, high sleeves and brocade have given way to skinny jeans and thigh-high boots, but the human craving to be noticed is evergreen.

What I am proposing is that what is really going on in PR is the kind of adaptation that is not a product of systems theory but of the dramaturgic nature of PR.

True, I have never filed my taxes as an actor. But no matter. I have been a paid, professional PR practitioner working in agency and corporate environments – as well as a magazine editor, a freelance writer and a college professor. When I was writing speeches, interviewing executives for the annual report and creating slide presentations for community relations, what I did was perform.

There is little likelihood that PR role theorists Dozier (1992) and Broom and Smith (1979) would agree with such a broad and unsystematic idea of the practitioner as actor. PR role theory has traditionally framed the practitioner's roles far more narrowly and discretely as managers and technicians. PR was narrowly defined within the activities of organizational life. Practitioner roles were itemized to "conceptualize the *problem-solving process facilitator*" (Dozier, 1992, p. 330). Such thinking, of course, tends to dismiss improvisation as irrelevant and, more important, unevolved.

But such a view misses a crucial point. Like other kinds of acting, whether on a theater stage or in a face-to-face interaction, PR is a problem-solving activity that requires what is commonly prized as "thinking on one's feet." Professional actors and practitioners perform on stages freighted with problems to be solved. Without a problem to resolve, there would be no drama of sufficient interest to hold our attention. The same is true of PR. Without problem solving there would be no PR.

As a practitioner, I prepared, in a fashion analogous to stage actors, to be credible and persuasive with my audience. I sought to suss out them (or him or her) in order to do what an actor seeks to accomplish: to be not only credible but interesting. To hold the audience's attention – even to be entertaining, at least to some extent.

Acting and truth

Performance theorists have categorized acting, helpfully, as a subcategory of performance and, as in the public relations of everything (PRe), inclusively, as in Henry Bial's (2004) discussion:

> For every kind of performance there is a different kind (and often many kinds) of performing. Performing happens in everyday life, in the home, in the workplace, in sports and games, in the arts, and in sacred and secular ritual. Any time you take on a role, tell a story, or simply enact a bit of restored behavior, you are performing. This does not mean you are "faking," or being untrue to your "real self" . . . performing often involves the utmost sincerity.
>
> (p. 183)

Can it be that the opposite of sincerity isn't insincerity but the ethics of professional and personal obligation? And can it also be that authenticity is, like symmetry, a normative ideal in the perception of the philosopher? If so, then can we say that the ethics of professionalism demands performative competency and client loyalty but not necessarily sincerity or authenticity? If this is so of professionalism, then we've identified a rift between the personal and professional. It is this rift – this division – which the sociologist Arlie Hochschild (1983) found to be emotionally turbulent, spiritually costly and ultimately problematic about the more intensively performed professions such as airline flight attendant and debt collector. That typology may be applied to PR practitioners, whose performance is to pitch, cold call, present, rebut and defend their clients' and their own faces.

To a significant extent, PR practitioners enact a performance of customer service, particularly to their clients. The PR practitioner's smile cannot, as Hochschild has said, merely be painted on. The "emotional cost" of this sort of Stanislavskian deep, as opposed to surface, acting was explored by management theorist Alicia Grandley (2003) in her analysis of the emotional tensions associated with customer-service delivery. Indeed, a PR practitioner in an asymmetric relationship with a client often must endure it with a smile. This is another demonstration of symmetry theory's flaws. Symmetry theory assumes that such relationships gravitate toward balance. But the odds are against such a balance when heading into the headwinds of immense power differences between the practitioner-server and the client served.

It is from a performative perspective that we are permitted to see the PR practitioner as more than the sum of her tactics. Something more is going on with her that is neither fake nor mechanical. Through the lens of cultural anthropology, yet other attributes of the practitioner and her practice come into view – their ambiguity and their aesthetics. The practitioner/boundary-spanning performer bears some resemblance to the anthropologist Victor Turner's (2004) liminal personae, or "threshold people," who

> are necessarily ambiguous, since this condition and these persons elude or slip through the network of classifications that normally locate states and positions in cultural space.
>
> (p. 79)

No matter how business-like and "serious" her performance, the practitioner must provide, at some level, entertainment or risk the boredom and disinterest of her constituents. What she writes, posts, tweets, pictures, directs, or produces may or may not be pretty. Even so, art is not always pretty. The practitioner probably will not consider herself an artist. But in her performance there is something of the aesthetic – something compelling if she succeeds, or stultifying when she fails. For Schechner (2013, p. 48),

> beauty is hard to define. Beauty is not equivalent to being "pretty." The ghastly, terrifying events of kabuki, Greek tragedy, Elizabethan theatre, and some performance art are not pretty. . . . But the skilled enactment of horrors can be beautiful and yield aesthetic pleasure.
>
> (p. 48)

The American Beat poet Lawrence Ferlinghetti (1958) portrayed the performer as a circus acrobat on tightrope, high above the audience, and "constantly risking absurdity" (p. 29).

PR's contested role

The literature of practitioners' roles is among the most copious and prolific of any topic in PR scholarly literature. Robert Kendall (1993) complained about Marvin Olasky's article on practitioners which "argues that PR suffers a reputation of being peopled with 'low life liers [sic],'" and that its reputation has been sullied in "aborting the debate over the nature of the field" because of "general agreement conceding that it [PR] is simply 'Machiavellian smartness'" (Section I).

The source of Kendall's complaint was not to dispute the bad reputation of PR but that Olasky's "reading of the literature is biased." But that bias happened to lead to a "worst case" conclusion, in Kendall's view: "that the field is ambiguous."

Yet Kendall's argument was itself caught in his own bias when he offered a "more realistic" reading of the literature that leaders "including Bernays, Vail, Page, Child, and the PRSA code of ethics give priority to the public interest in their understanding of PR."

The argument turns on two problems: one, that Kendall's critique is not really about whether Olasky's reading of the literature is "realistic" but that Olasky's conclusion was not to his liking. More problematical still is the way PR's obsession with its reputation tends to dominate investigations where that obsession is neither particularly germane nor salient.

What with the priority accorded by PR to its beleaguered reputation, it is understandable that there has been little interest in viewing its role through the unfamiliar lenses of performance, acting and aesthetics.

The ancient stage

Whatever it is, PR is, to echo Ecclesiastes, nothing new. The conventional and apparently commonsensical consensus of PR scholarship is that PR is indeed new, and referring to practices prior to the twentieth-century creation of a PR industry as merely "PR-like." Mine is the minority view: that the PR ideas and practices that existed before the twentieth century were not "like" PR – they *were* PR.

The historian and sociologist Elizabeth Burns (1973), influenced by the dramaturgical theory of Erving Goffman, offered no evidence of an interest in PR. Burns believed that there is a "line drawn between the two kinds of behavior, theatrical and untheatrical" that is related to the socialization of a particular social group – say, "a group of upper-class English people at a formal function" and "an Italian family greeting each other with kissing and hand-shaking" (p. 20). These are both theatrical; to assert they are not would be to make what she called a "moral vision conditioned by the process of socialization" (p. 20). In other words, people would rather not imagine themselves to be acting, but are able to recognize the acting of others.

In a deeply researched and insightful way, Burns traced the origins of that division between theatrical and untheatrical behavior to a place where the PR scholar Donn James Tilson (2011) goes: religion. For Tilson, in the rituals of sacred and celebrity theatricality can be found what he called a "covenantal" relationship of

PR. Specifically, in Burns, it is in the "dramatic tropes, which were introduced into the [Christian] service during the ninth century" (p. 24). What occurred in those religio-dramatic tropes articulated that division:

Thus for the duration of the performance the congregation's attention was given to observation of expressive action rather than to worship or prayer, which are forms of communication with God . . .

In this way began the long, slow process of structural division between actors and audience before drama can develop into a separate art.

(p. 24)

In a footnote, Burns pointed out that "the same process seems to have occurred in Ancient Greece" (p. 24).

Of course, I would hardly have thought to claim a religious deduction on the income tax form that identified me as a PR practitioner. In my current status as a university professor, what I report to the U.S. Treasury derives not from acting but from teaching, consulting, facilitating and writing. But I experience all of these doings as acting. Were I merely speaking or communicating, I would be unlikely to leave a classroom or boardroom or a new-business pitch feeling as if I had run a marathon. That which calls on such intense energies of the body, mind and voice I experience as a performance, as opposed to a conversation. This is what Merleau-Ponty (1964) seems to have meant by a phenomenology that has its source in the body and experiences life as art.

Despite the thoroughgoing secularism of the "communication management" school of PR scholarship, is it altogether unreasonable to rethink the origins of PR in ancient civilizations and early medieval performances? The modern university itself, after all, can trace its origins to the Church whose soaring architecture it has so often adopted.

I don't mean to diminish the compelling experience of acting by reducing it to a mere metaphor or analogy. Not at all. My experience in the classroom is the work I do to hold my students' attention. I experience that work as acting – not because I would prefer to imagine that I am a "real" actor, but because the work I am doing is an act. On a stage. In a series of scenes that demand different choices. The evaluation of me as a teacher is the evaluation of my performance; and it is on the performance of my students that I base my evaluation of them. We are thus engaged in a drama of mutually expressive action. It will come as no surprise to classroom teachers that students' engagement with their smartphones and other technological devices have all but overtaken students' interest in the traditional, unmediated expressive classroom communication. At the same time, the classroom teacher finds herself challenged to compete with the mediated offerings on the web: videos, music and tweets composed, clicked, shared and contemplated.

As actors, practitioners must be aware of their tools: voice and body. At the more senior levels, practitioners assume the roles of director, coaching other practitioners, or media-training their clients. As producers, practitioners scout locations for staging the special events that are crucial to the *mise-en-scène* of PR.

The visionary architect Buckminster Fuller liked to say "I am a verb." The PR actor-practitioner must be in command of tone, gesture and the rhythms of performance. Stella Adler (2000), the acting coach of many famous American actors, wrote that acting is *doing*. Every performance is an experiment. From the communication theorist Albert Mehrabian (1966), one learned uses of what he called "immediacy behaviors" such proxemics, or the strategic and rhetorical use of space. Practitioners need be spatially articulate. Such articulateness can take the form of moving the body closer to or farther from a single student or an entire class, strolling slowly forward as in a cinematographer's dolly shot.

PRe thus rethinks PR as no single thing but as an idea and an institution with multiple natures – political, poetic, dramatic. For PRe, PR is theater. It is a perspective that is at once humanistic, aesthetic and sociological in the dramaturgic tradition of Goffman, Geertz, Schechner, Turner and others. Following this path has led me to observe the practitioner as an actor. Not in the commonplace sense of faking or even pretending. But more in the sense of what professional actors actually do: prepare themselves to imagine, encounter and inhabit a character so that neither they nor the audience will experience their acting as anything other than authentic. For competent, professional actors, their work is authentic, at the very least. At the height of their art, it is irresistibly interesting. Not only is what actors do persuasive – it can be compelling, moving, memorable, inspiring and transformative for the audience as well as for themselves.

The problem with the conventional thinking, theory, tropes and vocabulary of PR is that it has had the effect of shrinking and flattening the experience of practitioners and the nature of PR. The only corrective is to reawaken PR scholarship to be more alive to the practice in fuller, more robust terms that avoid the pitfalls of a dry-as-dust portrayal of PR.

Perception as an art

Robert Leaf (2012), the retired former International Chairman of Burson-Marstellar, one of the world's largest PR agencies, recounted an experience at a conference in Moscow during the 1950s. The experience shaped his idea that "perception management" is the fundamental universal principle of PR (p. 3).

Facing a cordial audience of Soviet government officials, "there was still a belief among many Russians that Western marketing techniques were tools of capitalism," which raised questions of their appropriateness for a communist society. After his presentation, there was a question from a professor in the audience: "Mr. Leaf, how can you justify any social good in advertising?"

> I paused for a long moment while I studied the audience. After some careful thought I replied, "Let us say you are trying to sell harvesters you manufacture in Soviet plants to Egypt. And at the same time, Americans are also trying to sell them American-produced harvesters. If the Americans succeed in making the sale, the profits would usually go to individuals in private companies who

can use the money in any way they see fit and for their own pleasure. But if you sell the harvesters, you can use the money to build hospitals, improve roads, and provide a better life for the more impoverished. But to be able to do this first, you have to sell those harvesters. And if it is your advertising that helps you accomplish this, there is no question that it definitely has a social good."

The professor immediately replied, "Mr. Leaf, I can accept that completely." Looking out at the audience, I got the feeling that he was not the only one who bought my reply.

I've often thought about this meeting in later years and my response to the learned Russian gentleman's question and what it accomplished. I became more convinced than ever about a strong belief I had always held – about the key to successful communication, no matter who the audience is. That key is the need to manage perceptions and that belief is that the public relations business is, in reality, *perception management.*

(p. 3)

Storytelling

If practitioners typically resist the image of themselves as actors, they tend to cherish the description of themselves as storytellers.

In "Storytelling Can Bring Your PR Effort to Life," an article published in 2013 in *PR Tactics,* a Public Relations Society of America trade publication, Richard Pirozzolo, the founder of Pirozzolo Company Public Relations, advises practitioners to think and write like the authors of fiction:

Whatever we know and remember about whaling is probably thanks to Herman Melville's story of Ahab and the Great White Whale. We most likely didn't learn about whaling from thick history books, newspaper accounts and certainly not trade magazine articles in *Whaling Age* on the finer points of harpoon selection.

It's the great story – the narrative – that makes the events and reality more vivid and the details stick in our memory.

What does this have to do with public relations?

Consider the value of using the principles of fiction to tell our clients' stories. Consider the NASA space program for example. Sure, we saw and read about plenty of Space Shuttle launches and have seen scratchy news footage of the Mercury program and the lunar landing. But we got our *feeling* for the camaraderie, the teamwork, and the danger from the stories we read or movies we saw such as *The Right Stuff* or *Apollo 13.* Likewise, Tom Wolfe made the roots of NASCAR come alive in his account of Junior Johnson, "The Last American Hero," that he wrote for *Esquire.* Spies? Ian Fleming and John Le Carré made the intrigue – and tools of the trade – come alive for us.

(Pirozzolo, 2013)

The PR of everything, or PRe, observes the crucial literary elements of PR, which symmetry theory, in its attempt to scientificize PR, has all but deleted. As the practitioner Pirozzolo observed in a variety of blogs on his website, PR is advised to think in the literary terms of story, conflict, drama and humor, as well as thinking with the visual imagination that has become an increasingly central aesthetic in our intensely visual age.

That said, we come around to re-asking the question Goffman (1974/1986) posed in *Frame Analysis:* What is it that is really going on? For our purposes in examining what is really going with PR practitioners, we are rephrasing the question in several forms: What is it that PR practitioners really do? What is it that practitioners believe they are doing? What is it that PR practitioners advise other practitioners to do? What is it that practitioners believe is effective PR?

With their understandable concern to avoid the negative stereotype of the PR "spinner," practitioners cannot be blamed for questioning the sobriquet "actor." Far more appealing for the practitioner to describe his role either in the jargon of the profession, as a "social media manager," or more grandly, as a "chief rebranding officer." Still, as the sociologist Tom Burns (1973) reflected, "Few people like to believe they are acting all the time. This seems to be perceived as a charge of insincerity and even a denial of identity" (p. 20).

Acting's emotional cost

"In everyday life," the sociologist Arlie Russell Hochschild (1983) wrote, "we are all to some degree students of Stanislavsky" (p. 194).

Hochschild's critique of Goffman is not a rejection of the reality of acting, but of the cost of it. What Goffman's dramaturgy failed to account for was not the gestures on the outside but the feelings on the inside.

Hochschild's insights into the "commercialization of human feeling" confound the emotionless theory of symmetry with its faulty assumption that the powerful will be "willing to change" by negotiating with the relatively powerless.

As Hochschild observed, the Bureau of Labor Statistics categorizes mathematicians and diplomats as professionals. But emotional labor is critical to the professionalism of the diplomat, not to the professionalism of the mathematician (p. 148).

In the "image business" of PR, emotional labor is crucial to the professionalism of the PR practitioner. It's not enough if she merely engages in what Stanislavsky (1936/1976) called "surface acting" – raising an eyebrow, winking and nodding. To really succeed in the eyes of her managers and clients, she must do what Stanislavsky called "deep acting." The actor must develop deep feelings for the role she plays. She must *believe.*

Such a perspective reveals a dimension of dramaturgy that was left largely unexplored by Goffman. It is this emotional economics – the stressfulness of plunging into emotional debt – that gets to the heart of the practitioner's performance. It is what such nostrums as perception and symmetry ignore; but it is at the core of the practitioner's experience.

Where the PR executive memoirist Robert Leaf ends, Hochschild begins. That is, with perception – the "art" of it and the "management" of it. That PR begins and ends with perception is the conventional thinking of PR. But for Hochschild (1983), perception fails to account for what is really going on in interaction in that "perception is not all there is to emotion or feeling, nor is it its sole cause, but it is the principle according to which emotion and feeling are named" (p. 233).

For PR and its practitioners, it is hard to underestimate the distinction between perception and emotion, because the distinction points us to the problem with mechanical conceptualization of systems-theory-based PR. The campaign to reconstruct PR as a "science" has had the unintended (or perhaps intended) consequence of emptying PR of feeling, which is an extraordinary misunderstanding of practitioners' experience. The failure to understand, much less to value, the experience of practitioners is hardly a reliable basis for understanding PR itself.

Beyond managers and technicians

The conventional theory of PR roles – the hierarchical-and-task conception of strategic manager and creative technician – fails to grasp not only the emotionality and dramaturgy of the practitioner's experience but, in the title phrase of Sherry Turkle (1997), the practitioner's "life on the screen." Turkle wasn't addressing the screen lives of PR practitioners when she published her book on the problematic social and psychological effects of screen life immersion; the 1990s predated Facebook, Twitter and the welter of social media. The passage of time, with the PR industry's and the practitioner's increasing immersion in digital–social media has only served to underscore the relevance of Turkle's themes. One of the earliest thought leaders about the Internet and the web and their impacts, Turkle's views changed from her initial enthusiasm for the alchemically liberating empowering tools of technology to a recognition of the web and social media's darker sides – the loss of nurturing face-to-face contact, the erosion of mobile-phone-obsessed parents' attention to their children and the troubling perception among some Millennials that interaction with robots, although not the same as contact with real people, was good enough.

Glen Broom purported to discover five roles in PR practice; these five were eventually reduced to a pair – the strategic manager and the communication technician (Broom & Smith, 1979). What's missing from such a theory of roles is, among other things, the practitioner's experience of emotion as well as her activity as a performer and her imaginative play. The serious, even dour, idea of the practitioner's role skims the surface of what has been increasingly observable in the screen-mediated interactions of PR practitioners. For, like the rest of the wired world, practitioners live their lives on several screens and multiple platforms. Their roles are enacted not from the anchoring permanence of a single identity but with an actor's capacity to create, inhabit and project identities according to the requirements of the scene and the practitioner's motivation.

Although the institution of PR has embraced the cause branding and social responsibility ethos espoused by Carol Cone as living one's values, little scholarly attention has been paid to the role-expanding, boundary-spanning, identity-altering implications of that ethos (Cone et al., 2003). The role of a practitioner who is the "manager" of a campaign or, as a "technician," creates copy and posts images to an organizational blog, fails to account for her roles she plays on the deeper level of her identity. She conceives of her role in terms of her values – the *raison d'être* of her most important choices: her career and the culture of the organization that she believes will enable her to role-play her values. What is commonly called "making a difference" will be the actor's motivation that animates her choices and drives the energy with which she performs as technician or manager.

Role shapes, and is shaped by, the practitioner's encounters with her fluid multiple identities inside and outside the real and virtual space of the organizational stage. The "value-driven" practitioner, seen increasingly in a PR career, refuses to leave her values outside her cubicle. Textbooks such as Guth and Marsh's (2000) *Public Relations: A Value-Driven Approach,* have taught her that PR is, or ought to be, a profession that provides her with the opportunity to live her values. She comes to her job – her career, not only in nonprofit but corporate environments – prepared to live her values.

The historiographical foundation of value-driven textbooks is that the nature of PR has "evolved," a story of the triumph of ethics and professionalism. The implication for the practitioner is that the value-driven organization has evolved to enable her to live out her values and "make a difference." In her artful and artfully strategic presentation of her changing and changeable faces on Facebook, the boundary between her professional and private selves is subject to the face she prepares to meet the faces she meets. The boundaries do not need be spanned because they are porous, subject only to the practitioner's perception of herself and her situation. In Turkle's (1997) term, the individual does not engage in boundary spanning but "boundary negotiations" (p. 22).

In PRe, to grasp what is really going on, it is necessary to broaden the binary and hierarchical conventions of PR role theory. In the age of mediated, value-driven organizations and practitioners – and multiple identities on several screens – it will not do to consign the idea of identity to the organizational purgatory of metaphysics.

In such a world, Merleau-Ponty's idea of life as art is a more accurate guide to what is really going on in PR practice than the categorically constrained conventional role theory of symmetrically framed PR. There is more to the role of manager than managing; more to the role of technician than techniques.

Not only is there more to roles than manager and technician, there are more disciplinary perspectives from which to observe roles. Earlier chapters in this book have cited the anthropological perspectives of Victor Turner's (1988) "anthropology of performance" and Richard Schechner's performance theory, both acknowledging their debt to the dramaturgical microsociology of Erving Goffman. There is no doubt that PR can be taught profitably from such perspectives because they bear directly on the problems and strategies of PR, including crisis communication and marketing communications.

The specifics

Actors performing a play inherit the legacy of Stanislavsky, who taught that the actor must avoid approaching her role as the expression of some general motivation or objective, but rather begin by concentrating on the selection of a specific action. The play may be thematic, the playwright intellectual, but the acting must first be physical. "Generality," Stanislavsky wrote, "is the enemy of all art" (Harrop, 1992, p. 45).

If PR practitioners can be said to begin by addressing a problem or challenge, it is typically framed in general, abstract verbs indicating a categorical, but unspecific action or objective cast in the infinitive tense such as *to brand, to target, to reposition, to publicize*. These are the *whats* of PR. But the real actions of the practitioner are the *hows*. In my career, my most frequent request from a PR agency client was that I explain to practitioners how to deliver bad news.

The consultant's problem in addressing a PR agency request of that sort parallels the director's problem in addressing the needs of actors. What's really being asked is less a general approach than a range of specific, implementable actions of which the practitioner – and the stage actor – must be capable of doing or learning to do. In the tradition of Stanislavsky and his followers (Lee Strasberg, Stella Adler and Sandy Meisner among the best known), the actor must call on the tools in his possession – his voice and his body – not to perform, but to do something, to speak and move. The actor's choices will depend not only on her intelligence and commitment but ultimately on her capacity to wield her instrument just so.

The PR consultant does not enjoy the advantage of the stage actor and director. All their problems have reference to a particular play in hand – a play that has been written and shared with the cast. All attention can be focused on it. There is no such object of focus for the consultant and the practitioner. There is no text to thumb through – only the challenging, nebulous, contingent and ongoing nature of the situation. The situation may comprise a pile of texts – web sites, links, tweets, press releases, blogs, Facebook posts, anonymous critiques, voicemails and YouTube videos. The practitioner's response may be like the speaker in the Wallace Stevens (1959) poem who is overwhelmed by "the dreadful sundry of this world" (p. 27).

The situation of PR is a dreadful sundry of texts. From these and her experience and intelligence, the practitioner must call forth an approach, and that approach must begin with a specific action. Frequently, the practitioner's action calls on the same tools as the stage actor: voice and body. In the words of the influential acting coach, Stella Adler (2000), "You have come here to learn how to act, and I keep telling you I want to teach you how *not* to act – except in the very precise sense of performing actions" (p. 86).

Physicality

When PR practitioners are asked whether what they do could be called acting, their response is, unsurprisingly, emphatically and typically no. They are not acting – they are implementing a strategic plan. They are exceeding client expectations. They are responding, rebranding, repositioning.

What could account for this language of abstraction? For one thing, it is also a kind of disciplinary and theoretical language. This is true at the secondary level of abstraction – descriptions of actions devoid of physicality, such as "I wrote a crisis release," "I pitched a Mommy blogger," "I helped out with our brand journalism."

None of these descriptions is remotely like what Stanislavsky meant by the "circle of attention" – the exercise for an actor that forces her away from the Big Picture of the scene and into the smallest, nearest, most intimate and immediate physical action (Benedetti, 1998, p. 42). The actor who must get up off her chair and make her way across the room and to the door to exit has a great deal to think about. But she must do it – every movement of her body in that scene – in such a way that it will create the illusion for the audience that she is *not acting.* Everything she does in that scene must feel perfectly natural not only to her but also to her audience. Such is a paradox of the actor – or, perhaps, of the many generations of actors on stage and screen influenced by the theories of Constantin Stanislavsky.

But how can the actor accomplish this immense, do-or-die challenge? How can she not *act* but *be,* while managing to create the illusion necessary for the success of the performance and the response of the audience? The actor must, in a sense, pretend in order to convince the audience she isn't acting. This counterintuitive, contradictory task is the actor's art. By being "in the moment," in actor jargon, the audience, too, is scooped up into the moment. What the actor must do turns out not to be pretending at all. If it were, we – the audience – would throw rotten tomatoes, leave the theater and demand our money back.

Stanislavsky struggled with this problem and, in his autobiography, reported that he had an insight. He called it the *circle of concentration.* Sitting in her chair, the actor needs to focus on what is closest to her. Perhaps, it will be her own hand on the table. She must feel the tension in the muscles of her legs. It will not be by acting but by circling around her own kinesthetic physicality and focusing on the objects closest to her that the actor will be able to avoid the disaster of abstractly symbolizing a performance. (Adler, 2000, p. 199).

The serious and the silly

About that straw man of symmetry theory, P.T. Barnum, the usual objections have been to his ethics, or lack of them. But more rarely expressed are objections to his silliness. For PR scholars, Barnum's worst sin was not a lack of truth but a lack of seriousness. Bearded ladies, jumbo elephants, dwarfs and mermaids: such things lack the managerial propriety of "evolved" PR.

Such a lack of seriousness has been a common critique of the work of actors. After all, if the strong suit of PR as regarded by the PR profession is credibility, then mermaids and bearded ladies must be unacceptable, regardless of their ability to go viral. Converts to PR from careers as advertising theorists, Ries and Ries (2004) asserted PR's ascendancy in *The Fall of Advertising and the Rise of PR:* "advertising is funny, public relations is serious."

To rethink the practitioner as an actor is to risk discarding PR's trump card. Besides, outside the theater and the studio sound stage – in the boardroom, on the webinar, in a CFO conference call – acting will be understood to be lying. But that is precisely why the practitioner must be as effective at what he does as the stage actor. Both must do anything *but* act to create an illusion. It will be argued that this is where the analogy breaks down. The stage actor's illusion is pure entertainment in the cathartic interest of the audience, but the PR practitioner's illusion is nothing more than a scam.

But the objection is misleading. If the intention of the practitioner's media pitch is to perform the Joseph Conradian novelistic task of *making the journalist see* the value of the product, and if the journalist does his requisite double-and-triple sourcing and persuades his editor of the newsworthiness of the story, then both practitioner and journalist are acting in the best interest of their constituencies and engaging the public sphere ethically and professionally.

In such a scenario, the PR process can be understood not as a zero-sum game – a game where there are winners and losers – but as a game where all the players are winners. What contributes to this desirable outcome is the ability of the practitioner to act by appearing not to act. She succeeds by moving through a performance that feels comfortably natural both to her and her journalist audience.

The practitioner's tools are fundamentally the same as the actor's: the command of voice on the telephone; the control of body in dyadic, group and public encounters. None of this is intended to deny the critical importance to the practitioner of the suite of skills, including writing and technology. But if properly understood, the practitioner's command of acting is not merely intended as an analogy but as a counterintuitive and perhaps initially unwanted perspective that can help us move beyond the set of framing assumptions, tastes and distastes that comprise the conventional conceptions of PR and its practitioners.

In Goffman's term, practitioners must be dramatically disciplined. Both front stage and backstage, verbally and gesturally, in the tone of their speech and the rare instances of their silence, in their memos and pitch letters. Their performances must be smoothly enacted to please their constituent clients, reporters, bloggers and regulators, as well as their bosses.

Much attention has been paid to the digital–social media skills the practitioner must command. Far less attention has been paid to the practitioner as actor. But no matter the range of his or her skill set, incompetent actors fail. Although I know of no research that derives PR success or failure from the actor's skills of body and voice, their importance is mirrored in what the social sciences call *face validity*.

In the Stanislavskian sense of professional "method" acting, the practitioner is an actor who must "prepare" (Stanislavsky, 1936/1976):

His job is not to present merely the external life of his character. He must fit his own human qualities to the life of this other person, and pour into it all of his own soul. The fundamental aim of our art is the creation of this inner life of a human spirit, and its expression in artistic form.

(p. 14)

Clearly, however, the PR practitioner is not preparing to inhabit a scripted character. But neither does the practitioner prepare to be *herself.* That will not do because each client, each scene, each environment poses a different set of problems for the practitioner. Faced with the last-minute call to the set of a crisis, the practitioner, for all intents and purposes, will need to inhabit the role of crisis communicator. She may in fact find herself in the situation of actors who are benefitted and limited by being typecast. Like the working stage or movie actor, the practitioner engages an array of dramas, new sets and a shifting cast of actors, directors and producers

Like Stanislavsky's actor, the practitioner – and perhaps especially the value-driven practitioner – must not merely present the external life of her character but find within her own experience emotional connections to the role she performs.

Adding to the practitioner's challenge is that she will not only act; she will also consult, coach, train, facilitate and educate. In theatrical terms, she will be a director and a producer.

Even if the idea of acting avoids the ironic and subversive intention of Marlon Brando's remark that acting, not prostitution, is the "oldest profession" (Brando, 2013), it is clear that, like a "real" actor, the practitioner is creating a performance for someone – an audience, a client, a reporter, an organizational manager. Or, as the performance studies scholar Marvin Carlson (2004) observed,

> According to [Richard Bauman] all performance involves a consciousness of doubleness, through which the actual execution of an action is placed in mental comparison with a potential, an idea, or a remembered original model of that action. . . . Performance is always performance *for* someone, some audience that recognizes and validates it as performance, even when, as is occasionally the case, that audience is the self.
>
> (Carlson, p. 71)

The ancient and modern theater

For all its modernity, PR is nothing new under the sun. Two millennia ago, Saint Paul performed the role of what can be called an excellent and ethical PR practitioner (Brown, 2003). The intellectual shaper of a great religion made excellent use of targeting, market segmentation, special events, writing, publicity, public speaking, grassroots organizing and inspirational leadership. Indeed, the edifice of Christianity itself would rise for all times on the foundation of his performances. In nascent, first-century Christianity, there was compelling drama in Paul's conversion in Damascus and in his preaching the new religion's unique selling proposition of salvation to pagans, Jews and Jesu-cults of Corinth and Ephesus across the Roman roads. These roads were described by Marshall McLuhan (McCluhan, 1965, p. 90) as another extension of man – another form of media (1965, p. 90).

So it would be in the second millennium, as the historian Rosario Villari (1991) noted of the dramatics of Renaissance Christianity, that the preachers used a broad range of theatrical resources, and the missionary's reputation was linked to the success of such techniques (Villari, 1991, p. 185).

For PRe, PR needs to be rethought outside the box of organizations and their proprieties. PRe is an idea large enough for the persuasive styles of both Barnum and Paul. Whether approached from the perspective of the humanities or that of the sociologists, PRe is simply too large and dramatic for the container into which it has been squeezed.

References

Adler, S. (2000). *The art of acting.* (H. Kissell, Ed.). New York, NY: Applause Theatre and Cinema Books.

Benedetti, J. (1998). *Stanislavsky and the actor.* London, England: Routledge.

Bial, H. (Ed.). (2004). *The performance studies reader.* New York, NY: Routledge.

Brando, M. (2013). Acting, not prostitution, is the oldest profession in the world. In *fuckyeahbrando* [tumblr blog]. Retrieved from http://fuckyeahbrando.tumblr.com/post/528571035/acting-not-prostitution-is-the-oldest

Broom, G. T. & Smith, G. D. (1979). Testing the practitioner's impact on clients. *Public Relations Review,* 5(3), 47–59.

Brown, R. E. (2003). Saint Paul as a public relations practitioner. *Public Relations* Review, 29(1), 1–12.

Burns, E. (1973). *The sociology of literature and drama.* Baltimore, MD: Penguin Books.

Carlson, M. (1989). In E. Barnouw (Ed.), *International Encyclopedia of communications* (p. 185). New York, NY: Oxford University Press.

Carlson, M. (2004). What is performance? In H. Bial (Ed.), *The performance studies reader* (pp. 68–78). New York, NY: Routledge.

Cone, C. L., Feldman, F. M. A. & DaSilva, A. T. (2003). Causes and effects. *Harvard Business Review,* 81(7): 95–101.

De La Rochefoucauld, F. (1959). *The maxims of La Rochefoucauld* (L. Kronenberger, Trans.). New York, NY: Vintage.

Dozier, D. (1992). The organizational roles of communications and public relations practitioners. In J. E. Grunig (Ed.), *Excellence in public relations and communication management* (pp. 327–355). Mahwah, NJ: Erlbaum, 327–355.

Ferlinghetti, L. (1958). *A Coney Island of the mind: Poems by Lawrence Ferlinghetti.* New York, NY: New Directions.

Goffman, E. (1986). *Frame analysis: An essay on the organization of experience.* Boston, MA: Northeastern University Press.

Grandley, A. (2003). When the show must go on: Surface acting and deep acting as determinants of emotional exhaustion and peer-rated service delivery. *Academy of Management Journal,* 46(5), 86–96.

Guth, D. W. & Marsh, C. M. (2000). *Public relations: A value-driven approach.* Boston, MA: Allyn & Bacon.

Harrop, J. (1992). *Acting.* London, England: Routledge.

Hochschild, A. R. (1983). *The managed heart: Commercialization of human feeling.* Berkeley: University of California Press.

Kendall, R. L. (1993). [Untitled review]. In *The public relations body of knowledge* [Loose-leaf bound]. New York, NY: Public Relations Society of America.

Leaf, R. (2012). *The art of perception: Memoirs of a life in PR.* London, England: Atlantic Books.

McLuhan, M. (1965). *Understanding media.* New York: McGraw-Hill.

Mehrabian, A. (1966). Immediacy: An indicator of attitudes in linguistic communication. *Journal of Personality, 34,* 26–34.

Merleau-Ponty, M. (1964). *The primacy of perception.* Evanston, IL: Northwestern University Press.

Pirozzolo, R. (2013). Storytelling can bring your PR effort to life. *Public Relations Tactics,* 20(2), 17.

Ries, A. & Ries, L. (2004). The fall of advertising and the rise of PR. New York: HarperBusiness.

Schechner, R. (2013). *Performance studies: An introduction.* New York: Routledge.

Simmel, G. (1950). *The sociology of George Simmel* (K. H Wolff, Trans.). Glencoe, IL: Free Press.

Stanislavsky, C. (1976). *An actor prepares.* New York, NY: Theatre Arts Books.

Stevens, W. (1959). *Poems.* (H. Stevens, Ed.). New York, NY: Vintage Books.

Tilson, D. (2011). *The promotion of devotion: Saints celebrities and shrines.* Champaign, IL: Common Ground.

Turkle, S. (1997). *Life on the screen: Identity in the age of the Internet.* New York, NY: Touchstone.

Turner, V. (1988). *The anthropology of performance.* New York, NY: PAJ.

———. (2004). Liminality and communitas. In H. Bial (Ed.), *The performance studies reader* (pp. 79–87). New York, NY: Routledge.

Villari, R. (Ed.). (1991). *Baroque personnae* (L. G. Cochrane, Trans.). Chicago, IL: University of Chicago Press.

5   History

The history we read, though based on facts, is, strictly speaking, not factual at all, but a series of accepted judgments.

Geoffrey Barraclough

Attempts at periodization have obscured public relations and its history.

Lamme and Russell (2010, p. 281)

This chapter opens the closed, evolutionary, progressivist historiography that underlies most public relations (PR) textbooks and much scholarly research.

When Botan and Hazelton (1989) published their first of two collections on PR theory, their rationale was clear: PR was atheoretical. It lacked a theory base – its own theory base. Unlike cognate social sciences like sociology and psychology, PR would never be taken seriously by the scholarly and academic world in its then theory-less condition.

That was then. But it is no longer the case. In the quarter century since those theory-less days, there has been a bull market for PR theories. These theories underlie the lion's share of research published not only in the quantitatively oriented *Journal of Public Relations Research* but in the oldest peer-reviewed PR journal, the *Public Relations Review*, founded by Ray Hiebert, the PR historian and biographer of Ivy Lee.

Today, what characterizes PR is not any lack of interest in theory but its dismissal of history. In part, to account for this misperception and imbalance, this chapter begins by pondering PR's historical paucity and ends by proposing an unconventional historical perspective. The final third of the chapter examines how rethinking PR history reflects the practice's definitive strategic ambiguities.

PR's historical disinterest, combined with its increasing pace of theory building, raises questions of fact as well as opinion. Has PR ever given evidence of an interest in history? Is there a prevailing concept of history in PR scholarship? If PR had, at one time, an interest in history, when did that interest begin to decline? Are there problems associated with PR disinterest in history? Is there a relationship between the decline in historical interest and the growth of theory?

The history of PR scholarship during the Grunig era was to place PR as a "scientific" edifice. But there are many cracks in that edifice, including its spurious, truncated progressivist American-centric concept of history. Nevertheless, inferentially based social science methodologies such as content analysis would be one place to begin such an investigation. Of course, such an analysis would demonstrate the probability – but not the truth – of the thesis.

History and theory

Historian Bernays

The most ambitious and prolific scholar in twentieth-century PR, Edward Bernays (1923), appeared to want it both ways. (Bernays, 1923) He worked tirelessly to frame PR as a crystallizing, engineered, sociologically and psychologically legitimated science, as well as an "idea" (his word) and an institution whose history was as long as history itself. In his 60s, after he was well established as a thought leader who had been at the forefront of bringing PR from an idea to an industry, he published a book entitled simply *Public Relations* (1952). As Bernays explained in a preface, the book was not intended as a "how to," which Bernays believed sent the wrong message and failed to tell the real story:

> Since public relations rests fundamentally on ideas, not on mechanics, this [how-to] approach presents a distorted picture.
>
> (p. vii)

Instead, Bernays intended to write the history of PR "to show the reader that modern PR did not spring full-grown out of anybody's brain – that it has its own history and that it has evolved from earliest times out of the needs of human beings for leadership and integration" (p. vii).

Unlike the symmetrists, Bernays meant nothing quite so Darwinian about the adaptation and survival of PR. More significantly, though, Bernays's perspective of PR offers a pair of ideas that conventional, contemporary PR scholarship and textbooks have missed or abandoned: (a) that it is not only PR's "roots" that are ancient but its deepest and most basically human social and political sources, and (2) that what accounts for PR is a historical perspective that carefully parses its periodicity.

These ideas are both more interesting and more radical than PR scholarship has supposed. Although many textbooks continue to offer lip service to the "roots" of PR in antiquity and late modernity, the roots themselves are regarded as historical incidentals and thus disconnected from what PR "really" is – systematic management of applied social science phenomena.

But that is not how PR's first historian understood and explained PR. For Bernays, the way to understand the idea of PR was through its history. Notwithstanding Bernays's scientific ambitions, he understood science more as a historian with a keen interest in borrowing from scientific ideas and articulating them metaphorically. "Obviously," he wrote, "public relations is not an exact science. But the approach to the problems encountered [by society] can be scientific – social engineering, the engineering of consent, humanics, human relations, or whatever term we wish to give it" (p. 5).

Whatever term we wish to give it. Exactly. It wasn't a science that Bernays was creating. It was terms. Words. Ideas. It is in this sense that science was not, for Bernays, primary – at least, not for understanding the nature of the idea of PR.

The depth of Bernays's interest in the history of PR may be gauged by the amount of attention he devoted to it in *Public Relations*. The first two chapters ("Public Relations Today" and "Why Public Relations is Vital Today") take but eight pages. The history of PR, from its origins, which "go back to earliest times" (p. 11), to the mid-twentieth century, comprise the next nine chapters and 114 pages.

I will leave it to disciplinary historians to critique the amateur efforts of Bernays's commentary on the succession of civilizations from Sumeria, Babylonia, Assyria and Persia, to Egypt, Greece, Rome, the "Dark Ages," the Renaissance, Reformation, Counter-Reformation and onward to the Enlightenment and revolutions of the eighteenth century and the Napoleonic era, socialist movements, industrialization and growing mass literacy of the nineteenth century.

That breathless historical panoply, from the fourth millennium BC to the founding of colonial America, take but two chapters and 25 pages. The next seven chapters and 100 pages are devoted to American PR over three and half centuries. The perception – increasingly invalid with the globalization of communication and information – that PR is *sui generis* American has its origins, in no small part, in the prodigiously prolific reach of Bernays himself.

As historians well know, there are many approaches to writing history. If Bernays was not a scientist – and he was not – neither was he a historian, strictly speaking. That is, it wasn't history itself that preoccupied Bernays. It was that he saw history as the way to account for what PR really is – or was. No doubt professional historians would hardly deign to honor Bernays's chapter with the term *history*. Clearly, Bernays's accounts of complex civilizations over millennia are impressionistic. What is worth our attention, however, is what Bernays himself attended to: his thesis that from ancient to modern times, humans communicated.

It can be observed that Bernays's idea of history is partially, but not completely, *uniformitarian* – which is the belief in the stability of human nature permanently and universally. However, the complex and famous debates about the ideas of history, including historicism, are not altogether pertinent to the purposes of the current chapter. It is sufficient to note that the overarching historical perspective of Bernays (1952) in his storytelling of PR history revolves around the definition he offered of PR at the outset of his book: that PR is "(1) information given to the public; (2) persuasion directed at the public to modify attitudes and actions, and (3) efforts to integrate attitudes and actions of an institution with its publics and of publics with that institution" (p. 3).

PR scholars and students will recognize the persistence of these ideas in many current definitions of PR. However, the second idea – persuasion – was demoted to the status of "asymmetric" by the dominant theorists of PR, who theorized a more ethical and excellent model based on a more symmetric concepts such as negotiation and the "willingness to change."

As for a thesis of this chapter – the relationship between the decline of PR history and the rise of the social science approach – Bernays (1952) included "the development and acceptance of the social sciences" among the many reasons for "the rise of the new profession of adjustment" (p. 3).

Historically speaking, the uniformitarianism of Bernays's history of PR derives less from the close investigation of history itself than from Bernays's perspective that the principles of PR can be seen as embedded in societies throughout history. Unlike Grunig, who presumed to correct and improve upon Bernays's idea of PR, Bernays did not allow his passion for science and engineering to dwarf and minimize his respect for history.

Metatheory

As Botan and Taylor (2006) noted, the evidence indicates that PR theory is growing toward abundance. Ever since the early 1990s, when the PR academic discipline managed to establish itself as an applied social science, the dynamic of theory *building* became theory *competition*, according to Botan and Taylor:

> With about 250 [research and theory] papers presented to the public relations divisions in the Association for Education in Journalism and Mass Communication (AEJMC), the International Communication Association (ICA), the National Communication Association (NCA), and the International Public Relations Research Conference (IPRRC) in 2003, public relations may be poised to become one of the most researched areas of communication.
>
> (p. 1)

The same cannot be said of historical approaches to PR. If PR theory building has been a long bull market, the historical approach to the discipline has declined just as sharply, although from a much smaller base. In Heath and Toth's (1992) first collection of essays about rhetorical and critical approaches to PR, the index lists eight references, including five paradigms comprising progressives, counter-progressives, management, new left and new right. A generation later, Heath, Toth and Waymer (2009) indexed but a single reference to history: the "historical context" within the feminist approach to PR:

> Recently, feminists have begun to see the necessity of including historical contexts in their work" (Heath, Toth & Waymer, 2009 referencing Ashcraft & Mumby, 2004). As Laura Sjoberg (2006) indicated, "feminists see that history is the study of masculinity in global politics."
>
> (in Sjoberg, 2006, p. 292; in Heath et al., p. 113)

In other words, it has been feminists who almost, but not entirely, alone among PR scholars have recognized that the theoretical rigor of their research and the persuasiveness of their political, sociological and economic arguments could never abide the exclusion of history. It is the thesis of the historical sociologist Margaret Somers (1991, p. 7) that all social theory is historical and, consequently, needs to be historically grounded. Somers cited and quoted Terrence McDonald's (1996) observation of "the historic turn in the human sciences," which, according to Somers, is a question that "touches on some of the most critical and contested issues facing not just historical sociology but the social sciences across the board." (p. 7).

In the movement of the dominant coalition of PR scholars to reframe the discipline as an applied social science, the almost total lack of interest in history is highly problematic. PR theory is social theory and, as such, ignores history in its theory development at its own peril.

What is proposed in this chapter's extended reflection on the historical nature of PR is not an attempt to create a "scientific" theory of history on which to ground a theory of PR. Rather, it is to elaborate on what I have published in previous "meta-theoretical" reflections on certain extraordinarily influential individuals and historical periods that predate not only the PR tactics in nineteenth-century America of P.T. Barnum – PR history's straw man – but the founding of America itself. By *meta-theoretical* I mean a critical approach to theory that comments on, rather than develops, theory. Among previous considerations of extraordinarily influential figures have been Saint Paul and the popes of the Catholic Propagandio during the Catholic Reformation (or Counter-Reformation) of the seventeeth century (Brown, 2004). The coauthors of a multi-edition PR textbook, Newsom, Turk and Kruckerberg (1996) noted the historical source of PR in propaganda two centuries before the installation of Barnum in the PR textbook consensus. It was the establishment of the Catholic *Propagandio* (or "propagation of the faith") by Pope Gregory XV in 1622. Beginning in 1988, this PR organization renamed itself The Congregation for the Evangelization of Peoples (Vatican Museums, n.d.).

As for the inclusion of Saint Paul in the tradition of PR, the idea was suggested to me by the classicist Jeffrey Hart (2001) who reminded us that Paul was among the most highly influential figures in the history of Western civilization. The idea of *influence* seems to me inseparable from the reality of PR. But the inception and reception of symmetry theory has sought to exclude both influence and persuasion from the "excellent" and "ethical" practice of PR. Such an abandonment is not borne out in the day-to-day planning and implementation of PR, nor could it reasonably be argued that rejecting persuasion was what Bernays intended by promoting ethics and social responsibility. In contrast to symmetry's devaluation of history, the PR of everything offers an endorsement of the historical imagination. Such a perspective in no way implies the devaluation of science but rather an approach that avoids scientism at the expense of history.

Some examples may be offered of PR scholars' approach to PR's history. In *Public Relations: The Profession and the Practice,* the second edition of the textbook by Lattimore, et al. (2007), a chapter on history is the second of 17. In framing history as lessons for the study of PR, the authors diverged from the abandonment of history by PR scholars and practitioners. Yet for both scholars and practitioners, abandoning history is puzzling. For, as the authors noted, history offers the source of PR in the rhetorical approaches in Greece during the fifth century BC.

The now-current eleventh edition of the popular textbook by Fraser P. Seitel (2011), *The Practice of Public Relations,* also gives its second chapter over to history. The chapter is called "The History and Growth of Public Relations," a reference to the conventional historical trope of PR education and scholarship that frames the institution as essentially the invention of late modernity. That PR can be said to have "ancient beginnings" (Seitel, 2011, p. 23) somehow manages to leave unaltered the conviction that the institution is not only a creature of late modernity but an American innovation. It is worth noting that in the obligatory references to the Federalist Papers and to America's founding fathers, PR has framed itself as much in political as historical terms. That conventionally framed PR scholarship and textbooks have recognized the PR nature of particular movements and individuals in history but not other movements and individuals is an example of the failure of critical thinking. Why stop with the American Revolution when there's Saint Paul?

In Morris and Goldsworthy's (2012) textbook *PR Today: The Authoritative Guide to Public Relations,* PR history is entirely absent, save for a seven-page section in the first chapter subheaded "Lessons From History." The book was published in the United Kingdom, and the authors usefully included the Usual American Suspects (P.T. Barnum, Bernays, etc.) and a reference to Philip M. Taylor (2003), the public diplomacy scholar who wrote *Munitions of the Mind: A History of Propaganda From the Ancient World to the Present Era.* The *PR Today* textbook authors took pains to explain that Taylor's concept of propaganda, as a "deliberate attempt to persuade people to think and behave in a desired way," is in fact related to the deliberative process of PR (p. 11).

Although it is the prevailing, axiomatic assumption that PR and propaganda are mutually exclusive, the reality of their relationship is far more nuanced. Although PR's severest critics, such as Noam Chomsky, conflate PR with propaganda, blaming Bernays and his "engineering" and "manufacturing" of consent, perspectives not so biased are willing to grant that there are many essential distinctions between PR and propaganda. Nevertheless, the PR scholar Burton St. John (2006) made a persuasive case for the existence of "ethical propaganda" in the case of Ivy Lee's transparent approach to PR in an early twentieth century case involving the monopolist John D. Rockefeller and the American railroads.

Definitions

That said, we now turn to the matter of how history is defined. Definitions of history abound. For the purposes of this chapter, I follow historian John H. Arnold's (2000) interpretation of history as "the past itself as well as what historians write about the past" and historiography as "the process of writing history" (p. 5). That these definitions were intended by the author to encompass all of written history, from Herodotus to the present, is in keeping with the idea of PR as multidisciplinary and radically inclusive.

Legitimacy

The late, esteemed, and historically oriented PR scholar Ron Pearson (2009) wrote insightfully,

> If all writing about the past is partly an effort to understand the present, a confusing and contradictory present would seem to call more insistently for historical analysis and explanation. This is especially true for the profession and academic discipline of public relations.
>
> (p. 92)

In Pearson's recognition is the implication of the wholeness of PR, both as a social theory and as a basis of its ethical defense. Pearson cited PR historian Ray Hiebert, whose deep commitment to history included his standard biography of Ivy Lee. Hiebert noted that it was Ivy Lee who said, in 1921, that "Without public relations, democracy could not succeed in a mass society" (Pearson, p. 95).

Put another way, it is a PR historian's approach to PR that has mounted the ethical defense of PR as necessary to modern democratic societies, as opposed to the criticism of PR as an image-obsessed, pseudo-event-making, antidemocratic institution. Hiebert's Ivy Lee is a PR innovator whose sensibility was not that of a social scientist but more clearly political and historical. To understand Ivy Lee, for Hiebert, was to understand the inseparability of the historical and the political. It is from this holistic perspective that Americans speak of their presidents in terms of an enumerated historical succession from the first, George Washington, to the forty-fourth, Barack Obama. It is also from this perspective that Great Britain has educated its students in the much longer succession of monarchs and prime ministers, and Catholics with the most powerful of memories can name the historical succession of the papacy.

In his treatment of the historical approach to PR, Pearson's central concern was its legitimacy. Hiebert (1966) framed that legitimacy in distinctly historical and political terms – terms that implicitly suggest a justification of the ethics of PR. That justification rests on the kind of ambiguity discussed in the chapters in this volume on ethics and politics – the kind attributed (albeit, dubiously sourced) to Winston Churchill's oft-cited justification of democracy as the worst form of government, with the exception of all others.

A likely explanation of history's absence from PR thought is that PR has sought to include itself among the social sciences; history, classified as a humanity, has never been integrated into the decades-old theory-building project of PR. The abiding relationship of PR with the missions and practices of management, with its orientation to current accountability and future directions, is another likely reason for the perceived irrelevancy of history to organizational success. Lip service is paid, and special events are mounted, to recognize the value of "institutional memory" and the historical founding of organizations. However, in the perception of management, the value of PR can never be independent of persuasive evidence of PR's contribution to management's objectives. As a result, PR is expected to contribute to the marketing, economic and financial metrics of organizations. And because the dominant paradigm of PR regards PR as "communication manage-ment," PR has purchased the perception of its value at the cost of tethering itself to organizational managerialism. It is its relationship with management that calls into question the ability of PR to define itself as an independent entity or institu-tion. Its vaunted "distinctiveness" is limited to the larger and imposing power of the management to which the PR "function" is accountable.

Not every PR practitioner, agency or department would regard this organizational servitude (or consultant function) as a bad deal for PR. Rather, it is generally regarded as necessary and even axiomatic. Nor is PR's obedient asymmetry to senior management's power limited to the environments of corporate communica-tions or publicly held companies. Organizational management's perception of func-tions and subfunctions of PR is not essentially different in organizations classified as activist, nonprofit, higher education, health care, military – and, in what will seem a rather unsettling or outrageous notion – even terrorist environments. Are there not publicity and social media functionaries in the hierarchical, networked organization of global Al Qaeda? And is that question really so far-fetched?

In contrast to the prevailing scholarly assumption of PR as a child of exclusive modernity, PR's history will be understood in the broader context of a classical and continuing tradition.

Such a historical rethinking aligns far more easily with the rhetorical, critical, sociological and political sources of the discipline – and with the long flow of his-tory itself – than with what I have called "the myth of symmetry" (Brown, 2006). That theory posits PR as an "evolution" beginning with P.T. Barnum in the mid-nineteenth century and progresses liberally and ethically past the limits of persuasion toward an equitable balance.

Problematics

The perception of PR theoretical paucity is the consequence of four kinds of prob-lematics. One, the problem of interrelatedness: that the paucity of theory is related to the poverty of history. Two, the problem of academic sociology: the assumption that PR is an applied social science rather than an interdisciplinary study or a human-ity (L'Etang & Pieczka, 1996). That problem is, in turn, related to the official defi-nition of PR as "distinctive." Three, the problem of historiography: that PR history is modern history. This latter problem is, in turn, related to the assumption that PR is a collection of functions. Four, the problem of presentism and futurism bias: that PR is concerned not with the past but with the present and the future. The moder-nity bias of PR historiography accounts in part not only for the assumption that PR emerged and evolved from technology. This bias has also arbitrarily assigned the technological sources of PR to the nineteenth century, beginning with photography and moving with lightning speed to the Internet. What should be obvious to PR scholars who are familiar with Marshall McLuhan's ideas of technology is that technology did not begin in the nineteenth century but represents an extension of man, as the Roman Empire's roads were an extension of the legs of the Romans.

But as bias PR historian Andy Piasecki (2000) observed, PR was already sophisticated in the middle of the nineteenth century during the very period in which symmetry theory claims that PR was just beginning. As Piasecki wrote, "Public relations practices of the railroad companies during this [American frontier] era were sophisticated and managerial" (p. 1).

As Pearson (2009) observed, the interpretation of history must be understood as an expression of the beliefs of the historian:

> No single, obviously correct public relations history exists; rather there are a plurality of public relations histories.
>
> (p. 93)

This wired-in subjectivity "can be seen as a main conclusion following the themes of postmodern rhetorical theory" (p. 93).

The rejection of foundationalism – the belief in the reality of a true, objective history external to the colorations of subjectivity – is one of the sensibilities not only of postmodernity but of our own era. In this respect, our era may be contrasted, obviously, with the Enlightenment, or at least our era's subjective view of the Enlightenment's foundationalistic cast of mind. Lest these contrasts appear simplistic, it should be said that the skepticism of our times shares the stage uneasily with equally if not more powerful beliefs in technologically and engineering-driven solutionism as well as with various and sundry religious fundamentalisms.

From the early twentieth-century pioneering of Bernays to reframe PR from propaganda to the engineering of consent, PR has sought to wrap itself in the mantle of science and the language of statistical probabilism (Brown, 2004). However, by distancing itself from mere impressionism, PR has devalued history. Even when textbooks, rather than websites, are used to teach PR, the obligatory chapter on PR history is, at most, marginal to the pedagogy. Nor does PR textbook history interrogate the modernist assumptions of PR's evolutionary trope that has been called "the myth of symmetry" (Brown, 2006).

The theory-building project of PR has been patiently detailed in a pair of volumes edited by Carl Botan and Vincent Hazelton. The evidence of these volumes demonstrates virtually no interest in historical approaches. At the risk of exhausting the reader's patience with a list, here is the complete table of contents from the apparently exhaustive compendium of PR theories that have been developed in just the previous generation: The contents of Botan and Hazelton's (2010) *Public Relations Theory II* include, from the first essay to the last, theories of excellence, rhetoric, persuasion, roles, crisis, competence, grand strategy, corporate social responsibility, media relations, social capital, organizational communication, future tools, nation building, structuration, complexity, sense making, technology, government relations, general theory of relationship building, ethical community building and public affairs.

An automated search of the volume yields more than 40 uses of the word *history*, but none of them refer to historical approaches to theory building, and a similar search for *historiography* turns up not a single hit. It is reasonable to conclude that – at least from the perspective of Botan and Hazelton – when it comes to PR scholarship's theory building and conceptualizing about the field, history is simply not included. Nor, I suspect, in the digital–social era, would it be missed or mourned by students or practitioners.

Twenty years before Botan and Hazelton's collection of essays on theory, the admirably concise gathering of descriptions of PR research by John V. Pavlik (1987) did not include history among the thumbnails on research and theory of attitudes, roles and other nodes of the discipline of communication.

The loud silence around the matter of history raises questions, starting with why the disinterest? Is history irrelevant to PR? Should PR textbooks cease including an obligatory chapter about PR history?

Implications

The consequence of these problems is that both historical approaches to PR and scholarship about PR's historiography have been marginalized.

Few approaches to PR are less popular than history. Hamstrung by the assumption of PR as a very young, very modern institution with little more than a century of history, textbooks give history short shrift – sometimes a chapter, other times a glancing reference to the Usual Suspects: Bernays, Lee and Page. Recalling the scholarly writing on PR history, what comes to mind is the cursory outline of the history of PR in Bernays's (1952) textbook, Cutlip's (1994) book on PR's American history and a smattering of insightful work by Hiebert (1966), Marvin Olasky (1987), Ron Pearson (1992, 2009) and a few others.

It would appear that in light of the evidence that the scholars and practitioners of PR have long failed to show the slightest interest in history, the burden of proving history's relevance to PR is on those who, like me, continue to believe in its value.

In the subtitle of his study of PR's history, "The Unseen Power," Cutlip (1994) noted that a source of PR's extraordinary power is its invisibility. Bernays (1928), too, in *Propaganda,* had observed this attribute by calling PR practitioners "invisible wire pullers" (p. 5). From the perspective of the PR of everything, invisibility is no less crucial to the power of PR than the special event, the speech, the press conference and the parade. The imagery of invisibility calls to mind, at once, the social and political world to which Cutlip referred, and perhaps for Bernays, the murky invisibility of the unconscious explored by his famous uncle Sigmund Freud.

Ambiguity

The aforementioned Pearson (1992) usefully outlined five historical perspectives in the approaches to PR. These are indexed in Toth and Heath (1992) in the contrasting pairs of progressive and counterprogressive, new left and new right, as well as the management perspective. The contrasts consist not only of history but of politics, to which Pearson added yet another perspective: economics. In the subheaded section called "PR and the Specter of Socialism: Olasky," Pearson paired the PR historian Marvin Olasky's (1987) historical–critical deconstruction of PR as an institutional strategy to control markets with the business historian R. S. Tedlow's (1979) thesis that business was "secretive and insensitive, indeed contemptuous, of public opinion before the emergence of public relations" (Pearson, 1992, p. 120). As for the conventional trope of PR scholarship – that PR "evolved" – Tedlow adopted a position that resonates with one of the themes of this book's chapters on ethics and politics, namely that the ethics of PR is both complex and somewhat ambiguous:

> He suggested the story of public relations is much more complex and ambiguous.
>
> (Pearson, 1992, p. 121)

Notwithstanding the ambiguous nature of PR, the conventional history of PR is neither ambiguous nor complex but linear and vertical. What symmetry theory did to accommodate its conceptualization of PR that "evolved" in but a half a century from unethical to ethical and excellent was to create a mythical historiography characterized by an unstated nineteenth-century belief in a triumphal progressivism. In the view of the American historian Charles Beard, the idea and faith in progress, attributed to the Irish historian J.B. Bury (1932/1955), was broadly influential from the nineteenth to the twentieth century.

Management

A great deal has been said already about the managerial perspective that flourished in the 1980s with embrace of excellence theory by management culture. Now in its fourth edition, more than a million copies have been sold of Peters and Waterman's (1981) *In Search of Excellence*. The idea of excellence has spawned innumerable how-to books for countless uses extending far beyond business to dozens of environments, professions, teams, groups and individuals. So influential were the book's ideas about the philosophy of excellence and the idea that it could be quantified that by 1992, excellence theory became an equal ideological partner with the "ethics" of symmetry theory, as elaborated in the influential book edited by Grunig (1992) that sought to anatomize and promote excellence theory for PR. Historically speaking, the managerial perspective has held a dominant position in both the scholarly and practitioner worlds since the modern era of Page, Bernays and Lee.

Progressivism

The nineteenth century may not have innovated monetarism, behavioral economics or microfinance. But in the nineteenth century, economics was called *political economy*, indicating that economics was largely understood to be inseparable from politics. Although Pearson (1992) contrasted the critiques of PR from the New Left with those of the New Right, he believed their political disagreements amounted to less than their historical agreements. No matter the historical approach, all the historians

> agree on a number of basic facts. . . . Professionalized public relations is a practice that begins in the last decades of the nineteenth century and first two decades of the twentieth century and arises in the context of significant economic, technological, and social changes associated with that time period.
>
> (p. 126)

What were these "basic facts?" They were a combination of crises (e.g., monopoly capitalism) and progress (e.g., in levels of education, technology and egalitarianism; Pearson, 1992, p. 126). Referencing Hiebert, Pearson concluded that the historical meaning of these changes in PR terms was "the democratizing influence of public relations" (p. 126).

In other words, the idea of PR is bound up with the idea of progress and the political consequence. This, then, suggests that what drives the perspective of the PR history is a teleology whose engine is the idea of progress.

If there is a dominant consensus and perhaps general theory of PR – that of symmetry's equation of excellence and excellent – it is founded on a progressive theory of history. Nothing so animates the historiography of PR as progress. When PR scholars have stooped to consider not only the events of the past but their collective historical meaning, their voices have been nearly unanimous that things have been getting steadily better. The prevailing idea of PR history has it that PR has gone from bad to better – much better.

Casting doubt on this sunny historiography requires but a healthy skepticism. Some questions arise. What is the evidence for the bad-Barnum-to-ethical-excellence story? Does that reassuring historiography benefit the PR industry, and if so, how? What part, if any, does the textbook trope of "evolution" play in PR's ideas of its own history?

PR's ideology

Bernays set the tone for the little-noted but foundational historiography of what is referred to in this chapter as the *general theory of PR*. Except for taking issue with the ethics and efficacy of persuasion in Bernays's conception of PR, Grunig reiterated Bernays's progressive historiography, although without Bernays's respectful concern for history.

PR, in its rhetorical character, has absorbed and channeled three ideas: the triumph of positivism and science, the call to programmatic action and the improvement of human and social life.

These intellectual and ideological relationships appear in Grunig and Hunt's (1984) textbook *Managing Public Relations*. The title of the second chapter of this influential textbook – "Origins and Contemporary Structure of Public Relations" – offers a clue. It is interesting in that rather than proposing consideration of history and structure separately, Grunig and Hunt connected them in what contemporary Internet jargon refers to as a *mashup*. Thus connected, the authors proceeded to conceive the textbook version of what might be fairly described as a general theory of PR – a theory based on the idea of progress.

Putting aside, for a moment, that the authors of this general theory of PR would, under many critiques over several decades, back it down to a "willingness to change," what was left unchanged was its historiographical foundation.

What was that foundation? It was the idea that PR was (a) modern and (b) a series of four distinct and discrete worldviews: aethical and unprofessional press agentry; the more professional but ambiguously ethical information model; the yet more professional but ethically questionable persuasion model; and, last, the "normative" but ahistorical equation of excellence and ethics whose existence is outside the realm of both history and experience.

Critical questions arise. Why only four models, rather than, say, one or five or 20? What point is there in beginning with Barnum, other than to make him a straw man to project a progressive theory of PR? Does Barnum's use of newspaper publicity provide an adequate reason to cast him as PR's *ubermensch?* What, then, of the woodcut illustrations that abounded in the millions of printed persuasive pamphlets of the eras following Gutenberg and Luther and countered by the Catholic Reformation of the seventeenth century? What, then, of the more than half the New Testament that comprises the letters of Paul to the Jesus cults of the first century AD (Brown, 2003, 2004; Lamme & Russell, 2010; Tilson, 2011)? Were these, in the phrase of Grunig and Hunt (1984), merely "public relations-like activ-ities in history" (p. 14)? What makes the activities in history of Barnum "real" but the activities of the Catholic propagation of the faith not sufficiently real, other than the textbook authors' interest in developing a modernist and progressive theory of PR?

But rather than single out the historiography of Grunig and Hunt, it should be noted that they didn't invent the progressive wheel. It was set in motion by none other than Bernays (1952). The modernist and evolutionary historiography of PR is laid out in chapters three through 11 of *Public Relations.* By the time of publica-tion of that book, less than a decade after World War II, Bernays had long since made his reputation with the two seminal books he published in the decade fol-lowing World War I: *Crystallizing Public Opinion* (1923) and *Propaganda* (1928). But it was the publication of *Propaganda* – coming, as it did, in the wake of the historical darkening of the meaning of the term in the era of fascism – that repre-sented a sea change for Bernays and the idea of PR. In *Public Relations,* Bernays made a dozen references to *propaganda,* referencing its initial usage in the *propa-gandio* of the Catholic Reformation and referring to the propaganda of mid-nineteenth century Europe as "political propaganda of the dubious kind" (p. 48). In the fashion of the ethical ambiguity of PR (Chapter 5), Bernays offered a binary distinction between the "kind" of bad (or dubious) propaganda and the good and moral political propaganda of the American Committee on Public Information (or Creel Committee), meant simply and pro-ethically to influence public opinion

(p. 75). As Bernays reported it in *Public Relations,* the problem with American wartime propaganda wasn't ethics but "improvisation" (p. 75):

> Public relations activities in World War I never attained their full potential. They were never really co-ordinated or integrated in any country and were largely a matter of improvisation.
>
> (p. 75)

In Bernays's progressive historiography of PR, PR's "coming of age" was the period he designated beginning with 1929, the year immediately following 1928, when *Propaganda* was published. What Bernays did seemed nothing more than mere euphemism, which disgusted George Orwell who deconstructed propaganda's playing fast and loose with language in *Politics and the English Language* (1946/2006). Bernays deleted the word *propaganda* from the idea of PR and replaced it with the phrase *public relations counsel.* It was, in effect, an attempt to redact and rebrand PR itself. Public relations counselor: it was the phrase Bernays used to describe himself. He retained the phrase for the title of his memoir in 1965.

As for the period Bernays designated as PR's "coming of age," it is the idea of history framed as the idea of progress: "Carrying forward the tenets of the reform movements that had developed since the Civil War and had found expression in legislation under [Presidents Grover] Cleveland, Theodore Roosevelt, and [Woodrow] Wilson, President Franklin Roosevelt initiated far-reaching reforms" (p. 99).

The dominant general theory of PR, cast as normative (what should be) is a rhetorically hedged bet. By avoiding a direct and declarative "face claim" for the ethics and excellence of PR, the general theory has been able to take dominion over the uncomfortably ambiguous spaces of PR. Either explicitly or implicitly, the general theory continues to be endorsed by the industry's practitioners, academics and trade organizations such as the Public Relations Student Society of America (PRSSA). The endorsements have been enacted and expressed in programs of corporate social responsibility, cause branding and cobranding nonprofits, nongovernmental organizations and organizations of health care and the arts. The U.S. industry's trade organization, the Public Relations Society of America, is allied with the PRSSA, a sister organization for students. At the beginning of each academic year, these organizations publish a special issue of a newsletter themed around ethics.

Framing PR as an ethical profession is the practice's most reliably evergreen campaign message. PR's defense of itself, which wages the industry's continual war against its many critics, is targeted to, and communicated through, classroom teachers, practitioners and scholars. Much is at stake. PR professors benefit from evidence that supports the academic legitimacy of their discipline. Practitioners benefit from rhetoric and investments that burnish perceptions of PR practice among their constituencies. PR scholars benefit from the boost in academic legitimacy as well as the persuasive power associated with research conducted in the putatively testable framework of a social science.

Evolution

The idea that PR has "evolved" is a familiar trope for the classroom and the journal. The idea has been frequently challenged as a myth (Brown, 2006; L'Etang, 2008). The idea of PR's evolution is wired into PR's general (dominant) theory. Although evolution is a staple of PR textbooks, its acceptance has been uncritical. That PR is somehow better today than it was when it began appears too common-sensical to be challenged. But the challenges have been mounted, from several sources. The first of these critiques have come from the self-named, unofficial group of "radical PR" scholars (see their blog at http://radicalpr.wordpress.com/). Assembled for a 3-day conference at the Stirling University, Scotland, in July 2008, 31 PR scholars from Europe, South American, Australia and New Zealand presented papers. Each paper took a postsymmetry view of PR, approaching PR from rhetorical, feminist, postcolonial, ethnographic, sociological, historiographic and other qualitative methodologies.

Other sources, which amount to further expressions of the "radical" movement, can be identified in the postsymmetry scholarship of Lamme and Russell (2010), Tilson (2011). What unites these disparate and far-flung scholars is not only (or in every case) the rejection of the general theory's idea of "evolution," but their postsymmetric, qualititative, multidisiplinary approaches to PR. In "Removing the Spin: Toward a New Theory of Public Relations History," Lamme and Russell mounted a thesis that challenges PR's symmetry-based historiography, including its assumptions about periodization and its "functional" structure.

> In the absence of a general theory that describes the rise and growth of public relations, scholars have tended to organize public relations and its antecedents into time periods that present a progressive evolution from unsophisticated and unethical early roots to planned, strategic and ethical campaigns of the current day. We argue that such attempts at periodization have obscured our understanding of public relations and its history. Indeed, public relations historians have long called for such a departure, noting the constraints it has imposed on understanding the development of public relations in the United States and around the world.
>
> (Lamme & Russell, 2010, p. 281)

Lamme and Russell (2010) rejected symmetry's conception of PR for the way that the theory has limited our understanding of PR. What these scholars have done is to break away from misleading dependence on linear interpretations of the field's past and construct a long-term view of the development and institutionalization of persuasive organizational communication strategies and techniques (Aldoory, 2009, p. 113).

Breaking away from the constraints of an evolutionary historiography has enabled PR scholar Burton St. John (2006) to develop his idea of "ethical propaganda," and Tilson (2011) his idea of the profane, popular and sacred "covenant" that character-izes the nature of PR's relationships from ancient to contemporary times.

Rethinking functionalism

Like Lamme and Russell and others, Tilson adopted the postsymmetric nonevolu-tionary, nonperiodized, nonlinear idea of history. Others in the "radical" camp have moved the conversation about PR well outside the strict, internally self-referential theory building of the previous generation. The results have enriched the scholar-ship of PR from the perspectives of culture, discourse analysis, ethnography, reli-gion, internationalism, phenomenology and sociology. A benefit of such broadening could eventually be the admission of PR scholars to the conversations carried on without their participation by politicians, political scientists, historians, sociolo-gists and others in the social sciences and humanities.

A further critique of PR's conventional approach to history has been the result of rethinking its functionalism. Lamme and Russell (2010) proposed "that a new theory of the history of PR begin with the public relations function itself" (p. 355). In the view of those scholars, what has mattered historically is less about the "func-tions" of PR and more, in a broader and simpler sense, about "what they knew to do" (p. 356). What they knew "might well have been grounded in religion, politics, and reform, rather than in business" (p. 356).

Ultimately, that rethinking led the scholars to the thesis of this book's argument against the prevailing idea of PR as an essentially modern institution:

> The public relations function has remained remarkably consistent over time, even without the twentieth century rules of engagement.
>
> (p. 356)

If I have any quibble with Lamme and Russell, it is perhaps a small one: I fail to see the need to continue describing PR in functional terms. A more "radical" question would ask why PR scholarship even needs a theory of history. Three reasons come to mind. The first is intuitive: that history infuses the meaning of everything – of our experience of the world and ourselves, and the sense making we bring to that experience and this world. Context, is has been said, gives mean-ing, and as long as the quest for meaning is meaningful for us, context, background and origins will continue to interest us.

The second narrower and more specific rationale for the importance of history to PR scholarship comes from the discipline of historical sociology, which says that all social theory is historical. Where PR history has been focused almost exclusively on cases, campaigns, events and individuals of modernity, virtually no attention has been paid to the theoretical and sociological underpinning of histori-cal thinking.

The third reason for restoring a deeper, critical concern for history to PR schol-arship is that for better or worse, PR scholarship will continue to rely upon some idea of history. Far better, then, for PR to embrace and rethink its history than to accept symmetry's simplistic version or dismiss it altogether.

It is also true, however, that practitioners may have little or no use for PR history outside of institutional memory of organizational culture, cases, failures, and successes. They may well look upon PR scholarship with some degree of ambivalence, depending on their perception of its value to their daily needs, strategies and plans.

That iconic modernist Gertrude Stein (1990) famously remarked of Ezra Pound that he was "a village explainer, excellent if you were a village, if not, not." Without a cash-value relevance that contributes to organizational return on investment, much scholarly thinking in a theoretical vein is destined to be regarded as village explaining. But on the upside, many practitioners, as we see in Chapter 8 of this volume, not only appreciate ideas about their practice but have what could be called a history of putting those ideas into practice.

References

Aldoory, L. (2009). Feminist criticism in public relations: How gender can impact public relations and texts and contexts. In R. L. Heath, E. L. Toth & D. Waymer (Eds.), *Rhetorical and critical approaches to public relations* (pp. 110–123). New York, NY: Routledge.

Arnold, J. H. (2000). *History: A very short introduction.* Oxford, England: Oxford University Press.

Ashcraft, K. L. & Mumby, D. K. (2004). Organizing a critical communicology of gender and work. *International Journal of the Sociology of Language, 166,* 19–43.

Bernays, E. L. (1923). *Crystallizing public relations.* Brooklyn, NY: Ig Publishers.

———. (1928). *Propaganda.* New York, NY: Horace Liveright.

———. (1952). *Public relations.* Norman: University of Oklahoma Press.

Botan, C. H. & Hazelton, V., Jr. (Eds.). (1989). *Public relations theory.* New York, NY: Routledge.

Botan, C. H., & Hazelton, V.(2010). *Public relations theory II.* New York: Routledge.

Botan, C. H. & Taylor, M. (2006). The state of the field. *Journal of Communication, 54*(4), 645–661.

Brown, R. E. (2003). Saint Paul as a public relations practitioner: A metatheoretical speculation on messianic communication and symmetry. *Public Relations Review, 29,* 229–240.

———. (2004). The propagation of awe: Public relations, art and belief in reformation Europe. *Public Relations Review, 30,* 381–389.

———. (2006). The myth of symmetry: Public relations as cultural styles. *Public relations Review, 32*(3), 206–212

Bury, J.B. (1955). *The idea of progress: An inquiry into its growth and origin.* New York, NY: Dover.

Cutlip, S. (1994). *Public relations history: The unseen power.* Mahwah, NH: Erlbaum.

Hart, J. (2001). *Smiling through the apocalypse: Toward the revival of higher education.* New Haven, CT: Yale University Press.

Grunig, J. E., (Ed). (1992). Excellence in public relations and communication management. New York: Routledge.

Grunig, J. E. & Hunt, T. (1984). *Managing public relations.* Fort Worth, TX: Holt, Rinehart & Winston.

Heath, R. L., Toth, E. L. & Waymer, D. (Eds.). (2009). *Rhetorical and critical approaches to public relations II.* New York, NY: Routledge.

Hiebert, R. E. (1966). *Courtier to the crowd. The story of Ivy Lee and the development of public relations.* Ames: Iowa State University Press.

Lamme, M. O. & Russell, K. M. (2010). Removing the spin: Toward a new theory of public relations history. *Journalism Communication Monographs* 11(4), 280–362.

Lattimore, D., Baskin, O., Heiman, S. & Toth, E. L. (2007). *Public relations: The profession and the practice*. New York, NY: McGraw-Hill.

L'Etang, J. (2008). *Public relations: Concepts, practice and critique*. London, England: Sage.

L'Etang, J. & Pieczka, M. (1996). *Critical perspectives in public relations*. London, England: International Thomson Business Press.

McDonald, T. (1996). *The historic turn in the human sciences*. Ann Arbor, MI: University of Michigan Press.

Morris, T. & Goldsworthy, S. (2012). *PR Today: The authoritative guide to public relations*. Houndsmill, England: Palgrave.

Newsom, D., Turk, J. V. & Kruckeberg, D. (1996). *This is PR: The realities of public relations*. Belmont, CA: Wadsworth.

Olasky, M. N. (1987). *Corporate public relations and American private enterprise: A new historical perspective*. Hillsdale, NJ: Erlbaum.

Orwell, G. (1946/2006). *Politics and the English language*. Peterborough, Ontario, Canada: Broadview Press.

Pavlik, J. V. (1987). *Public relations: What the research tells us*. Thousand Oaks, CA: Sage.

Piasecki, A. (2000). Blowing the railroad trumpet: Public relations on the American frontier. *Public Relations Review, 26*(1), 53–65.

Pearson, R. (1992). Perspectives on public relations history. In E. L. Toth & R. L. Heath (Eds.), *Rhetorical and critical approaches to public relations* (pp. 111–130). Hillsdale, NJ: Erlbaum.

———. (2009). Perspectives on public relations history. In R. L. Heath, E. L. Toth & D. Waymer (Eds.), *Rhetorical and critical approaches to public relations II* (pp. 93–109). New York, NY: Routledge.

Seitel, F. (2011). *The practice of public relations* (11th ed.). Upper Saddle River, NJ: Prentice-Hall.

Sjoberg, L. (2006). Gendered realities of the immunity principle. Why gender analysis needs feminism. *International Studies Quarterly, 50*, 889–910.

Somers, M. R. (1991). We're no angels: Realism, rational choice, and rationality. *American Journal of Sociology, 97*, 1.

Stein, G. (1990). *The autobiography of Alice B. Toklas*. New York: Vintage.

St. John, B. (2006). The case for ethical propaganda within a democracy: Ivy Lee's successful 1913–1914 railroad rate campaign. *Public Relations Review, 32*, 221–228.

Taylor, P. M. (2003). *Munitions of the mind: A history of propaganda*. Manchester, England: Manchester University Press.

Tedlow, R. S. (1979). *Keeping the corporate image: Public relations and business. 1900–1950*. Greenwich, CT: JAI.

Toth, E. L. & Heath, R. L. (Eds.). (1992). *Rhetorical and critical approaches to public relations*. Hillsdale, NJ: Erlbaum.

Tilson, D. (2011). *The promotion of devotion: Saints, celebrities and shrines*. Champaign, IL: Common Ground.

Vatican Museums. (n.d.). *Propaganda fide*. Retrieved from http://mv.vatican.va/3_EN/pages/x-Schede/METs/METs_Main_06.html

Part II

The humanities of public relations

6   Voices

A pair of related themes animate this chapter. The first concerns the problematic retreat from historical thinking that has characterized public relations (PR) scholarship in the symmetry era. The second is about a way in which history of PR can be rethought in cultural terms as what has been called "cultural styles" (Brown, 2006; O'Malley, 2004). What can help remediate the scholarly silence on PR history is an approach to history that makes PR audible as a series of voices. What follows may be thought of as a historiographical typology of four voices of PR: prophetic, academic, humanistic and artistic.

The idea of the PR voice can be understood to resonate with the PR face, explored in Chapter 3. Together, voice and face flesh out the embodiment of PR.

The term *cultural styles* is the coinage of a scholar from the margins of the PR discipline. The cultural–historical schema is modestly referred to as a "device" by its author, J. W. O'Malley (2004), a historian of Christianity. O'Malley did not propose his "device" as a metanarrative but as an exploration of history from multiple perspectives. It is not, strictly speaking, a religious or spiritual perspective, but an inclusive, aesthetic and humanistic one.

The historiographical schema in this chapter is more conceptual than theoretical, if theory means scientific methodology. The cultural-styles device conceives history outside the conventions of periodization. Instead, the device's operative principle permits ancient speech to occupy the same historiographical space as modern and postmodern speech. It is a historiography absent the dubious conceits of symmetry theory's "evolution." It has neither symmetry's defensive teleology nor its unstated assumption of nineteenth-century progressivist ideology (Brown, 2006). What follows may be understood as intellectual history.

O'Malley's (2004) schema of Western civilization classifies history into four cultural styles: prophesy and reform; the academy and the professions; poetry, rhetoric and the common good; and art and performance. These styles offer distinctive and often sharply divergent ways of thinking about the same matters. Communications scholars are likely to be quite familiar with such variations in attitudes, beliefs and opinions. Philosophers are well acquainted with variant epistemological perspectives.

Before overlaying examples from PR history and PR's voices onto O'Malley's four cultural styles, a description of those styles is warranted. Two advantages provide a rationale for rethinking PR history and voices in terms of cultural styles. First, doing so offers a corrective of the flawed historical foundations of symmetry theory. Second, doing so revalues history as a way of accounting for, researching and theorizing about PR.

The relationship of culture to voice may be understood historically as the characteristic sensibility or way of thinking and speaking. It is the voice of a culture that arises from the way it understands the world and its place in it.

Culture 1: The prophetic voice

The sword of the Lord is filled with blood.

Isaiah: 34:6

The digitization of everything, especially "the media," has rendered long-standing ways of organizing working, communicating, and competing obsolete.

Larry Weber (2009, p. ix)

Culture 1 is the voice of terror and transcendence. It is oracular. It addresses mystery and paradox.

O'Malley (2004) identified in this voice "the otherness of God" (p. 6). For the historian of religion, these are the voices of Isaiah, Paul and Luther. These are the voices of Jerusalem and its strange sound that combined frightful and stern tones with the transcendent harmonies of a heavenly choir. In PR terms, Culture 1 is rallies and protests rather than subtleties and negotiation. It is the culture of the protest march for social justice in the resounding oratory of Martin Luther King Jr.'s "I Have a Dream" speech and Nelson Mandela's stirring call for brotherhood before his sentence to years in a South African prison. It is O'Malley's "post-Enlightenment" culture (p. 7). It is a culture that "decries its times" but "must hold out promise of better times to come" (p. 7). These are voices that are "beyond argument" (p. 7); the bringers of good and bad news (p. 7). It is a "message [that] demands conversion, reform, and utter commitment." Taken together, this is the voice of Jerusalem, not the voice of Athens.

Culture 1: Public relations

PR should be familiar with the prophetic voice, for it has become the voice of the digital–social era. It is the voice of innovation, of this-changes-everything! In his theatrical, semicomic, operatic, perambulatory stage presentations, Brian Solis (2011), one of the most widely followed American opinion leaders in marketing communications, channels Isaiah, sounding a warning to businesses that this is the end of business as usual. Failure to embrace new technologies will lead to destruction; salvation lies in abandoning traditional ways of thinking.

Solis's Twitter followers number in the hundreds of thousands. His blog's language is that of apocalypse, transformation and vision. His voice is that of the apocalyptically oracular voice of Culture 1. In *The End of Business as Usual* (2011) he addressed the "youthquake" that has already brought about the destruction of traditional top-down communication. Solis brings a sword to PR's cherished notion of its own definitive distinctiveness. What's really happening is that convergence has all but overwhelmed any solipsistic notions of uniqueness. Where the industry and scholars of PR have sought to defeat such heretical threats as integrated marketing communications and the conflation of marketing and PR, the prophetic voice of the digital–social era's thought leaders see PR's claim to distinctiveness as fruitless in the pivotal inflection of convergence.

The prophetic voice of Charlene Li (Li & Bernoff, 2008) identified this convergence as a "groundswell." Social media has upended the top-down power of Lipmannian–Bernaysian; the old hierarchy has been overthrown. The social–digital web generates power from the ground up. Clay Shirkey (2008), an organizational theorist, entitled his explanation of social media *Here Comes Everybody*, echoing a pun in *Finnegan's Wake*, James Joyce's (1930) convention-shattering novel. Guy Kawasaki (2000) is another technology prophet in Culture 1. He entitled a book *Rules for Revolutionaries*. Howard Rheingold (2002) spoke many years ago of virtual communities and the infiltration, amplification and transformation of media. Taken together, these voices can be heard in the mockingly prophetic songs of Bob Dylan (1965) such as the lyric in "Ballad of a Thin Man":

> Because something is happening here
> And you don't know what it is
> Do you, Mr. Jones?

Not that these prophets predict the end of capitalism. What they prophesize is its transformation and redemption. PR's prophetic voice of End Times typically amounts to a promotional strategy for redeemed organizations to generate new customers, new clients, new brands and new reputations. What the digital–social prophets bring is not a vision of salvation in the afterlife but the promise of happiness in this one. As in the prophetic gospel, the way up is the way down, and the organization must lose its life to gain everlasting life.

The prophetic influence is plain to see in the digitalized and social-mediated shape of PR campaigns. The website of Hill & Knowlton-UK (www.hillandknowlton.co.uk) speaks of "demystifying digital" and has a pull-down tab for social media. In Boston, an agency practicing PR changed its name from Mullen to Mullen PR-Social, with the awareness that its brand-name clients such as Southwest Airlines, Zappos (the online shoe marketer) and Olympus (the camera maker) are eager to be known for innovation. Organizations famous and obscure alike are embracing the prophetic voice of the social–digital revolution by mounting viral marketing, a groundswell of customer-generated Facebook posts, tweets, and other ways to reinvent PR via the advice of Brian Solis's (2010) book title, *Engage!*

PR's Culture 1 prophetic voice echoes down the halls of the agencies created in the image of the Internet god by Larry Weber, the founder of Racepoint, with its click-on site for the digital consumer, and Weber-Shandwick. Weber is occasionally credited with being the first PR entrepreneur in the United States to recognize, as early as the 1980s, the transformative potential of the web. Weber's (2009) call to action, *Sticks & Stones,* is apocalyptically subtitled: *How Digital Business Reputations Are Created Over Time and Lost in a Click.* The ephemeral nature of reputation recalls the centrality of crisis in the culture of PR, which has been elaborated in Chapter 2.

Culture 2: The academic voice

This is the voice of the scholar, the professor and the university. Its tone is rational, empirical, orderly and even-tempered.

If the Biblical prophets were typically eccentrics and freelancers, the academics of Culture 2 are tribal and professional. In O'Malley's (2004) device, Culture 2 is that of Aristotle and Plato, the "school of Athens" (p. 20). It is the voice of Athens, and the voice of science, contrasted with the voice of Culture 1, that of religion (p. 21). The voices of Culture 2 are "analytical, questioning, restless, and relentless" (p. 21). They are the voices of the medieval universities – "rigorous, reflective, and aggressive" (p. 21). In speaking of this as the culture of science, O'Malley used the term culture interchangeably with *philosophy*. Culture 2 was the "triumph of philosophy" (p. 14). Thinking on these matters, the poet T. S. Eliot (1921) identified what he called a "dissociation of sensibility" with the coming of the metaphysical poets of the seventeenth century, a schism that had been the subject of a famous debate in the 1930s about the relative claims of science and modernism, advanced by C. P. Snow, versus those of the literature and tradition, championed by F. R. Leavis (Colini, 2013). No such schism characterizes Culture 2. Its voices are heard in "Descartes, Galileo, Kant, Freud, Einstein, Derrida" (O'Malley, 2004, p. 14) – philosophers all. Although the Leavis–Snow debate has faded into historical obscurity, it signaled how passionate would be the battle for intellectual dominance between Snow's scientific sensibility and Leavis's humanistic sensibility. In the social–digital era, the debate has resurfaced as technorati versus literati and screen culture versus book culture.

Culture 2: Public relations

This academic voice of PR has been particularly strong in PR's twentieth-century modernist period. Among the most prominent voices of PR are the Americans, Grunig and Heath. Each has influenced the ways in which PR's trade organizations, such as Public Relations Society of America, think about PR. Both are identified with one or more than one academic institution. The same can be said for the vast majority of PR scholars, whose relationship to PR is not primarily to practice it but to probe and prescribe it.

Culture 2 is the "triumph of philosophy." We may understand philosophy in its most inclusive sense of embracing the humanities as well as the sciences. The sensibility of the Grunigian symmetrists is scientific in its ambition, approaching PR with the sensibility of the singular hedgehog: quantitatively. The sensibility of the Heathean wranglers is multiple, critical, rhetorical, historical methodologies of the humanities. It is the sensibility of the fox who, in the fable of Archilochus, "knows many things."

In contrast to the Culture 2 philosophers of academia, PR's day-to-day practitioners have typically little or less use for the academic voice, living as they do in a world of intense competition for pitching and keeping clients. It is an environment that favors the fast and pragmatic over the ponderous and normative. With their investment in efficiencies, Culture 2 practitioners have been drawn to systems. This valence may account for the appeal of symmetry with its systems-based foundation. Systematic approaches are not limited to Grunig's popular general theory of PR. Heath's rhetorical approach has generated typologies rather than systems, which can be seen in the typological categories of crisis in Coombs's (2012) situational crisis communication theory.

Despite Heath's rejection of Grunig's symmetry theory, the two philosophers speak in the voice of Culture 2. Each of these academics probes meticulously and advocates a pro-ethical and professional approach to the practice of PR. Their similarities are nothing if not echoes of the similarities of those uber-Culture 2 voices, Plato and Aristotle.

Culture 3: The humanistic voice

How beauteous mankind is!

Shakespeare's Miranda, *The Tempest*

Both Harold and Bill [Burson and Marsteller, co-founders of the eponymous global PR firm] were excellent writers. . . . "There were," Bill wrote, "tall words, short words, fat words, skinny words, boy words, girl words, and so on."

Leaf, 2012 (p. 30)

In Culture 3 we hear the voices of poets and rhetoricians.

Culture 3 was built on the foundation of Isocrates and the Sophists (O'Malley, 2004, p. 14) and the voices of "Cicero, Virgil, St. Ambrose, and St. Augustine" (O'Malley, 2004, p. 14). It is the culture of "poetry, drama, history, and rhetoric (oratory) – which would come to be called a humanistic education" (O'Malley, 2004, p. 14). It was Culture 3 that triumphed in the Renaissance (p. 15), surpassing the academicism of Culture 2.

In modernity, as in ancient times, Culture 3 is evident in

the humanists [who] also created a powerful machine of indoctrination and propagation, the humanistic secondary school, which was variously known as the *Gymnasium,* the *Lycee,* the *Liceo,* the Public School (in England), the Grammar School, and, eventually, the Young Ladies Academy. . . . The ideals

held high in this culture [Culture 3] were embodied and exemplified in literature, which begins with poetry. Homer was the schoolmaster of Greece. In
poetry, the reasons of the heart prevail, in a form of discourse that is more
circular than linear.

(O'Malley, 2004, p. 15)

Culture 3 is the voice of the poet John Keats's (1958) *negative capability,* his
argument that the poet is capable of remaining in doubt, mystery and uncertainty.
In Keats's poetics, Culture 3 anticipates Culture 4's emphasis on the aesthetic and
the beautiful, as it purports to see a different value than that of Culture 2:

Whereas the culture [Culture 2: Academic and Professional] represented by
Plato and Aristotle ends up pursuing Truth, the culture represented by Isocrates
and his followers is more intent upon the Good.

(p. 17)

Where Culture 1 courts innovation, Culture 3's approach is not "original
thought" so much as "the wisdom that knows how to make old truths effective in
new ways" (p. 17). Culture 3 produced Eleanor Roosevelt and Winston Churchill
(p. 19).

Culture 3: Public relations

A culture that prizes the wisdom of the past is, in PR terms, a culture that approaches
PR historically, which is to say unconventionally. Culture 3 PR is Heathean rather
than Grunigian. Because *historically* is an intellectually inclusive term, its meth-
odologies align with the traditions of rhetorical–historical–critical methodologies.
Culture 3 PR scholars tend to publish in the *Public Relations Review* and *Public
Relations Inquiry.* PR scholars with Culture 2 inflections tend to be drawn to the
Journal of Public Relations Research.

In PR terms, Culture 3 is a style that prizes the rhetorical endeavors of speechwriting, phrase making, and wordsmithing. Where Culture 4 will feature the visual,
Culture 3 is steeped in the verbal (as are Cultures 1 and 2.) Culture 3 PR practitioners
are people of the word, a sensibility that resonates with the prophets of Culture 1.
It was from a Culture 3 verbal sensibility that my former boss, the senior writer at
Atlantic Richfield (ARCO; energy, chemicals and transportation), described ARCO
not as an oil company but as "an earth resources company." Of course, PR's antagonists, inspired by the likes of Boorstin (1992) and Chomsky, view *earth resources*
as mere spin.

Gender notwithstanding, one man's rhetoric is another man's spin. From a cultural-
styles perspective, an important issue goes unheard in the argument over the
meaning of *spin.* The harshest critics of PR tend to be Culture 1 prophets, voices
crying out in the wilderness against the degradation of both the language and truth
itself. Orwell's (2013) famous essay on "politics and the English language" is
among the best modern examples of Culture 1's disgust with Culture 3's

rhetoricians. Such attacks, echoed in the dismissive tone of the "objective" voices of some journalists, are typically deconstructed in PR textbooks as the result of ignorance, bias or both.

Plato, a Culture 3 philosopher-academic, sought to reveal the problematically rhetorical spin of sophistry as well as the grave threat that poetry posed to the free citizens of the republic. Plato's pupil, Aristotle, as we know, turned in a very different direction, linking rhetoric to the health of the polis and sourcing Homer and the poets as the foundation of rhetoric.

Plato's rejection of most, if not all, rhetoric may be traced to epistemological questions about the relationship between mind and body. To Plato, these were fundamentally distinct and separate entities, the mind posited normatively as the vigilant controller of the base, irrational energies of the body. In modern communication theory, this mind–body dualism surfaces in the conventional theory that "receivers" process information preferably through their above-ground rational channels or, problematically, through underground, irrational processing channels. Saint Paul's concept of sin channels much of the philosopher's distaste for the low, irrational and destructive energies of the body.

Classical Greece itself was divided on dualism. When the dramatist Euripides represented reality in "The Bacchae," the real was not mind over body but the ritual dismembering of the body of King Pentheus by wild women possessed by Dionysian forces. (The Greeks called that violent ritual *sparagmos.*) But one could argue that the Maenads were as much objects of terror for Euripides as for Plato. Still, there is a point to be made here. What's at issue is not whether Euripides preferred the Dionysian to the Apollonian. Rather, it's the problem of dualism – the Platonic epistemology that insists on the separation of the bad body from the good mind. The mind–body problem surfaces when we rethink PR through the metaphor of the theater, the concept of dramatic discipline and the imaginatively compelling art of writing (Dillon, 2002, pp. 142–143).

In modernity, one could fairly claim to witness the epistemic convergence of mind and body. Henry David Thoreau confided to his journal in 1851 that "the body, the senses, must conspire with the mind" (Shepard, 1961, p. 51). More notoriously perhaps, a generation after Thoreau, Freud made the body and its drives the centerpiece of psychoanalysis. The twentieth century might well be said to have begun a major shift from dualism to holism in the epistemological orientation of Western civilization, generated by a deeper understanding of Eastern philosophies.

In my salad days as a speechwriter drafting a talk for the CEO of W.R. Grace & Co., an American chemical company, I was encouraged by the CEO's chief of staff to "make it sing." Melody can be crucial to the emotional impact of a persuasive speech. Singing, which requires the convergent participation of body and mind, is a phenomenon of Culture 3 PR. As Aristotle understood from his readings of cunning Odysseus in the *Iliad,* a melodious speech was likely to prove persuasive.

And there it is: the artifice problem that bedevils ethically obsessed PR. Culture 3 PR is neither fake nor artificial. It is an artifice, and as such as anticipates Culture 4's emphasis on art and beauty. The speech, or poem, is a construction made of words, much as the poet William Carlos Williams (1944) described the sentence as a machine made of words. In his hermit's cabin, the American proto environmentalist and devoted ethicist Thoreau loved to listen to the singing strings of the lyre. During the annual February celebration of Black History Month in America, Martin Luther King's "I Have a Dream" speech is aired frequently. Many historians rank it as the most influential American speech of the twentieth century. Delivered in the summer of 1963 to an estimated quarter of a million people in the nation's capital, King's speech has entered the canon of American literature, along with Abraham Lincoln's Gettysburg address and the Thomas Jefferson's Declaration of Independence. In the nonperiodized historical device of cultural styles and voices, Dr. King's speech belongs in the humanistic space of Culture 3, along with Saint Paul's "through a glass darkly" passage in I Corinthians 13 and Jesus's Sermon on the Mount. Of course, in their prophetic capacities, Jesus, Paul and King belong to Culture 1 (Brown, 2003). But their majestic poetry, rhetorical gifts and humanistic sensibilities grant them dual citizenship in Cultures 1 and 3.

As a PR practitioner in the environments of a public corporation and a PR agency, I performed my role primarily as a writer. That conventional PR theory classifying writers as "technicians" has always struck me as both reductive and a bit sad. Don Stacks of the University of Miami conducted research with PR practitioners and academics in the first decade of the twenty-first century. They told him that of the many skills associated with the practice of PR, the most valuable of all is writing (Drake, 2006). In light of Stacks's finding, the theory that reduces writing to a technical function is simply misleading.

Culture 4: The artistic voice

Beauty is truth, truth beauty . . .

John Keats (1958, p. 208)

Awareness of the transforming power of the photo is often embodied in popular stories like this one about the admiring friend who said, "My, that's a fine child you have there!" Mother: "Oh, that's nothing. You should see his photograph."

Marshall McLuhan (1965, p. 188)

Unlike Cultures 1, 2 and 3, which are verbal, Culture 4 is visual. It is the culture of beauty and performance

that expresses itself in ritual performance like coronation rites, graduation ceremonies, and Veterans' Day parades. It is the culture of dance, painting, sculpture, music, and architecture.

(O'Malley, 2004, p. 19)

Culture 4 is theatrical. Its theatricality and the gestures of its actors were closely observed in Erving Goffman's (1959) "presentation of self in everyday life," as elaborated in Chapter 3 on "face." Both practitioners of PR and individuals in their daily lives must do what professional actors say they do. They must be "in the moment," and therefore they must be prepared to improvise and react because the actor's situation is a stage of perpetual uncertainties. Culture 4 is the dance of improvisation. It requires of the actor what the crisis management scholar Ian Mitroff (2004) called, in the subtitle of his book *Crisis Leadership,* "planning for the unthinkable."

There's the central paradox of crisis communication. Everything must be planned, although nothing is certain. In Culture 4, the visual presents both the opportunity to raise an audience's awareness and the threat of an embarrassing photo or video going viral. In Culture 4, the PR adage that perception is reality becomes primarily a matter for the eyes. As for crisis, it is as common to Culture 4 as it is to the verbal Cultures 1, 2, and 3.

For O'Malley (2004), Culture 4 is the "intensely visual culture" into which Christianity was born – a culture of images. The Roman Empire "was a world of public rituals and public spectacles, chariot races, gladiatorial contests, street per-formances, religious rites" (p. 19). It was the world of the mass (p. 21). Culture 4's ritualistic nature is found in the Chapter 2 (Crisis) discussions of the anthropologist Victor Turner's theory of crisis as a ritual that begins with a breach, widens to a crisis and proceeds into a liminal space, after which comes remedial performances and gestures that either resolve the crisis or unravel the community.

Culture 4: Public relations

In Culture 4, we meet P.T. Barnum, PR's historiographical straw man and sym-metry theory's whipping boy. Culture 4 PR is the Barnum & Bailey ringmaster. As a practitioner of PR, Barnum was theatrical, presenting the spectacle of "jumbo" elephants, dwarfs, bearded ladies and South Sea mermaids. Barnum's Culture 4 is an engaging village of arenas, museums, displays and exhibitions. It is the theat-ricality of the beautiful young lady defying sudden death on the flying trapeze.

But if the public-be-damned Barnum is a creature of Culture 4, so are the artisti-cally minded popes of the Catholic *Propagandio.* It was Julius who hired Michel-angelo to paint the Sistine Chapel ceiling. In both the sacred cathedral and the profane circus tent, eyes were raised to the beauty far above.

Culture 4 is the gloomy projection of PR's disapproving critics. It is PR Culture 4 that Guy Debord (2000) indicted as "the society of the spectacle." It is the theatricality of the "pseudo-event" that Boorstin coined as PR's corrupt staging of fake reality. In these detractors' views, acting is implicitly condemned as pretend-ing rather than being. Critics of Culture 4 echo the Platonic disparagement of poetry and rhetoric. Not only is spin a fake – but acting is even more egregious. Where "real" professional actors serve the socially beneficial function of entertain-ment, the fake acting of PR practitioners serves only to corrupt the channels of communication.

The critique of Culture 4 PR recalls the heyday of the now outdated magic bullet theory of communication effects that asserted the essential passivity of people receiving mediated information. The information consumer was believed to be little more than a soft target without a will, an automaton that was powerless to resist the message of the marketer or corporation or politician's bullet.

In Culture 4 can be found the colorful posters and ritualistic performances of the Zapatistas, the Mexican revolutionaries who mounted a campaign that featured a deeply problematic combination of beauty and violence. In Culture 4 is found the films of Leni Riefenstahl, the innovative creator of the documentary "The Triumph of the Will" whose patron was the Nazi party and whose executive producer was none other than Hitler himself. It is hardly surprising that the very notion of classifying Nazi propaganda as art is a matter of controversy. But Riefenstahl's film belongs, however disconcertingly, in Culture 4 with Barnum's freak museum and the popes' ceiling. In Culture 4, we find what I have previously identified as "the propagation of awe" (Brown, 2004). In certain contexts, PR generates an awe that is typically visual and dramatic. Whether that awe crosses the boundary from PR to propaganda is an ethical question.

Although I stipulate here that whether a film or a ceiling is visual is a matter of fact, not a question of ethics, I am well aware of the controversy surrounding the films of Riefenstahl. Among the most passionate and compelling arguments against the idea of Riefenstahl's Nazi-funded films as art was mounted by the American culture critic Susan Sontag, who dismissed "Triumph of the Will" as "fascinating Fascism" (Sontag, 1975). The controversy breaches the complexities the surround the question of PR ethics, a subject treated at length in a later chapter of this book. But to put the matter succinctly, I have treated the matter of PR ethics more as a paradox than in the conventional fashion that emphasizes ethical distinctions over complexities and problematics.

If PR's cultural style in Culture 4 can be seen to propagate awe, it once again raises questions about the thesis of symmetry theory: that "excellent" PR is not about persuasion and winning but about an organization's "willingness to change." Symmetry seeks to expunge the assertive and dynamic energy of PR and prefers that it be perceived as complaisant and relatively passive. Such a reframing would enable PR to displace any of its historical aggressiveness onto that un-PR known as propaganda. It is not surprising that practitioners of PR would prefer to be seen as the "conscience of the organization." In practice, however, the huge disparities in power that inhere between a paying client and a PR professional makes it difficult, if not impossible, for PR to perform as a conscience. The structural relationship of PR performance is more accurately described as a drama of complexities, challenges, tensions and ambiguities. These complexities are most obvious in the practices of corporate communications, public affairs and press agents. Despite all the theatrical gallantry of corporate social responsibility and cause branding, these strategies in no way relieve PR of its ethical problems, nor do they transform PR into an institutional conscience.

The scholarship of PR continues to distance itself from history, PR's as well as the rest of history. If, however, an increasing number of PR scholars pivot toward engaging with historical thinking, we are likely to learn more about the relationship between PR and the public spheres of the humanities, the arts and religions.

By reimagining the history of PR through the lens of a cultural device, PR can reclaim the vast space of history that lies beyond the constricted space of conventional PR theories.

References

Boorstin, D. J. (1992). *The image: A guide to pseudo-events in America.* New York: Vintage.

Brown, R. E. (2003). Saint Paul as a public relations practitioner: A metatheoretical speculation on messianic communication and symmetry. *Public Relations Review,* 29, 229–240.

————. (2004).The propagation of awe. *Public Relations Review, 30*(4): 381–389.

————. (2006). The myth of symmetry: Public relations as cultural styles. *Public relations Review,* 32(3), 206–212

Colini, S. (2013). *Leavis-Snow: the two-cultures bust-up 50 years on.* Retrieved at www.theguardian.com/books/2013/aug/16/leavis-snow-two-cultures-bust.

Coombs, T. (2012). *Ongoing crisis communication.* Thousand Oaks, CA: Sage.

Debord, G. (2000). *Society of the spectacle.* St. Petersburg, FL: Red & Black.

Dillon, M. (2002). *Girls and women in Greek religion.* London, England: Routledge.

Drake, J. L. (2006). One size doesn't fit all in Master's programs. Retrieved at www.prsa.org/Intelligence/Tactics/Articles/view/566/101/One_size_doesn_t_fit_all_in_ma *ster_s_ programs_Comm#.U9VUykivyqQ.*

Dylan, B. (1965). Ballad of a thin man. On *Highway 61 Revisited* [Record]. New York, NY: Columbia Records.

Eliot, T. S. (1921, October). Review of metaphysical lyrics and poems of the seventeenth century: Donne to Butler, selected and edited, with an essay by Herbert J. C. Grierson. *Times Literary Supplement.*

Goffman, E. (1959). *The presentation of self in everyday life.* New York, NY: Anchor Books.

Joyce, J. (1930). *Finnegan's wake.* London: Faber and Faber.

Kawasaki, G. (2000). *Rules for revolutionaries: The capitalist manifesto for creating new products and services.* New York: HarperBusiness.

Keats, J. (1958). *Selected letters of John Keats,* G. F. Scott (Ed.). Cambridge, MA: Harvard University Press.

Leaf, R. (2012). *The art of perception: Memoirs of a life in PR.* London, England: Atlantic Books.

Li, C. & Bernoff, J. (2008). *Groundswell: Winning in a world transformed by social media.* Cambridge, MA: Harvard Business School Press.

O'Malley, J. W. (2004). *Four cultures of the* West. Cambridge, MA: Harvard University Press.

Orwell, G. (2013). *Politics and the English language.* New York: Penguin

Mitroff, I. (2004). *Crisis leadership: Planning for the unthinkable.* New York, NY: Wiley.

Rheingold, H. (2002), *Smart mobs: The next social revolution.* New York, NY: Basic Books.

Shepard, O. (Ed.). (1961). *The heart of Thoreau's journals.* Mineola, NY: Dover Books.

Shirkey, C. (2008). *Here comes everybody: The power of organizing without organizations.* New York, NY: Penguin.

Solis, B. (2010). *Engage!: The complete guide for brands and businesses to build, cultivate, and measure success in the new web.* Hoboken, NJ: John Wiley.

———. (2011). *The end of business as usual: Rewire the way you work to succeed in the customer revolution.* New York, NY: Wiley.

Sontag, S. (1975, February 6). Fascinating fascism. *New York Review of Books,* 22(1). Retrieved from www.nybooks.com/articles/archives/1975/feb/06/fascinating-fascism/

Weber, L. (2009). *Sticks and stones: How digital business reputations are created over time and lost in a click.* New York, NY: Wiley.

Williams, W. C. (1944). Introduction to *The Wedge.* Cummington, MA: Cummington Press.

7 Persuasion

> She was utterly essential in democratic states, where persuasion, rather than violence, was the ideal.
>
> Helen F. North (1993, p. 408, Speaking of Peitho,
> the Greek goddess of persuasion)

> He spoke, and sorrow for his own father
> Welled up in Achilles. He took Priam's hand
> And gently pushed the old man away.
> The two of them remembered. Priam,
> Huddled in grief at Achilles' feet, cried
> And moaned softly for his man-slaying Hector.
> And Achilles cried for his father and
> For Patroclus. The sound filled the room.
>
> Homer, *Iliad.* Book 24: 444–451.

Symmetry theory's persuasion problem

What is persuasion, and why has symmetry theory sought to expunge it from PR? Persuasion theorists Frymier and Nadler (2007, p. 4) stressed what for them is essential about persuasion: its grounding in ethics. The authors cited five authorial perspectives on the definition of persuasion ranging from 1981 to 2002. Bostrom (2003) emphasized that the purpose of persuasion is changing or shaping attitudes or behavior of the receivers (p. 11). Petty and Cacioppo (1981) also identified change as definitive but added the relativistic corollary that "one person's propaganda may be another person's education" (p. 4). Larson (1995) backed away from change, presumably with its implication of manipulation, and replaced it with the idea that persuasion results from "co-creation" and "alignment" resulting from symbolic interaction (p. 9). Perloff (1993) kept change as definitive but added the requirement that the persuadee has "freedom of choice," an opportunity not present, presumably, in propaganda (p. 14). O'Keefe (2002) defined persuasion in terms of the effort to "influence another's mental state" provided the persuadee has freedom of choice" (p. 5).

There are numerous other variables and subtleties that would satisfy Frymier and Nadler (2007), such as that persuasion need not be successful, and that the purpose of the persuasion need not be change but reinforcement (p. 5). But equally important for Frymier and Nadler, and a matter of consensus among persuasion theorists and researchers, is the unshakable ethical principle of free will.

The principle of the persuadee's free choice is intended both as an ethical boundary and an expressive reaction to the noxious political history of twentieth-century totalitarian propaganda. With our benefit of hindsight, identifying the blatantly deceptive and brutal communication strategies of Nazi Germany and Fascism as propaganda is unlikely to present a challenge to most twenty-first-century perceivers. The definition of *propaganda* was radically altered in the twentieth century from what it had meant during the era of the Catholic Reformation's propagation of the true faith. For one thing, propaganda became an evil thing; for another, it became understood as a political matter.

But the nature of propaganda and its relationship to PR presents a far more nuanced and thorny challenge. Frymier and Nadler (2007) were content to agree that the practices of PR, such as media relations, are wrongly assumed by readers to be the result of objective journalism rather than agenda-shaping PR. Nevertheless, Frymier and Nadler indicated that media relations does meet the "established requirements for persuasion" in that "they all involve an agreed on verbal and nonverbal symbol system, intent is clearly present in the hiring of PR professionals, the level of success varies, and the targeted result includes changing, shaping, and reinforcing responses from the receivers" (p. 10). But even if we accept the judgment of these scholars, the matter leaves a critical thinker viewing the matter less as black and white than as an ethically and epistemologically gray area. The persuasive process that leads from PR's advocacy to a gatekeeper's "objective" publication is typical of the kinds of ethical ambiguities inherent in the practices of PR.

The flawed logic of symmetry's evasion

Although for Frymier and Nadler (2007), readers' unawareness of the PR source invisibility did not cross the barrier from persuasion to manipulation or propaganda, it became a very different sort of disturbance for symmetry theory. For symmetrists, the critical issue wasn't whether PR met the criteria for persuasion. It was that persuasion itself did not meet the criteria for ethical and excellent PR. Following the symmetrist's logic, to be ethical and excellent, PR had not only to divorce itself from such noxious practices as political propaganda and manipulation, but from persuasion itself. PR could no longer allow itself to be persuasive or be perceived as persuasive. But in their attempt to erase persuasion from the realities of PR practice, the symmetry theorists fell into fallacious thinking that could not be rescued even with the label of "normative" they attached to it.

It would be difficult to imagine a PR practitioner telling a prospective client not to expect her work to persuade anyone. Nor would a practitioner's denial of persuasive skills be likely to lead to any sort of alignment or what Heath and Coombs

(2005, p. 282) coined as the "co-creation" of practitioner and client. That a client would be delighted to hire an unpersuasive PR practitioner beggars the imagination. Among the most serious problems with systems-based symmetry theory is its attempt to consign persuasion to an ethical purgatory it unwisely dismisses as asymmetry. Symmetry's attempt to dethrone persuasion and replace it with the quantitative mechanics of "symmetry–excellence" is reductive; offers a rather arbitrary, misleading and ethnocentric notion of history; substitutes teleology and progressivism for description; and demonstrates a naiveté or evasion of the realities of unequally distributed power among the parties to the public relations (PR) process. The problems with such thinking are numerous.

From the perspective of the public relations of everything (PRe), PR is, was, and will continue to be a form of persuasion. The general theory's campaign to expunge *persuasion* from the PR vocabulary defies history, logic, experience and common sense. It is one of the ironies of symmetry theory that by positing the exclusion of persuasion from the practice of PR, it engages in a deceptive practice, however unintentionally. Symmetry theory's retreat from persuasion recalls nothing more than the ancient Platonic antipathy to rhetoric. Like Plato, the modern symmetrist's objection is revealed to be, in essence, distaste.

Neopersuasion in the social–digital era

There has come into existence what has been called an economy of "likes." Facebook's "like" button has become a currency, as valuable as any other currency, to organizations, companies and their brands. In the digital–social era, the marketing and PR strategies of brands, nations, celebrities and individuals is increasingly dependent on the aggregation of hundreds, thousands and even millions of clicks on Facebook's "like" button, along with Twitter's retweet (RT), the reblog button and other instant affirmations of consumer approval. In the era of engagement, conversation and sharing, reputations are created, burnished, threatened and managed by paying the closest attention to the dynamics of what the social media analyst Brian Carter (2013) called in the title of his book the "like economy." It is no longer feasible for organizations in the wrangle of the marketplace to be ignorant of the carrots and sticks of the like economy, nor is its influence lost on nations or individuals.

Call it *neopersuasion*. It is how one may understand persuasion in the social–digital era, where visuality and screen culture have become the dominant coalition of persuasion. It operates persuasively and influentially within the hyperdynamics of the like economy. These operations are further proof that persuasion is alive and well in the postsymmetry era. How else to account for the profusion of persuasive strategies in an era when we inhabit four screens – television, laptop, tablet and mobile phone?

Not that ours is the first and only age of visuality. To a significant extent, visuality has always been a rhetorical expression, a means of persuasion. The shield of Achilles, in *The Iliad,* is hardly less visual than Vermeer's "Girl With a Pearl Earring."

What is at work in the digital–social culture is the pixelated, cinematographic visuality designed to be seen on screens, whether in movie theaters or on an iPhone. For PR, this is an era when a team of students and their professor at a college in Boston created a crisis-management-and-rebranding campaign to persuade 30 million Southern Californians to return to the ocean-side city of Rosarito Beach, Mexico. After having been a popular travel and tourist destination in the 1990s, the pretty city of 80,000 lost 80 percent of its tourist revenue during the decade of narcotic gang violence that claimed 30,000 lives in Juarez, a Mexican city a thousand miles and a sea away from Rosarito Beach. In my case study of the PR campaign to persuade tourists to return to Rosarito Beach, I cited the visual and event strategies that were the heart of the rebranding campaign: a student-created series of films and a film festival that offered up imagery of sunsets over the Pacific Ocean, chilled glasses of margaritas and couples dancing into the wee hours (Brown, 2012b).

The paradigm's background

PR's negative reputation in the wider world is a chronic challenge to the practice. In the last two decades of the twentieth century, the creators of symmetry theory and symmetry–excellence launched what amounted to campaign to repair PR's image. The symmetrists' strategy began with a diagnosis that a major source of PR's image problem was its adherence to persuasion. Having identified the suspected bacillus, Grunig and Hunt (1984) sought to destroy it with a booster injection of an ingredient they called *two-way symmetry.*

This powerful antibiotic, an amalgam of dialogue, negotiation and an authentic concern to get beyond persuasion's manipulativeness, was marketed along with a compelling proposition: Its validity and reliability could be statistically demonstrated.

The theory was not entirely new to PR. Conceptualizing PR as negotiation was among Bernays's (1928) notions more than 50 years before Grunig and Hunt published their theory in 1984. Goldman (1948) was quite specific about the nature of PR's dialogue when he used the memorable phrase, "a two-way street." Scott Cutlip, a widely followed and influential PR theorist and historian, was reported (perhaps apocryphally) to begin his lectures by chalking a line with arrows pointing in two directions on a blackboard. Thayer (1968), an organizational theorist, distinguished between so-called *monochronic,* or one-way communication, and *synchronic,* a superior two-way approach that corresponded to the difference between monologue and dialog (Brown, 2010). Bertalanffy (1976), a biologist, enabled the symmetrists to wrap their theory in the impressive foundation of general systems theory.

Symmetry theory amounted to nothing less than multifront assault on the concept and practice of PR. The implications of that assault appeared to sweep the basic concepts, practices and assumptions of PR into irrelevance. Against symmetry's putative science, rhetorical approaches looked impressionistic and quaint. Contrasted with symmetry's mechanical system of ethical balances, persuasion was suspect. Up against symmetry's quantitative methodology, all other approaches, including historical, critical, rhetorical and ethnographic, appeared painfully innumerate. Little wonder, then, that symmetry theory came quickly to be regarded as PR's dominant paradigm.

The assault on persuasion

Dethroning persuasion as the normative model for PR was both "symmetry" theory's central idea and its most problematic one. But can persuasion be dethroned when there are so many kinds of persuasion? Consider this recent cautionary e-mail to the editorial board members of the *Public Relations Review* from Ray Hiebert, the biographer of Ivy Lee and the journal's distinguished editor for four decades – printed here with his permission:

> I should point out that we are getting an increased number of manuscripts that deal with persuasion – especially those researching social media. Not all forms of persuasion are public relations, which is a unique form of persuasion. A lot of the use of social media should more accurately be defined as advertising or marketing. And "corporate social responsibility" is not necessarily synonymous with public relations.
>
> (R. Hiebert, personal communication, [March 2014])

But definitions themselves emerge from the soil of advocacy and argument that oils or clogs the gears of politics – small *p* and large *P*. Although it makes little sense to me to offer a blanket opposition to the making of definitions and their delineation of disciplinary boundaries, it does make sense to pose a critique and present alternative perspectives.

What's unexpressed but implicit in Hiebert's concerns about the proper disciplinary and intellectual frame for social media and corporate social responsibility is the force of convergence that is driving these practices together. Social media is especially problematic for PR because PR has worked so strenuously to define itself as a "distinctive management function." Like the Counter-Reformation Catholic Church with its *Propagandio de fides,* PR has invested much effort battling heretics and insurgencies from advertising, marketing and sales promotion to integrated marketing communication. Many PR textbooks can hardly wait in their first chapter to warn readers against confusing those practices with PR.

Social media – indeed, the Internet and the web – has become extremely problematic for PR. Which is ironic in that PR has rushed to embrace social media and rebrand itself in the hyphenated way that one of New England's prominent and long-established PR agencies, Mullen, has done. Beginning a few years after the advent of Facebook and Twitter, Mullen renamed the PR division of the agency Mullen PR-Social. Similarly, far from distinguishing itself from corporate social responsibility, PR has imbibed and adopted corporate social responsibility with enthusiastically reported programs of all kinds.

The concept of persuasion, however, presents more of a challenge to PR scholars who are met with the Grunigian orthodoxy and eschewed persuasion as unethical. That PR and persuasion are not the same thing, as Hiebert observed, does not negate the persuasive (indeed, the rhetorical) effects we humans experience daily and from our encounters not only with each other but from the compelling force of cathedrals, theatricals, symphonies, paintings and poems. The digital–social media era of PR abounds with examples of theatrical and compelling events whose motivation is persuasion. In the United States, AT&T staged a comic version of a failed flash mob whose plot showed how, in the middle of busy Grand Central Station, one man began dancing in the mistaken impression that he would be joined by the rest of the flash mob of dancers. But when he saw that he was embarrassingly alone, he pulled out his mobile phone and saw that the reason for his mistake was that he didn't have the right product, which would of course be a cellphone served by AT&T.

Such a broad interpretation of persuasion is bound to be rejected out of hand by none other than persuasion scholars. Richard M. Perloff (2003) offered a synthetic definition of *persuasion* that would exclude any such frame as one that contains cathedrals and symphonies. For Perloff, persuasion is

> a symbolic process by which communicators try to convince other people to change their attitudes or behavior regarding an issue through transmission of a message, in a atmosphere or free choice.
>
> (p. 8)

But what such an exclusion of theatrical persuasion fails to recognize is that the special event is, and has always been, one of the definitively persuasive strategies of PR. It makes little sense to exclude such strategies from the domain of persuasion unless one is content to exclude much of PR from the domain of persuasion. The thesis of this chapter is that the dominant, or symmetry theory of PR went overboard in the attempt to reframe PR as a softer, kinder, gentler PR, a PR free of the unpleasant realities not only of winning and competition but of persuasion. Any theory of PR "excellence" that omits and rejects the role of persuasion is both unrealistic and misleading. In the competitive world of industry, which Robert Heath (2001, p. 29), borrowing a phrase from Kenneth Burke, has described as a "wrangle in the market place," persuasive communication has always been, and continues to be, a crucial strategy. The popularity of corporate social responsibility (CSR), cause branding and the engaging tools of social media have in no way replaced persuasion. Quite the contrary. They've enriched its varieties.

For starters, we might permit ourselves the freedom (such a key word in Perloff's definition) to think about persuasion from the perspective of the performance, the theater, the aesthetic, the emotional – all of which raise red flags for persuasion theorists. Surely, affect must be excluded from "the atmosphere of free choice." But to what extent? Is the theater that dangerous a place to free choice? Why, exactly? Are emotion and aesthetics the enemies of freedom? Always? Sometimes?

Symmetry as myth making

Scholarly reputations are often made by demolishing paradigms and their creators. In just this way did the symmetry–excellence theory-building coalition seek to reject Bernays's persuasion-and-influence paradigm as asymmetric. What the theorists constructed in its place was what I have called "the myth of symmetry" (Brown, 2006). That mythic structure was founded on a modernist, American-centric historiography more or less borrowed from Bernays himself.

In the "normative" ethical-excellence space of symmetry theory, the strategic cause branding of Unilever and the strategic corporate social responsibility of Adidas would have to take ethical precedence over asymmetric persuaders such as Saint Paul and Abraham Lincoln. But the idea that Unilever and Adidas are more ethical than the saint and Mr. Lincoln defy common sense. Such a ranking could make sense in the aspirational no-place of symmetry.

Replacing speech

Persuasion isn't the only paradigm that came under attack during the previous generation or two. So did speech. From its origins in 1914 as a scholarly associa-tion of "public speaking," and soon after as "speech communication," the Speech Communication Association was rebranded as the National Communication Asso-ciation. In PR terms, the dominant coalition of scholars came to regard speech as having become too small a frame for what the research was all about.

Speeches make up much of the *Iliad,* and among the most compelling of all is old Priam's moving plea to the fierce and unpredictable Achilles to permit the grief-stricken father to take possession of his son Hector's body.

The exquisite speech, performed under intense pressure and uncertainty, is noth-ing if not a dramatic triumph and a work of art. It is most assuredly persuasive. What is really going on within Achilles in this scene tells us far more about the nature of persuasion than how the dominant PR theory describes it as a "willingness to change." The failure of that theory to capture the nature of persuasion can be attributed to the theory's abstract, colorless, flat, mechanical and dehumanized language. Persuasion has a heart as well as a mind – something that Aristotle makes abundantly clear by making Homer and the other poets the foundation of the *Rhetoric* (1997).

PR practitioners do not appear to find persuasion problematic, but it makes many PR scholars uneasy. The argument of this chapter understands persuasion as Winston Churchill saw democracy: as the worst of ideas except for the alternatives. In what follows, persuasion is examined from several sharply differing perspec-tives, including symmetry's. The chapter closes with a reflection on certain epis-temological and historical sources that may account for scholarly PR's discomfort with persuasion.

Whether they're permitted to be included in the official, sanctioned definitions of PR, persuasion and influence remain what they are and have always been: attri-butes of PR. That they are problematic attributes is consistent with the ambiguities wired into PR. It is not surprising that scholars have tried to downplay or even banish persuasion and influence, just as Bernays did with propaganda. Our response to ambiguity is often ambivalence. In his case for what he called "ethical propaganda," St. John (2006) either muddied the waters or indicated the ambigui-ties surrounding PR and propaganda.

If PR is rethought from the vastly more inclusive perspective of an "everything," the effect on persuasion is to expand its scope, size and inclusiveness. What such a broadened view enables the PR scholar to see is the sheer variety and diversity of persuasion rather than to accept the contemporary conventional trope of persuasion as ethically and professionally inferior to symmetric alternatives such as negotiation. Persuasion, properly understood and performed, enables negotiation rather than excluding it. A broader understanding of persuasion is relatively free of unwarranted anxieties of art, architecture, music, emotion and the body. This must not be construed as an argument for intellectual naiveté or mindless promiscuity but for the understanding and embrace of the arts and humanities in the ethical and historical idea and practice of PR.

PRe rethinks PR and its attribute, persuasion, in the earthy terms of the humanities, the arts, performance, painting, architecture and theatricality. For PRe, persuasion needs to be understood in its radical, bodily sense, whether sponsored by a corporation or performed by a dancer, an actor or a musician. The famous "I Have a Dream" speech by Dr. Martin Luther King Jr., which ends in a lyrical, songlike coda of eloquence, was intended to persuade a segregated nation to live out the dream of America's founders. One of the principles of PRe, itemized in the first chapter of this book, references the spectacularly compelling and persuasive Christian message of the soaring basilicas and cathedrals of the medieval and Renaissance architects.

In the light of this theatrical, profound and moving imagery, how then shall we confine our concept of persuasion to the limits of disembodied, intellectual argument on the debate stage and printed page? To do so is to choose that ghost in the machine, the Platonic dualism of the austere mind floating above the lowly body.

To rethink PR as persuasive is to reflect on the relationship of persuasion to what I have identified as "the propagation of awe" (Brown, 2004). During the Catholic Reformation (or Counter-Reformation to stem the Protestant insurgency), the popes marshaled all their powers, borrowing the famous phrases of Bernays, to crystallize Christian opinion and engineer consent. But although it is accurate to characterize the papal strategies in these modern PR terms, what the popes did was exponentially more crystallizing and engineered. They combined the aesthetic with the spiritual into a rhetorically compelling case for Catholicism. How? They hired what PR role theorists have called a "technician" whose name was Michelangelo. Citing the historians Paola Barocchi and Lucilla Bardeschi Ciulich's *I Ricordi di Michelangelo,* King (2003) noted a momentous day in the histories of religion, art and PR:

> On this day, May 10, 1508, I Michelangelo, sculptor have received on account from our Holy Lord Pope Julius II five hundred papal ducats toward the painting of the ceiling of the papal Sistine Chapel, on which I am beginning work today.
>
> (p. 44)

It will be objected that all this had nothing to do with either persuasion or PR – that at most, this was merely a PR-like action because Pope Julius wasn't the CEO of a global corporation or a PR agency. Of course not – literally. But soon after the publication of my article "The Propagation of Awe" in the *Public Relations Review* (Brown, 2004), a warmly praising, if succinct e-mail arrived in my inbox . It was from Robert Dilenschneider, the chief executive of The Dilenschneider Group and the former CEO of Hill & Knowlton, one of the nation's largest PR firms. It would appear likely that Dilenschneider was struck by the resonant relevance of PR's centuries-old historical foundations.

Historically, the dominant paradigm of PR has distanced itself normatively from persuasion and influence. Those strategies long ago took root in the cognate disciplines of political communication and political science. Yet they persist in the everyday practice of PR – for practitioners, clients and constituencies. But persuasion, like influence, is not so easily disposed of; see, for example, the first lines of a William Carlos Williams (2001) poem, "The Pink Locust":

> I'm persistent as the pink locust,
> once admitted
> to the garden,
> you will not easily get rid of it.
> (p. 299)

In that poem, the pink locust is the poet himself; indeed, it is poetry itself. It is not at all something to be gotten rid of.

Pity the poor PR practitioner whose performances are neither persuasive nor influential. To borrow a textbook phrase, the "realities" of PR all but assume that PR comprises, among other things, persuasion and influence. From the vertiginous ethical height of normative modeling, however, these realities can more or less disappear or be viewed as obstacles to be overcome. From this perspective, absent its actuality, the normative dissolves into the unsubstantial.

Influence and persuasion have tended to be researched if not interchangeably then from closely related disciplinary perspectives. In his review of social influence literature, the social psychologist John Turner (1991) defined *social influence* as "the processes whereby people directly or indirectly influence the thoughts, feelings, and actions of others" (p. 1). For Turner, influence comprises "the processes whereby people agree or disagree about appropriate behavior, [and] form, maintain, or change social norms and the social conditions that give rise to, and the effects of, such norms" (p. 2).

If the theoretical perspective of social psychologists like Turner assumes the presence of other persons as a first principle, social movement theorists do the same but emphasize the critical importance of power. In framing the dynamics of social movements, Stewart, Smith and Denton (2007) observed the challenges faced by "uninstitutionalized" social movements (e.g., groups around the abortion issue who are prolife and prochoice). The severity of the obstacles facing these movements has created a situation that necessitated the "pervasiveness of persuasion in social movement" (p. 22). The authors noted that "persuasion is the primary agency for satisfying requirements and meeting obstacles" (p. 21). These authors defined *persuasion* as "the use of verbal and nonverbal symbols to affect audience perceptions and thus to bring about changes in thinking, feeling, and/or acting" (p. 21).

Unlike symmetrist PR scholars, social movement theorists are inclined to recognize the overlap between persuasion and coercion. Stewart et al. (2007) quoted Turner and Killian (1972), who observed that "nonviolence always couples persuasive strategy to coercion" (p. 22). Turner and Killian went on to reject the idea of "mechanical systems" as a valid basis for understanding human influence because such a mechanistic view abandons results in the human capacity to choose being "endangered" (p. 34). Such a view is, or borders on, humanism, although it doesn't situate the discipline of social movement theory with the humanities.

In problematizing mechanistic systems in this fashion, these social movement theorists are mirroring the critique of symmetry theory's mechanistic assumptions about humanity and society. In addition, the social movement theory perspective of Turner and Killian avoids the categorical rigidity of the kind of PR theory that fails to acknowledge the overlap of PR's problematical and controversial areas (e.g., persuasion, coercion) from its unobjectionable ones (e.g., negotiation, conversation, willingness to change).

Where the "everything" perspective of PR departs from social movement theory and social psychology is that PRe takes the imaginative leap of recognizing the influential agency of things that don't imply immediate presence of people as do social movement and social psychology perspectives. In PRe, as elaborated in the Chapter 1 in this book, an agency is assigned to objects of all sorts that exert influence – cathedrals, rainforests or a universe of objects that have the power to compel and even transform attitude, belief, opinion and action.

Such a view does not seek the legitimacy of the "scientific" and may be seen by critics as bordering on the metaphysical. But this perspective does underscore PR's foundations in the aesthetic, spiritual and symbolic senses that comprise what I have called "the propagation of awe" (Brown, 2004).

The indirectness of influence

It is unlikely that a theorist would be met with as much resistance to expanding the scope of *persuasion* as to expanding the scope of *influence*. Although the conventionally accepted dominant paradigm of PR sought to reject persuasion as a normative model of PR, the concept of persuasion has a constituency of theorists outside the scholarly company of PR. Persuasion theorists demonstrate little or no interest in PR per se, and persuasion theorists do not share symmetry theorists' agenda to deconstruct persuasion.

The idea of influence has a somewhat overlapping scholarly constituency. Brian Solis, a widely followed thought leader of digital–social trends, offered this definition: "Influence is the ability to cause desirable and measurable actions and outcomes" (Solis, 2010).

The etymology of *influence* is Middle English, from Old French or from Medieval Latin, *influential,* from Latin for *in* plus *fluere*, "to flow into." It was scholastic Latin that established the sense of "imperceptible or indirect action exerted to cause changes" (Oxford Dictionaries, 2014). A definition more compatible with the indirectness and imperceptibility of PR can hardly be imagined. The etymology of *persuade* (or *persuasion*) dates back to the late-fifteenth-century term, *persuadere*. *Per* means thought to completion; *suedere* means to advise. The sense is "to cause someone to do something through reasoning or argument" (Oxford Dictionaries, 2014).

But much of the persuasive power of PR derives less from argument than from art; less from directness than from indirectness. As Shakespeare wrote in his great drama of ambiguity and ambivalence, *Hamlet*: "By indirections find directions out" (Act 2 Scene 3; Shakespeare, 1936). PRe diverges from the conventional bifurcation of persuasion into higher rational and lower emotional routes. Such a hierarchy masks the ancient mind–body dualism founded on the bias against the sinfulness of the body compared to the holiness of the mind. It is that bias that animates symmetry theory's failed attempt to erase persuasion from the "normative" practice of PR.

The persuasive wrangle

Borrowing from Kenneth Burke, the rhetorically minded PR scholar Robert Heath (2009) has written that PR is a "wrangle in the marketplace" (Heath, 2001, p. 16). Marketplace dynamics are applicable to the competition for dominance among theories, definitions, ideas, tastes and values. It should not be surprising to discover that like defining PR, defining persuasion begins the question of its meaning as opposed to ending it. By *meaning*, we ask, "What is really going on here?" If, on one level, that's an abstract-sounding question of epistemology, on another level, it's a question of everyday experience.

Let us return to the normative space of symmetry's ethics excellence (the way things ought to be.) As in David Vogel's (2005) idea of CSR – that it exists in a "marketplace for virtue" (the title of his book on CSR) – definition making is a wrangle in the marketplace of meaning. This is so because the nature of meaning is as contestable as PR itself.

How persuasion is defined depends on who defines it. It depends their intellectual perspective and discipline and their worldview: their cultural envelope, their demographics, their psychographics. Colloquially speaking, it depends on "where they're coming from." Communication theorists oriented to inferentially quantified methodologies contextualize persuasion in statistically operational terms. Infante, et al.'s (2003), for example, defined *persuasion* as "attitude change toward a source's proposal that results from a message designed to alter beliefs about a proposal" (p. 102). *Attitude* was defined as "how favorably we evaluate something" (p. 102). A *belief* is "a perception of how two or more things are related" (p. 102). *Beliefs* are related to persuasion as the "consequences of a proposal" (p. 102). *Influence* is related to persuasion strategically as [what] "a persuader wants to do is to influence a favorable attitude" (p. 102).

These communication theorists framed persuasion as ethically neutral rather than as problematic or negative. Where a more negative and problematic coloration begins is with their definition of *compliance*, which "involves more subtle forms of psychological pressure" (p. 103). In other words, the ethical boundary is framed in terms of the visibility or invisibility that attends the relational logistics in a specific instance of persuasion. The boundary is a particularly interesting one for PR, which deploys a panoply of actions that range from invisible to subtle to overt to spectacular. Communication theorists see persuasion beginning to become ethically problematic as it moves from the overt to the covert. But postsymmetry PR scholars have adopted a less tolerant or even intolerant view of persuasion as asymmetric rather than dialogic. In doing so, postsymmetry scholarship and other groups of PR scholars have rejected Heath's and Burke's "wrangle," Hiebert's prodemocratic idea of PR and Aristotle's ethical understanding of rhetoric. PR neoconventional scholarship has replaced these perspectives with a form of Platonic nullification.

Although Infante et al.'s (2003) view of persuasion isn't negative, that is how it is viewed not only by dominant-theory scholars but by ethics-and-values scholars as well as by critical-thinking scholars.

Aspirational PR

PR's own reputational deficits are well known and long established. As a result, the PR industry – its trade organizations, scholars and practitioners – have labored to repair, rebrand and reframe PR in a favorable light. Among PR scholars who could be called *ethics-and-values* scholars, PR ethics is derived from two major sources: symmetry theory and the PR industry codes. Guth and Marsh (2000) boiled down the ethical perspective of surveyed practitioners to saying "their role was to develop 'mutual understanding' between management and the public' "(p. 8). Guth and Marsh were less comfortable endorsing persuasion because unlike the Grunig and Hunt (1984) model of two-way symmetry's "willingness to listen" (Guth & Marsh, 2000, p. 147), persuasion is "linked to one-way communication which tends to ignore a central tenet of motivation, that people act in their own interests" (p. 147). The fly in the ointment of persuasion is human nature from a certain psychological perspective. In a sense, then, this is a way of saying that people are not to be trusted with persuasion.

Persuasion, or persuasive communication, has been perceived as problematic because of the track record of its possible consequences. Absent skepticism or critical thinking or even common sense, people have gambled themselves into bankruptcy, sworn allegiance to dictators and been left at the altar. That much we do know about human nature, even without the benefit of neuroscience or algorithms. However, it may not be persuasion but something else – manipulation, coercion, distraction – that could account for an imprudent gamble.

Nevertheless, persuasion is commonly associated with the bearing of rumor, character assassination, lies, flattery or seduction, as the French sociologist Jean Beaudrillard (1991) has shown. We teach our children not to get into a car with a stranger, and reporters are still trained in rigorous fact checking to triple-source their stories. Biblical texts are severe about the evils of rumor and gossip, but there are no such moral restrictions against persuasion.

Contemporary calls for organizational "transparency" point to a widespread suspicion of the opposite strategies such as hiding, silence and the guilty ring of "no comment." A half century ago, a book entitled *The Hidden Persuaders* (Packard, 1959) purported to unmask the "real" power of advertising as a raid on the unconscious and uncontrollable.

By itself, transparency cannot be relied on as a guarantor of ethics – not without the accompaniment of a courageous candor that braves the loss of face. The problematic nature of persuasion and influence is structural – in a sense, geological. Persuasion's agency – its power – is related to models of the self's composition as above- and below ground: conscious and unconscious. Similarly, communication theory has identified two contrasting routes by which persuasive communication is processed: above-ground logic and judgment and below-ground processing that bypasses judgment and is triggered by emotion, bias and irrationality.

Media effects theory has served to underscore the continuing problem PR scholars have had with persuasion. Although there is not sufficient space here for a robust and full discussion of Petty and Cacioppo's (1986) elaboration likelihood model, what needs to be said is that their theory, complex and elegant as it may be, manages to echo the ancient bias for the rational over the emotional and for higher mind over the lower body (p. 129).

After reigning as PR's paradigm for anywhere from half a century to several millennia, persuasion was demoted to second-class citizenship as *asymmetrical*. It was replaced with a succession of purported testable abstractions: two-way symmetry (1984), "excellence" theory (1992) and, ultimately, no more than a willingness to change.

The modern history of totalitarianism and propaganda appears to offer the likely reason that persuasion's stock fell so hard with most late-twentieth-century PR scholars. In the twenty-first century, there appears to be even more short sellers of persuasion – notably, the lions of the digital–social web who have promoted the idea that persuasion is not only passé but ill-mannered and that what matters now is a familiar litany of engagement, conversation and sharing.

But the rush to judgment on persuasion raises many questions that should make PR and its scholars take a far more critical second look. Although he has attempted to soften persuasion with notions like "co-creation," the weight of Heath's approach to PR places him on the side of persuasion. I know of no professional PR practitioner who has ever rejected the idea of negotiation, or "partnering" with a client, or cooperating with the media and other constituencies: not to do so would be impractically impolitic. But that "partnering" in no way excludes the centrality of persuasion to the practice of PR.

In Aristotelian terms, rhetoric is the best ethical means of persuasion. What's implied by the rhetorical approaches of Heath and Burke is an idea fundamental to a PRe: that inherent in a PR that serves the public good is a wrangle, a conflict. PR is fundamentally dramatic. Such a perspective has none of symmetry's anxieties about zero-sum games of winners and losers. A persuasion-based PR can be used to defend the value of PR in the same way as a trial by jury – a trial based on the most vigorous kind of advocacy and argument. Sociologically speaking, for

Goffman (1959) and a cadre of micro-sociologists, cultural anthropologists, performance theorists and political communication theorists, drama is fundamental to what Heath has called a fully functioning society.

As a rhetorically and historically based social institution, PR is inherently dramatic: what PR generates is a marketplace for hard-wrangling competition, not a normative space where parties are willing to change. Even that great anti-rhetorician Plato had to invent the noble lie for the philosopher king. In *The Republic,* Socrates explained that to keep the classes of citizens in harmonious relationship to each other, it would be necessary to invent a noble lie to prevent the destabilizing effects of one class from attempting to do the work of another class. The question of the noble lie has been among the most controversial and hotly debated questions bearing on ancient and modern interpretations of the complex interplay of ethics and politics.

Advancing a persuasion-based concept of PR is to defend PR against its critics for whom *public relations, propaganda, manipulation* and *capitalism* are more or less interchangeable terms. The attempt to dethrone persuasion and redescribe it as negotiation is, to coin a term, unpersuasive. Not only do PR's critics dismiss this rebranding attempt; so do PR's critical thinkers. Which is not to imply that the critical thinkers of PR are all that comfortable with the persuasion model; neither are they at ease with uncritical alternatives to displace it.

Recognizing the value of PR is not intellectually possible without accepting the central and continuing role of persuasion.

Persuasion or propaganda

Definitions are generally regarded as attempts to clarify meaning, although even that is an aspirational outcome. A certain level of rhetoric is inevitable. (The cynical, who style themselves as realists, would call it spin.) Nowhere are these shifts in denotation and connotation more striking than in definitions of persuasion, propaganda, and PR. In a sense, then, definitions can be about the competition for the terrain of meaning and significance. For example, Jowett and O'Donnell (1992) approached their definition this way: "Persuasion *as a subset of communication* is *usually defined* as a communicative process to *influence* others" (p. 21, italics mine).

To affirm the role that influence plays in PR campaigns is not to dismiss the reality of a bad influence. But in seeking to cleanse the persistently negative reputation of PR, symmetry–excellence theory and its adherents have attempted to create a persuasionless and influence-free PR. It just won't do. For, as Ronald D. Smith (2009) observed in *Strategic Planning for Public Relations,* "Persuasion is an inherent part of social interaction, something people everywhere do. Persuasion is deception, which relies on miscommunication" (p. 138). Jowett and O'Donnell's *Propaganda and Persuasion* noted the "transactional" nature of persuasion:

> People respond to persuasion that promises to help them in some way by satisfying their wants or needs.
>
> (p. 21)

The practices of social interaction and the transactional nature of persuasion are embedded in PR. If the personal is political, definitions themselves are, too. This is true especially in the humanities and social sciences. These issues are, in essence, epistemological well as political. But their complexity forces a scholar to recognize the transrational effects of history, ideology and emotion on the aspirational rationality of definitions.

Persuasion in the digital–social era

In the digital–social "revolution," PR's response to persuasion is an eye-roll and a yawn. In the perspective of digital–social media visionaries such as Brian Solis of PR 2.0, the problem with persuasion is not that it's unethical but that it's irritating, boring and passé. In the era of screens and innovation technologies, persuasion sounds passé – an anathema to PR firms that aspire to be ahead of the proverbial curve. For the American PR entrepreneur Larry Weber (2009) and a generation of similarly minded new media visionaries, the old PR of news releases is either dead or moribund. But a closer reading of Weber's sweeping pronouncement reveals its context. In the digital–social era, reputations that were created over time can be damaged by going viral on YouTube. Weber was describing how social media has led to an era of apocalyptic frailty for reputation, an unforgiving racetrack of microseconds on which the horse-and-buggy press release is left in the dust.

But if all this speed leaves the press release behind, it in no way diminishes the role of persuasion and influence. Whether the digital–social era has affected the natures of persuasion and influence or their process is a different matter than the continuing vigor of their relevance in PR.

The attempt to flee from persuasion is nothing new under the sun. It has been a staple of modernist PR, whose beginnings might perhaps be found in the following from Bernays's (1928) *Propaganda:*

New activities call for new nomenclature. The propagandist who specializes in interpreting enterprises and ideas to the public, and in interpreting the public to promulgators of new enterprises and ideas has *come to be known* by the name of "public relations counsel."

(1928, p. 37, italics mine, quotation marks his)

Thus began PR's long and arduous retreat from propaganda, which was extended by symmetry theory to include propaganda's putative association with persuasion. By the italicized phrase, I indicate that Bernays does not take direct credit for the innovation of a "new" sort of propagandist – only for wordsmithing its name. Bernays attributed the rise of the new propagandist impersonally – that is, to history and sociology ("the increasing complexity of modern life and the consequent necessity for making the actions of one part of the public understandable to other sectors of the public"; Bernays, 1928, pp. 37–38). If Bernays even mentioned persuasion in his treatise on propaganda, I could not discover it. (The book has no index.) The point is not that Bernays had no interest in persuasion, but rather that his attention was focused elsewhere, including distinguishing the directness of advertising from the indirectness of PR. It would be for other theorists with other perspectives – historical, political, social movement, psychological, psychoanalytical, speech, communication – to tackle persuasion head on.

The frequently cited definition of PR, curated by modern pioneer Rex Harlow in 1976, and cited in Grunig and Hunt's influential textbook in 1984, contains 472 words – none of them are any variant of *persuasion*. But just seven words into Harlow's word collage of definitions, there is this phrase: "which helps establish and maintain mutual lines of communication between and organization and its publics" (Grunig & Hunt, 1984, p. 7). The following subhead in the Grunig and Hunt text announces a turning point in the theory of PR: "Need for Mutual Understanding." It is not clear whether the subhead was the work of the authors or the editor, but the theme of mutuality is clearly established.

The turn away from persuasion was evident in what followed in Grunig and Hunt. The authors quoted a persuasion-based definition of PR from a textbook by L. W. Nolte (1979), published 5 years before theirs. Nolte's definition of PR suggests mutuality and dialogue but makes persuasion an explicit component:

This implies two types of activity. First, the public relations practitioner must persuade management to do the things to the organization that will make it worthy of public approval. Second, the public relations practitioner must convince the public that that organization deserves its approval.

(p. 7)

Grunig and Hunt (1984) followed by posing this question: "These definitions sound fine, you may think. What's wrong with them then?" (p. 8). Their objection is that the existing definitions failed to account for the linkage between three elements: "what public relations practitioners *do*," its effect and whether it's done "responsibly" (p. 8). The authors combined these three elements – activities, effects and ethics – into the succinct definition of PR as "the management of communication between and organization and its publics" (p. 8).

Not only does that definition contain no reference to persuasion, it serves as the basis for their idea that was the foundation of the theory of symmetry: systems theory. PR practitioners were styled as "boundary personnel [that] support other organizational subsystems" toward "helping that subsystem promote products or services" (p. 9). The authors traced the beginning of this system to "about the end of the nineteenth and the beginning of the twentieth century" (p. 9).

Thus described in managerialist organizational systems-theory terms, PR was framed as definitively other than persuasive communication, and imbued with the primacy of mutuality and ethics that would develop in less than a decade into the elaboration of systems theory and managerial theory of "excellence." At the same time, PR was putatively divorced from the alternate complexities of humanities perspectives – its history truncated, its scope narrowed to organizational communication. In order to accomplish this, the historiography of PR from ancient times through modernity had to be dismissed as "public relations-like activities"

(Grunig & Hunt, 1984, p. 14). A half a century after Bernays (1928) framed PR in sociological and historical terms, Grunig and Hunt refined and narrowed Bernays's reflections with the concepts and terminology of mechanistic, posthumanities systems theory that rendered persuasion not only objectionable, but obsolete.

System and scientism

Bernays, an enthusiastic admirer of science, nevertheless wrote that PR could never be an "exact science." The subsequent generation of PR scholars, led by Grunig, disagreed. Grunig, Hunt, and the scholars they influenced have devoted their lives to the proposition that PR is indeed an exact science. A half century before the unveiling of systems theory, Bernays framed PR in the social science concepts of nineteenth-century herd sociology. In turn, Grunig, Hunt, Dozier and other followers reconstructed PR theory as a quantifiably verifiable system.

This ambitious attempt has failed, not because symmetry–excellence hasn't been widely popular, adopted, preached, researched and published. It has failed because it is quite simply an overreach. There is a name for the belief that science (i.e., the methodology of science) is the only way of knowing fact and truth). The name for such a belief is *scientism*.

But scientism is a belief system, and one fraught with reductivist, problematic and even mythical thinking. The self-named "radical" scholars of PR – the diverse, international generation of philosophers, historians, cultural theorists, critical thinkers, feminists, phenomenologists, rhetoricians, action PR theorists and sociologists – have demurred. Heath, L'Etang, McKie, Ihlen, Fawkes, Fitch, Janonsoozi, Pieczka, Demetrious and numerous others have rejected the univocalism of systems-based symmetry for a variety of reasons. Singly and collectively, these postsymmetry scholars have deconstructed symmetry for its naiveté about the realities of power, culture, ethnocentrism, gender, history and epistemology (Brown, 2010). For these and other reasons, the scientism of symmetry theory has been called a "myth" (Brown, 2006).

Among the unintended consequences of a scientistic general theory of PR is that it has alienated PR from its sources in the humanities. Scientistic PR has intellectually impoverished PR. But a new generation of postsymmetry scholars have brought new and novel insights from humanistic, religious, aesthetic, anthropological and historiographical perspectives to the scholarship of PR.

Metaphorical physics

The impact of this new systems theorizing was a game changer for PR – a new language. Systems theory's mechanistic perspective on organizations became the new paradigm and PR scholarship's conventional wisdom. Reaction was swift. Almost immediately with Grunig's (1992) publication of "excellence", a robust alternative critique sprang up. In Europe, L'Etang and Pieczka (1996) published searching deconstructions of system theory from a variety of perspectives – historical, epistemological, ethnographic, discourse analytical, phenomenological and political.

What followed in the twenty-first century have been critiques from still other perspectives – from global, religious and spiritual directions, including Tilson's (2011) association of public relationships with religious covenants. And in the postmodern, digital–social era, the discourse about PR has superseded systems theorizing and organizational perspectives. These perspectives have been replaced with broader, theatrical, performative, historiographical, emotion-laden concepts of today's communications mantra: engagement, conversation and sharing.

Metaphorically (rather than astrophysically!) speaking, these changes describe the physics of PR – what has occurred and is occurring in our PR galaxy. This is the physics of convergence that has been described in previous chapters. The centripetal movement of crisis communications from outer orbit to the center of the galaxy; the convergence of once "distinctive management functions" of marketing, advertising, sales and PR. Even the "integration" of those functions – the trope of integrated marketing communications in the 1990s – has come to sound rather passé in our explosive era of instantaneous, continuous and algorithmically quantified measurement. And as in any idea of physics, it makes little sense to portray the movements as having begun in the mid- or late nineteenth century. In this way, metaphorical physics furnishes a more realistic idea of the history of PR than do PR textbooks that simply repeat the Barnum-to-Bernays-to-Facebook story.

The immanence of influence

As a judge in a variety of PR awards programs, I've observed, discussed and evaluated a variety of campaigns. It goes almost without saying that the concept of influence, like a river, ran through them. Over the years, as a judge of PR campaigns, I have been the target of persuasive communication by the authors of PR campaign narratives with such terms as *enhance, strategy, drive awareness* and with traditional and new-media tools (media relations, publicity, social media, video). But beyond those clichés, what has been compellingly persuasive to me has been the evidence of imagination, idea and performance gracefully executed to produce a demonstrable result.

Peitho: Persuasion embodied

"Love's mysteries in souls does grow," wrote the poet John Donne in "The Ecstacy." "But the body is his book" (1905, p. 44).

PR has many books. But does it have a body? Is it a body of knowledge? Or, on another level, is PR an embodied practice? If so, in what ways?

These odd-sounding questions are posed because of the body's agency in the theater of human interaction, conversation, negotiation, influence, and persuasion. How, then, can we understand what is going on in PR if the body were to be wished away, neglected, censored, restricted, obscured?

On the isle of Megra, in the Aegean Sea, classical Greek civilization created a shrine that embodied one of its most cherished ideals – persuasion. She was the goddess Peitho.

The details of her Olympian lineage are generally known, although imprecisely. She seems to have been the daughter of Aphrodite, the goddess of love. Her father may have been Hermes, that Greek bike messenger and, so to speak, web master, a fleet-footed transmitter of gossip. Hermes was known for playing fast and loose with the truth, a mediator with questionable ethics. He not only guided messages; he sometimes redirected them and misled their recipients.

The daughter of a beautiful but dangerous goddess and a brilliant but unreliable communicator, Peitho inherited Olympian genes for compelling speech and sexual adventurousness. The source of her persuasive powers was a potent mixture of words and flesh. Peitho's art (*peithein*) was holistic. The Greeks of antiquity located the source of persuasion in the body, with all the body's rhetorical and sexual valence (Buxton, 1982).

To recognize the bodily source of persuasion is to rethink PR in the spirit of an *everything* – holistically, as it were, rather than as Platonic epistemological dualism. Ancient Greek culture appears to have worshipped Peitho not because she was "manipulative" or "unethical" but because she represented the enchanting power that could overcome divisions between persons and bring them together. For this reason, Peitho was called upon in prayerful supplication. To rethink persuasion as *peithein* resonates with Tilson's (2011) "covenantal" or spiritual idea of PR from the worship of Christian saints to contemporary celebrities.

Peitho was a cult figure, like Madonna and Cleopatra, as the American culture critic Camille Paglia described them. Unrequited lovers called on her to break down the walls of a beloved's resistance. Gorgias, a founder of Greek rhetoric, was no less aware than we are that sex sells; that words hold an erotically persuasive charge. In his encomium to Helen of Troy – who was herself tragically persuaded by handsome Paris – Gorgias wrote that "language is a powerful ruler who, with a tiny and invisible body, accomplishes deeds most divine" (Buxton, p. 31). Small body or not, rhetoric was imagined in holistic way that Plato, who preferred to divorce the body from the mind and soul, found deeply objectionable. The debate has never ceased.

The classical historian F. M. Cornford observed that the ancient Greeks had two definitive attributes: competitiveness and loquaciousness (Cornford, 1932/1961). The Greeks institutionalized those traits in the Olympics, the tragic theater and in the oratory of real men like Demosthenes and fictive men like Odysseus.

Greek Olympian and dramatic oratory managed to forge a holistic unity of two seemingly irreconcilable aspects of the self: mind and body. That dualism is associated with Plato, who was ever suspicious that the *peithein,* or persuasive powers, of the poets and rhetoricians would blind human beings to the numinous, noncorporeal truth. Inspired by Peitho, rhetoricians and poets fused sexuality with intellectuality and were able to rouse (and arouse) their listeners to conviction, purpose and action. Sometimes to adultery. Sometimes to war. Sometimes to noble courage. At times, even to the brink of divinity. The sainted Jew, Saul of Tarsus, who became known as Paul after his conversion on the road to Damascus, was just such a classically trained rhetorician. The creator of incipient global Christianity, Paul travelled for two decades on Roman highways spreading the gospel 20 years before Matthew, Mark, Luke and John wrote their accounts. (Akenson, 2000; Brown, 2003; Wilson, 1997; Winter, 1997). Paul knew his Homer and his Aristotle and could skillfully target his audiences of pagans and Jews with a well-turned antithesis and a lovely metaphor. Before Paul's martyrdom took his head, he turned Rome's head toward Christianity and altered the course of history.

Poetry's foundation in metaphor is assumed, as is its foundation in rhetoric. Nevertheless, the debt PR owes to poetry and metaphor is scarcely, if ever, noted – except perhaps in PRe. But the definitive attributes of indirectness and invisibility that lend PR much of its power can be found in Homer and Shakespeare.

Notwithstanding its conventionally intellectual associations, persuasion's source is the body. In Plato's time, rhetoric was taught in the same space as athletic training, at a *palestra* or gym. There, young athletes learned physical moves and rhythms that paralleled the verbal elegance of synecdoche, anaphora, metaphor and irony:

> As locations of physical training – young boys learned and practiced running, jumping, wrestling and boxing, for starters – the gymnasia were already important sites for the production of citizen subjects, and moreover, the production took place in a decidedly corporeal style. From this spatial intermingling of practices there emerged a curious syncretism between athletics and rhetoric. . . . In the gym, over the sound of the bagpipe-like instruments called *auloi,* mind and body were but a single sweating thinking substance.
>
> (Hawhee, 2002, pp. 144, 146)

Despite its association with the evils of manipulation, persuasion is, at heart, a spiritual matter. As the ancient Greek rhetoricians observed, persuasion begins in the body. Persuasion is a matter of breath and sound, an oral emanation and an aural reception. The ancient source of persuasion is speech, which the rhetoricians raised to the level of the art of oratory. Music, with its with its melody, rhythm and percussion, informs and animates speech. Where manipulation defines for us the disconnection between persons, persuasion's original purpose was to connect persons and bond them as free citizens to their community.

Persuasive speech is a matter of enchantment. Referring to Plato's dialogue, *Phaedrus,* a pair of rhetorical scholars described persuasion's body:

> In the first place, discourse is carefully constructed 'like a living creature, with its own body, as it were; it must not lack either head or feet; it must have a middle and extremities so composed as to suit each other and the whole work.
>
> (Thomas & Webb, 1994, p. 21)

Having learned the art of rhetoric, the orator had a noble purpose, whether as an advocate in court, a senator in the forum, or as one who simply came to praise. As with the achievement of excellence in any art, intensive study was necessary for the aspiring persuader. Aristotle's *Ars Rhetorica,* rhetoric's seminal manual, explained how the disposition of an audience could be analyzed as well as how best to express character, logic and emotion.

For the ethical rhetoricians whom Aristotle taught, the motivating force of persuasion was not manipulation, but magic. It was about enchantment, rooted in the poetry of Homer and the inspired, persuasive speeches of Odysseus and a legion of speakers. What these persuaders created in their listeners and readers was most certainly as sense of awe. That, and not manipulation, is the truth at the heart of Peitho.

The melody and magic of *peithein* (or the bodily energy of persuasion), which pours forth from Peitho's body, is an expression of authenticity – a sacred force that connects whole persons to each other.

PR scholarship's problem with persuasion is not that persuasion and influence are bad – they're simply not good enough. Not good enough to the gold standard of symmetry. Although this is certainly the explicit case against persuasion and influence, it does not account fully for the scholarly distancing. Looked at from a historical, interdisciplinary perspective, persuasion is neither unethical nor excellent. It's ambiguous, complex and dramatic. These definitive attributes pose significant problems of measurement and conception for symmetrical, quantitative and aspirationally scientific PR scholars. Experience, drama and art do not lend themselves to inferentially statistical methodologies. Fundamental to PR are events – trade fairs, concerts, conventions. All of these have historical foundations in messianic religious pageants; medieval morality plays; the Sistine Chapel ceiling; the classical music composed by Haydn, Mozart and others to their client patrons; the poems of Enlightenment poets dedicated to their patrons. These are the precursors of 1960s street theater "happenings" and the videos of General Mills that promoted its Chex cereal on the company's website. The argument that Homer, Haydn and Michelangelo are somehow irrelevant to the history of PR is an unpersuasive feature of modernist and symmetry theory PR.

Persuasion and influence are complex, worrisome, problematic and ambiguous. In part, their perceptual complexities can be traced to the checkered history of perceptions of the human body. Humanity, and perhaps especially Pauline Christian humanity, has been ever anxious about the body. The body remains a thorny, problematic, worrisome proposition. Unlike symmetry theory's mechanical system, the human body cannot be quite so easily managed. Bodies are paradoxical, at once compelling and repulsing desire. The body's anarchy flies in face of the managerial illusion while at the same time demanding one's attention to experience. For phenomenology, the body is the very source of what we can know.

Early psychoanalytic theory, particularly that branch influenced by Freud, theorized a dynamic that was self-driven, and often undone, by forces he called *ego*, *superego* and *id*. The psychoanalytical geology of the self was modeled in a form that recalled the tripartite hierarchical model of the great chain of being. Medieval man occupied a spiritual middle ground between the angels above and the devils below. His (and her) very nature was roiled by not only by the contingencies of fate but by the dark energies of desire – the legacy of humanity's lapsarian origins.

In this psychoanalytical theater, existence was governed by a drama generated by three ideas: the anarchic desiring id, the existence of an unconscious and the mechanism of repression that served to keep the anarchic forces underground.

From this perspective, our belief that we can manage others or institutions or organizations amount to a delusion: we cannot ultimately manage ourselves. Such a view can range from the tragedies of Oedipus and Othello to the farces of Molière and Monty Python.

Persuasion and influence have two faces – one light, one dark. There's the body problem. From Plato to Freud and beyond, the body has remained a troubling idea. Its problematic nature is no less so for the social scientists whose special focus is persuasion. The scholarly consensus on persuasion is deeply Platonic, or dualistic. Persuasion is a mental phenomenon. Persuasion is rational; the body irrational. Persuasion is processual, slow, deliberative. The body is troublingly improvisational and sudden, full of illogical but compelling agonies. Persuasion is negotiated, mutual, fair and just. The body has none of persuasion's accountability. Having been deprived of its body in the pages of textbooks, persuasion emerges decently clothed and properly mental. No longer connected with Peitho, persuasion has lost its gendered pronoun and become a neutered "it."

Persuasion as manipulation

Among the most cited persuasion scholars, Robert Cialdini (1985) has approached persuasion from the methodology of experimental social science. Collectively, the findings of his experiments have led him to frame persuasion in the ethically problematic sense of compliance. In studying a professional subgroup he called "compliance professionals" – that company of advertisers, salespersons and marketers – he concluded that they are more apt to be compliant than they are to be willing to change. In a book he coauthored (Goldstein, Martin & Cialdini, 2008), Cialdini and his partners identified six particular principles: reciprocity, commitment, social proof, liking, authority and scarcity.

In the hands of a managerial approach to PR, these are not the foundations of an ethical and excellent willingness to change, but a series of techniques that weaponize the wellspring of PR's general theory: negotiation. Harvard University Law School's Program on Negotiation views the negotiation process not in the softer sense of the dominant theory's willingness to change but as way to "enhance the perception of fairness" (Harvard, 2014).

The compliance gaining and weaponizing of negotiation undermines the simplistic idea of negotiation in PR theory. Cialdini's findings, translated into the mechanistic language of managerial control, derive from one of the central problems with PR thought: that perception is reality (Brown, 2012). This is a time-honored adage of PR that can and has been used in very different ways – as manipulative compliance gaining or as the foundation of Coombs's (2012) ethically normative, perceptually based situation crisis communication theory, in which a crisis is said to exist because it is perceived to exist by stakeholders – whether it exists or not.

Not only do persuasion and compliance partake of ambiguity and complexity – they would appear to lead down an Alice-in-Wonderland epistemological rabbit hole where things appear to be something they either are or are not.

Rethinking persuasion

PR scholars, practitioners and new-media visionaries need to rethink their flight from persuasion and influence. Persuasion need not be relegated to second-class status in theory building or left exclusively in the disciplines of political communication and political science. In the practice of PR, persuasion and influence are fundamental realities not subject to theoretical replacements or evasions.

PR will continue to wrestle with the problem of persuasion and influence. From the perspective of the humanities, the ambiguities of these concepts must be recognized along with our ambivalence toward them as strategies, theater and consequences.

On a personal note, I have preferred that my students experience me as likeable rather than wax indifferent. In the argument that my likeability will empower their learning, it is hard to miss the self-serving rationalization. Likeability has been reliably correlated with strongly positive evaluations of teachers. It is also a principle of what I have characterized as the darker, mechanistic, manipulative dimension of persuasion and one of Cialdini's principles of the psychology of compliance. What I learned about nonverbal expression from conversations at UCLA with the communications theorist Albert Mehrabian – the persuasive efficacy of a variety of nonverbal immediate behaviors like proxemics and smiling – I have sought to deploy both in the classroom and in everyday life.

Smiling, however, turns out to be no less ambiguous or differently processed than any other strategy of persuasion. As the historian of art Angus Trumble (2004) noted in *A Brief History of the Smile,*

> The term "smile" can be applied to numerous phenomena relating to the movement of the lips and the contraction of various muscles of the face, ranging from the involuntary reflect of the neonate to the mask of comedy, from the contemplative smile of the Buddha to the chilly rictus of the news anchor, and a vast assortment of smiles in between. A smile may seem friendly to one person and insane to somebody else.
>
> (p. xliii)

I would not be utterly surprised to learn that my smiles have been cognitively processed across that astonishing spectrum.

Such lessons and their uses have convinced me of the inseparability of PR from the experience of everyday life that expands the concept of PR well beyond the conventional disciplinary attempt to limit it to communication management.

References

Akenson, D. H. (2000). *Saint Paul: A skeletal key to the historical Jesus.* New York, NY: Oxford University Press.

Beaudrillard, J. (1991). *Seduction.* New York: Palgrave Macmillan.

Bernays, E. L. (1928). *Propaganda.* New York, NY: Horace Liveright.

Bertalanffy, L. V. (1976). *Perspectives on general system theory: Scientific–philosophical study.* New York, NY: George Braziller.

Bostrom, R. N. (2003). *Persuasion.* Englewood Cliffs, NJ: Prentice-Hall.

Brown, R. E. (2003). Saint Paul as a public relations practitioner. *Public Relations Review,* 29(1), 1–12.

————. (2004). The propagation of awe: Public relations, art and belief in Reformation Europe. *Public Relations Review,* 30(4), 381–389.

————. (2006). The myth of symmetry: Public relations as cultural styles. *Public Relations Review,* 32(3), 206–212.

————. (2010). Symmetry and its critics: Antecedents, prospects, and implications in a post-symmetry era. In R. L. Heath (Ed.), *The Sage handbook of public relations* (pp. 277–292). Thousand Oaks, CA: Sage.

————. (2012a). Epistemological modesty: Critical reflections on public relations thought. *Public Relations Inquiry,* 1(1), 89–105.

————. (2012b). Rosarito Beach: Mediated reality and the rebranding of a Mexican border city. In A. M George & C. B. Pratt (Eds.), *Case studies in crisis communication: International perspectives on hits and misses* (pp. 419–436). New York, NY and London, England: Routledge.

Buxton, R.G.A. (1982). *Persuasion in Greek tragedy: A study of Peitho.* London, England: Cambridge University Press.

Carter, B. (2013). *The like economy: How businesses make money with Facebook.* Indianapolis, IN: Que.

Cialdini, R. (1985). *Influence: How and why people agree to things.* Kent, UK: Quill.

Coombs, W. T. (2012). *Ongoing crisis communication.* Thousand Oaks, CA: Sage.

Cornford, F. M. (1961). Before and after Socrates. London, England: Cambridge University Press.

Donne, J. (1905). *The love poems of John Donne.* C. E. Norton, ed. Cambridge, MA: Houghton Mifflin.

Frymier, A. B. & Nadler, M. K. (2007). *Persuasion: Integrating theory and research.* Dubuque, IA: Kendall-Hunt.

Goffman, E. (1959). *The presentation of self in everyday life.* New York: Anchor.

Goldman, E. (1948). *Two-way street: The emergence of the public relations counsel.* New York, NY: Bellman.

Goldstein, N. H., Martin, S. J. & Cialdini, R. B. (2008) *Yes! 50 scientifically proven ways to be persuasive.* New York, NY: Basic Books.

Grunig, J. E. (1992). *Excellence in public relations and communications management.* New York: Routledge.

Grunig, J. E. & Hunt, T. (1984). *Managing public relations.* Mahwah, NJ: Lawrence Erlbaum.

Guth, D. W. & Marsh, C. (2000). *Public relations: A value-driven approach.* Upper Saddle River, NJ: Pearson.

Harvard. (2014). *Program on negotiation.* Retrieved from www.pon.harvard.edu/

Hawhee, D. (2002). Bodily pedagogies: Rhetoric, athletics and the Sophists three R's. *College English,* 65(2), 143–156.

Heath, R. L. (Ed.) (2001). *Handbook of public relations.* Thousand Oaks, CA: Sage.

Heath, R. L. & Coombs, W. T. (2005). *Today's public relations.* Thousand Oaks, CAL Sage.

Heath, R. L., Toth, E. L. & Waymer, D. (2009). (Eds.) *Rhetorical and critical approaches to public relations* II. New York: Routledge

Homer. (1997). *Iliad* (S. Lombardo, Trans.). Indianapolis, IN: Hackett.

Infante, D. A., Rancer, A. S. & Womack, D. F. (2003). *Building communication theory.* Long Grove, IL: Waveland.

Jowett, G. S. & O'Donnell, V (1992). *Propaganda and persuasion.* Thousand Oaks, CA: Sage.

King, R. (2003). *Michelangelo and the Pope's ceiling.* New York, NY: Penguin.

Larson, C. U. (1995). *Persuasion: Reception and responsibility.* Belmont, CA: Wadsworth.

L'Etang, J. & Pieczka, M. (1996). *Critical perspectives in public relations:* London, England: International Thomson Business Press.

Nolte, L. W. (1979). *Fundamentals of public relations: Professional guidelines, concepts and integrations.* London, England: Pergamon.

North, H.F. (1993). Emblems of eloquence. *Proceedings of the American Philosophical Society* 137(3), 406–430.

O'Keefe, D. J. (2002). *Persuasion: Theory and research.* Thousand Oaks, CA: Sage.

Oxford Dictionaries. (2014). *Definition of* influence. Retrieved from http://oxforddictionaries. com/us/definition/american_english/influence

Packard, V. O. (1959). *The hidden persuaders.* New York: Pocket Books.

Perloff, R. M. (1993). *The dynamics of persuasion.* Hillsdale, NJ: Erlbaum.

———. (2003). *The dynamics of persuasion: Communication and attitudes in the 21st century.* Mahwah, NJ: Erlbaum.

Petty, R. E. & Cacioppo, J. T. (1981). *Attitudes and persuasion: Classic and contemporary approaches.* Dubuque, IA: Brown Company.

———. (1986). *Communication and persuasion: Central and peripheral routes to attitude change.* New York, NY: Springer-Verlag.

Shakespeare, W. (1936). *Complete works of Shakespeare* (G. L. Kittredge, Ed.). New York, NY: Ginn & Company.

Smith, R. D. (2009). *Strategic planning for public relations.* New York, NY: Routledge.

Solis, B. (2010, September 29). *Exploring and defining influence: A new study.* Retrieved from www.briansolis.com/2010/09/exploring-and-defining-influence-a-new-study

Stewart, C. J, Smith, C. A. & Denton, R. E., Jr. (2007). *Persuasion and social movements.* Long Grove, IL: Waveland.

St. John, B. (2006). The case for ethical propaganda: Ivy Lee's successful 1913–1914 railroad rates campaign. *Public Relations Review* 32(3), 221–228.

Thayer, L. (1968). *Communication and communication systems: In organizations, management and interpersonal relations.* Homewood, IL: Richard D. Irwin.

Thomas, C. G & Webb, E. K. (1994). From orality to rhetoric: Greek intellectual transformation. In I. Worthington (Ed.), *Persuasion: Greek rhetoric in action* (pp. 3–25). London, England: Routledge.

Tilson, D. J. (2011). *The promotion of devotion: Saints, celebrities and shrines.* Champagne, IL: Common Ground.

Trumble, A. (2005). *A brief history of the smile.* New York, NY: Basic Books.

Turner, J. W. (1991). *Social influence.* Belmont, CA: Wadsworth

Turner, R. H. & Killian, L. M. (1972). *Collective behavior.* Englewood Cliffs, NJ: Prentice-Hall.

Weber, L. (2009).*Sticks and stones: How digital business reputations are created over time and lost in a click.* New York: Wiley.

Williams, W. C. (2001). *The collected poems: Vol. II: 1939–1962* (C. McGowan, Ed.). New York, NY: New Directions.

Wilson, A. N. (1997). *Paul: The mind of the apostle.* New York, NY: Norton.

Winter, B. W. (1997). *Philo and Paul among the Sophists.* New York, NY: Cambridge University Press.

Vogel, D. (2005). *The market for virtue: The potential and limits of corporate social responsibility.* Washington, DC: Brookings Institution Press.

8 Politics

Man is, by nature, a political animal.

Aristotle

Aristotle's observation applies not only to man but the social institutions created by man. These include, of course, public relations. The perspective of the public relations of everything (Pre) is that public relations (PR) shares with politics a commitment to persuasion. Unlike the bloodless intellectuality of symmetry theory, Pre makes room for the passions.

Pre recognizes what Heath and others have called the *postsymmetry era* (Brown, 2010). In doing so, Pre identifies and critiques symmetry theory's problematic attempt to remove persuasion from PR, along with all of PR's harder realities, and replace them with a softer alternative that foregrounds corporate responsibility and expels from the fields of "excellence" the persuasive, victory-seeking political nature of PR.

The advocates of the soft-edged PR soon discovered that symmetric PR, unburdened by the realities of persuasion and power, was a great deal easier to advocate. If PR were to be posited as the equivalent of corporate social responsibility (CSR) and corporate citizenship rather than corporate victory through persuasion, perhaps PR's negative image could be redeemed.

Symmetry's redemptive rebranding has turned out to be very popular with undergraduates of the millennial generation who seek work that would enable them to "live their values," in the words of American PR entrepreneurs. Symmetric PR has also been warmly received by corporations, which welcomed the opportunity to "give back" and "do well by doing good" by strategically budgeting programs of philanthropy, advocacy and partnerships with charitable organizations. Brown and Rancer (1993) did a quantitative, cross-cultural comparison of U.S. and U.K. PR agency preferences for asymmetric and symmetric models of PR. Unsurprisingly, both U.S. and U.K. PR firms reported what was a statistically significant preference for symmetric strategies. In the United States, CSR reporting spiked among the larger corporations from around 500 programs in 1999 to 3,500 in 2010 (Newell, 2012).

The glaring problem with such preferences is that they can be so easily anticipated. PR firms, like other organizations, would prefer to frame their mission and

their practices in the softer light of symmetric PR than the harsh light of persuasion. They would rather be viewed, and view themselves, as large-hearted negotia-
tors than as small-minded tacticians.

What, then, could be wrong with this picture? Simply this: it tells only a rather
small fraction of the nature of PR. This is not to say that the "real" nature of PR is
the caricature of cold-hearted, power-mad greed or flimflammery as its critics such
as Chomsky and Boorstin have long insisted. But PRe critiques symmetry theory's
willingness to accept the self-serving popularity of the symmetric model as evidence that PR has gotten past persuasion. What symmetry has gotten past has been
a more thoughtful concept of persuasion. What symmetry has substituted for such
a concept has been the simplistic equivalence of persuasion with manipulation.
That persuasion *can* be manipulative is not in question. What is problematic is that
symmetry theory expresses or implies that persuasion *is* manipulation. What is also
problematic is that symmetry theory purports to define the many kinds of persuasion that occur in the practices of PR as somehow less than ethical or excellent.

What is further problematic is for symmetry theory to ignore the inconvenient
truth that the historic standard for programs of CSR have been but a fraction of a
corporation's net profits. For example, Dayton–Hudson Corporation, one of the
thought leaders and early adopters of CSR in the 1960s, set for itself a standard of
budgeting 5 percent of its net profit for CSR. Not 5 percent of total revenues; 5
percent of net profits, a far more modest investment.

Was Dayton–Hudson engaging in flimflammery or a gross distortion of its
"true" rapacious soul? Hardly. But allowing that the company was engaging in
socially and economically admirable behavior, it does not follow that the company
had moved beyond persuasion in all its strategies and operations. Nor is PRe's
critique diminished by symmetry theory's rejoinder that the "willingness to
change" is normative rather than descriptive. Not to seem unkind, but such a
defense strikes me as a bit of a dodge. PRe prefers to observe the world that is
rather than avert one's eyes and reconstruct the world that ought to be.

PRe both understands and accepts the persuasive and thus political nature of PR.
Among the most obvious places to identify the political nature of PR is in the mission and operations of its subdisciplinary applications of public affairs and government relations. The knowledge of politics and its logistics – issues, advocacy,
argument, conflict, negotiation, resolution – is such a well-established template for
the practice of PR that there exists a well-traveled career pathway between politicians, lobbyists and the agencies and departments of PR.

Not only are there shared sensibilities; skills sets are also shared. In the U.S.
Presidential campaign of 2012, the reelection victory of the incumbent president,
Obama, was widely credited to his campaign's vastly superior skills in the deployment of digital–social tools, targeting and analytics found in the most competitive
and successful PR agencies and departments. In the marketplace wrangle that is
PR, organizations use digital–social tools and knowledge to gain competitive
advantage by identifying target consumers and influencing leaders. They use these
new analytics tools to collect, record, interpret and report their successes and failures to senior management.

But if analytics-based performance offers a quantitative commonality between PR and politics, the two professions share a different kind of commonality – the theatrical skill of acting. Like a politician on the campaign trail, the PR practitioner must prepare for, face, engage and win over audiences. Although contemporary PR theory has sought to replace the model of persuasion and winning with symmetrical softness, PR agencies and departments are not judged as effective unless their pitches get the results they were intended to get. Press releases, stories pitched to journalists and presentations by PR agencies to gain new clients are all, in their own ways, acting performances. For the PR industry, which is what economists call a highly unconcentrated industry different from, say, telecommunications, a multitude of small PR firms live and die in the attempt to acquire new clients. A PR agency's objective in pitching what is known as "new business" is to win new clients, not simply to engage them in conversation. That an agency may approach this challenge with so-called "win–win" strategies that create client opportunities for CSR does not represent a sea change in the nature of PR but merely a strategy. The agency intends to be sufficiently persuasive to win a client whose business is typically the object of intense competition. The reality of this contest resonates not with symmetry theory, but Heath's (2001, p. 39) description of PR as a "wrangle in the marketplace."

PR's propaganda problem

Looked at from the perspective of PRe, PR is a narrative that takes PR from the dark rigidities of propaganda to the sunny malleability of CSR. Aristotle and Plato understood politics as an argument to be won or lost, not a conversation over dinner. As F. M. Cornford (1932) observed of Greek civilization, among its most definitive features was its passion for competition that took shape in two places: politics and the Olympics.

When it came to politics and persuasion, Plato and Aristotle approached those matters quite differently. Aristotle's *Rhetoric* can be understood as a seminal text of PR in which persuasion is the basic and ethical foundation. Plato, however, was deeply skeptical of rhetoric, notably of the Sophists. His skepticism is echoed in that of PR itself. These opposing Classical approaches are echoed in the pro-rhetorical approaches of postsymmetry PR scholars and in symmetry theory's attempt to define and quantify the one true form of PR excellence.

Fast forward to the Catholic anti-Protestant Reformation of the seventeenth century. The word *propagandio* is used by the Catholic Church as the name for what was, in effect, a highly sophisticated PR agency created to stem the rising insurgency of Protestantism in Europe. But in the vision of the popes, and the understanding of a holy mission to burnish the true faith, the term *propagandio* meant nothing more or less than the propagation, or passionate advocacy, of Catholic doctrines and institutions. It wasn't until the rise of twentieth-century totalitarian fascism and communism that *propaganda* acquired the noxious meaning it retains today: that is, of lies, distortions, gross mythologizing, racism, suppression and censorship in the service of a corrupt political regime.

By the middle of the twentieth century, a layer of cultural noxiousness was deposited onto that of the specifically political. After the conclusion of World War II, Guy Debord (1967/1994), among other continental cultural theorists, as well as observers of American advertising and PR, began to frame PR and advertising as forms of cultural propaganda, with all the negative associations of lying, distortion and mythologizing in the service of a corrupt and corrupting consumerist capitalism.

In the middle of the twentieth century, the philosopher Jacques Ellul (1965) mashed up Platonic skepticism with French continental cultural criticism with his thesis that there had emerged a new and noxious form of sociological propaganda that came to be called "persuasion from within" (Black, 2001, p. 125). This was a kind of propaganda imbibed by individuals and groups unconsciously. By mid-century, persuasion was joining propaganda on the list of cultural evils, paving the way for the antipersuasion theory of symmetry.

PR and advertising were easy targets for this propagandistic framing. After all, it was the PR pioneer Bernays who, in 1928, titled his book about the new profession *Propaganda*. Bernays would regret that title and spend the rest of his career in an attempt to rebrand PR in a host of positive ways, as socially responsible, professional and scientific. He signaled as much when he changed the name of his business from the Propaganda Bureau to the Public Relations Consultancy. In so doing, Bernays was not only seeking to distance himself and PR from propaganda but to identify PR with the worlds of business management, political advising, public policy and international diplomacy (Bernays, 1965).

As late in PR's "evolution" as the 1920s, in the era of George Creel's wartime Committee on Information, PR could easily have been mistaken for propaganda. It is a moral, tactical and even national equation that persists in the minds of PR's harshest critics. Whether propaganda itself could ever be "good" is yet another matter explored in a series of reflections on PR thought (Brown, 2012). The conclusion of St. John (2006) is: yes, there *is* such a thing as good propaganda, an example of which can be found in Ivy Lee's pro-ethical propaganda campaigns to gain support for a rate increase for his client, the Pennsylvania Railroad, in the first decades of the modern PR industry. St. John argued that

> beneficial and ethical propaganda can serve to move audiences to consensus and action within a democracy.
>
> (p. 221)

What is striking about such an argument is what it has in common with a number of PR scholarly defenses of the pro-social and ethical capacities of PR: virtually all of them frame arguments that are political – that link PR to democratic societies in which choices are made by the ballot, not the bullet.

In this fashion, both the scholarly critiques and defenses of PR have been typically, if not always, couched in political terms. It is in this sense, then, that PRe sees *more* of PR in political terms. To some extent, the argument of this chapter can be seen not as reductive or eccentric but as resonating with the broad spectrum of PR scholarship that has sought to defend or critique PR in the political terms that support the idea of PR's political nature.

The political nature of corporations

As a speechwriter for an oil ("earth resources") company and a chemical conglomerate in the 1980s, I discovered the political nature of PR to be a daily and continuing urgency. Practitioners wrote Q&A pamphlets to rebut congressional calls for an "excess profits tax" on oil companies. Slide shows were prepared for the incoming Reagan administration on the costs–benefits of alternate energy systems. The risks and rewards of operating in Saudi Arabia and Indonesia were debated. The practitioner's life – my workaday life – could be described as a series of political campaigns. I was called on to argue and advocate on virtually every imaginable issue in the *polis*.

Although not pointedly or specifically political, Heath's (2010, p. 6) "fully functioning society theory" comes to mind here because its broad perspective of PR seems to be inescapably political (p. 10). The stage upon which the oil and the chemical company played their parts could be fairly characterized as political, with the companies' passionate immersion in issues. As for poetry and rhetoric, I will not forget the refrain from a corporate vice president of W.R. Grace & Co., which was the coda to his memos meant to motivate me to rise to the occasion of my speechwriting art: "Make it sing!" Like me, the VP would have had to put his resume out on the street in Platonic state.

Multinational corporations are as populous as small cities. For example, 99,100 souls were reported as employees of Exxon-Mobil (Global 500, 2014; see also www.exxonmobil.com/USA). The impact their corporations make on society is no less political than economic or social. In David Vogel's (1980) foreword to *Corporations and Their Critics,* a collection of essays about corporate responsibility he coedited with the then-CEO of Atlantic Richfield Company (ARCO), he identified the nature of giant corporations in political terms:

> Just as the governments of fifty states differ in their administrative competence, concern for the less fortunate, and degree of corruption, so do *the nation's large private governments – its corporations –* vary in their treatment of their employees, relationship to surrounding communities, and concern for the environment.
>
> (p. vii, italics mine)

Political ambiguity

Convergence is not the only structural characteristic of the political nature of politics. Nor are power or asymmetry or performance. Politics is ambiguous. In *Politics and Ambiguity,* the political theorist William Connolly (1987) elaborated on the ambiguity of democracy. Connolly's thesis is of particular relevance to scholars of PR who, like Hiebert, view PR as uniquely suited to democratic soil:

Politics and authority stand in a relation of interdependence and opposition to each other. And this ambiguity, too, must be kept alive, for without authority, politics degenerates into violence or coercion, but politics also provides an indispensable barrier to the intensification and overextension of authority.

(p. 141)

The ambiguity of this condition should resonate with PR scholars who have defended the value of PR by reference to its thriving in democratic soil. That is essentially a *better-than-the-alternatives* defense – the alternatives being "violence or coercion" in Connolly's terms. While the ambiguities of politics are not those of PR, there are significant parallels, particularly in the context of their overall convergent similarities. Both politics and PR require the dramatic discipline of an "on-message" performance. Both politics and PR rely on artful tailoring of multiple messages by means of a granular, carefully toned and – especially in the era of "big data" – algorithmic analysis of socioeconomic segments. Both institutional practices can be understood rhetorically and dramaturgically. And, as a consequence, both politics and PR have faced fierce impeachments of their legitimacy, authenticity and ethics.

Not that Ivy Lee, Edward Bernays and other "pioneers" of twentieth-century mass communication theories and PR were at all devoid of interest in, or the practice of, politics. On the contrary, they were immersed in it. Famously or notoriously, Joseph Goebbels, the Nazi Minister of Public Enlightenment and Propaganda, was sufficiently impressed by Bernays's theories of mass communication to attempt, without success, to hire him as a consultant. Instead, he had to be content with Bernays's (1923) *Crystallizing Public Opinion* and his *Propaganda* (1928). The Nazis were more successful in the case of Ivy Lee, and their success in hiring Lee's firm had unfortunate consequences for Lee's reputation. Although he was not a PR practitioner but a journalist, Walter Lippmann has been considered among the "pioneers" of modern PR. Bernays liberally credited Lippmann's *Public Opinion* (1922) with influencing his own theories just 3 years after the publication of Lippmann's classic.

The history of political theory (e.g., Plato, Aristotle, Augustine, Machiavelli, Hobbes, Locke, Rousseau, Burke, Jefferson, Tocqueville, Marx, Benjamin, Friedrich, Strauss, Arendt, Sartre) provides ample evidence of striking resonances with PR. The theory of public opinion, for example, is among the most central and abiding interests of politics and PR. That public opinion has become a "science" is more a reflection of the continuing division of sensibilities between the sciences and the humanities than a persuasive rebuttal of the profoundly political nature of PR.

Duality

Among the most salient resonances between politics and PR is to be found in the schismatic condition of their epistemology. A Platonic-like dualism can be adduced to account for the ambiguities and tensions of both politics and PR. That both politics and PR so passionately attempt to identify the legitimate wholeness of their practices is an indication of their need for legitimacy amid potent attempts to discredit the legitimacy of their face claims. The rhetoric of political authority has been famously visualized as the binding together of sticks, a Great (and a Berlin) Wall. The rhetoric of the resolution of political distinctions has been depicted as a rainbow, a blindfolded lady balancing opposing arguments and, in some imagery, wielding a double-edged sword. Both politics and PR simultaneously – and paradoxically – acknowledge and deny their doubleness, preferring to redescribe it not as duplicity but as *statecraft, real politic* or *symmetry.* But what's at the core of these framings is the ambiguous attitude of both politics and PR to epistemological duality. For its part, in the twentieth century and our own, PR has undertaken strenuous efforts to either deny its dualities or resolve them by means of investments in programs of corporate social responsibility and cause branding. These efforts are often created through strategic alliances with well-reputed nonprofits, nongovernmental organizations and government initiatives such as "clean" energy and recycling.

Few political theorists are as frequently invoked than Niccolo Machiavelli, the figure widely credited with being the first modern political theorist and who has been famously misread and oversimplified. Perhaps what makes Machiavelli strike us as a figure of modernity has its source in the complexity of his ideas about politics. Reading him more critically than the superficial bumper sticker of ends justifying means, we discern in his advice to the Prince the assertion of the tensions, doubleness and ambiguity surrounding the relationship of politics to power. Indeed, the Prince is directed to be a kind of Stanislavskian method actor if he wants to become an *effective* Prince. Like the actor, the Prince is not directed to "be himself" but to fully inhabit a role on whose professionalism will rest the foundation of a coherent and peaceful nation-state. How the Prince must perform, Machiavelli explained, "is by *virtu* and the force of one's own arms" (Machiavelli, 2003, p. xi). It is thus not by transparency and directness – those shibboleths of PR – that a political practitioner becomes effective. Rather, it is by means of a dramatically disciplined, situationally contextualized, artfully compartmentalized and staged performance.

The effective (if not "symmetrical") Prince must be an excellent actor, capable of achieving Machiavelli's concept of balancing generosity and meanness (Machiavelli, 2003, Chapter 16). He must grasp "how a ruler should act to gain a reputation" (Machiavelli, 2003, Chapter 21). He should know how to *seem* for the telos of the effectively ruled, stable and peaceable civil society.

As an aside, it should be noted (if it is not contextually apparent in such a comparison between deeply disparate historical eras) that unlike "method acting" developed by Constantin Stanislavski and Lee Strasberg in the mid-twentieth century for professional actors, Machiavelli did not advise the Prince to tap into the inner core of his most private and painful experiences and memories, although the outrageousness of the idea is amusing. The point of such a comparison is, at once behavioral, dramaturgic and metaphoric. Effective governance for the Prince demanded the dramatic discipline of binding together opposites into an apparent whole. Such a performance calls to mind, however anachronistically, the adage that perception is reality. Indeed, one may argue that such an equation may not be subject to the usual objection of anachronism but would be offered instead as a transhistorical feature of social and political life.

What Machiavelli sought to teach the Prince was that the powerful leader has no shape – that power is in the performance, but competent acting would require every bit of the Prince's commitment to do what was necessary. That, of course, is not what is meant by "Machiavellian." And although Bernays and other modern pioneers would hardly have cited Machiavelli as their inspirational mentor, they understood that their practice demands more than what we call "communication competence" – it demands dramatic discipline. Dramatic discipline demands more than what we call "audience analysis" – it requires what actors on stage must do: watch, listen, read and respond to the other actor, the situation, the problem. In this way, dramatic discipline and finely attuned attention generate those private opinions that are the seeds of public opinion.

Nothing is more central to PR than public opinion, the truth of which was driven home in Walter Lippmann's classic analysis. In her essay, "Public Relations and Public Opinion," Magda Pieczka (1996) explored the development of a contentious disagreement in public opinion research during the middle third of the twentieth century. The controversy surrounded the rising popularity of public opinion polls supported by the newly influential group of empiricists (Pieczka, 1996, pp. 58–64). Although the details of those arguments are too technical to permit a full treatment in these pages, Pieczka's speculations are of interest here. Pieczka did not attempt to referee the debate about empiricism but to point out that these arguments are relevant "at a time when clear aspirations to a social-scientific status have been expressed in the field" (p. 58).

Pieczka (1996) located the core issue in the attachment of PR theory to Grunig and Hunt's situational theory of publics and the co-orientation theory as the basis of "excellence" (p. 63). The definition of public opinion formation was expressed, in PR theorist William Ehling's terms, as "a dialogue and argument about politics and issues that goes beyond the revealing of private opinion to the forming of public opinion," consistent with Jurgen Habermas's idea of public opinion (Ehling cited by Pieczka, 1996, p. 63). Finally, Pieczka raised a question crucial to our understanding of the place of PR in the academy, which shall be more fully explored in Chapter 10 on the humanities:

> Public relations, in this definition, seems to act as the enabling mechanism for public debate, therefore for public opinion and the public sphere. If this is how the practice appears, where then should the study of public relations as a discipline be located in the social sciences?
>
> (p. 64)

The answer was offered by L'Etang and Pieczka (1996): PR belongs to interdisciplinary studies, rather than strictly and solely to the social sciences or the professions (pp. 9–13).

The cadre of "radical PR" has been, in its critiques of PR, keenly aware of those asymmetries of power and influence that can be said to be clearly political (rather than solely commercial) in nature. A century ago, it was Bernays's strategy to redescribe PR as commerce rather than propaganda, as if the two were mutually exclusive and their political nature could be redacted.

The so-called "radical PR" scholars in the postsymmetry era have critiqued conventional PR theory precisely on the grounds that it has avoided or minimized the political nature of PR and the vast inequities of power in relations among genders, races and nations, as well as within organizations. Thoughtful analyses of the political nature of PR can be found in Charles Taylor's (2010) analysis of the formation of civil society and PR scholar David McKie's (2010) identification of political power asymmetries between indigenous and colonialist populations in New Zealand.

In the wake of the oil-price spikes of the 1970s by the OPEC cartel and the devastating effect on the public image of oil companies, I was hired by an "earth resources" multinational company, as were other new editorial hires, because I was a professional, published writer. ARCO also hired television producers, graphic designers and economists. When I began my career in PR, it was in Editorial Services, a department whose "editorial" function contained numerous subfunctions, including writing for the *ARCO Spark*, the company's internal newspaper; writing for the company's annual report, which was itself a tactic or tool of the investor relations function; and writing planning scenarios developed by senior management to "manage" social, economic and political trends.

Within a short time, I was promoted to a function grandly known as *executive communication* and commonly understood as *speechwriting*. It was as a speechwriter that the broad and deep political nature of this corporation and its peer corporations became evident to me. My initial experience as a PR practitioner called for my becoming immersed in the political environment of a giant "earth resources" (oil) corporation. This meant dealing with the issues it sought to "manage" and the crises that threatened the way many external, internal, domestic and international constituencies perceived the corporation.

The most pressing concerns of the company's CEO and other top management revealed the corporation's umbilical connection between operational success and the public's perception of the company as a political entity. The corporation's viability didn't merely depend on having mutually beneficial relationships with society in general. Its viability depended on the quality of its relationships that orbited around political relationships with government and communities.

True, a giant corporation is political in a way that smaller, less visible, less environmentally impactful organizations are not. But it is no less true that every organization, large or small, bears a relationship to society that is at once persuasive and political.

Politics, legitimacy, entertainment and the public square

In a frame other than systems theory, politics can be understood as more than a mere "function" of PR. In the largest, most visible, publicly held corporations, the political assumes a huge presence. The philosopher of science, Gaston Bachelard (1965), made the poetic observation that nests take their shape from the breasts of birds. So too do organizational "houses" take their shape from the impress of what inhabits them. At ARCO in last third of the twentieth century, the impact of politics – issues,

visibility, controversy about oil companies – was the architect of a sizable department of public affairs. With symbolic significance, the PR department – publicity,
graphic design, corporate ID – occupied the sixteenth floor of the 52-floor ARCO
Tower, but the public affairs department had the fortieth floor. Up there, politics was
that much closer to the topmost floor, where the CEO and president did their thinking in the stratosphere.

The PR adage that perception is reality is embedded with matters of judgment,
class, status, gender and, thus, politics. Wealthy and ambitious companies – and
companies whose operations are threaded through the everyday experiences of
people – are more political than other, smaller, less visible companies. The combination of everyday familiarity, visibility in the media and economic and environmental impact make behemoth companies emphatically political. In the
crosshairs of public opinion, ARCO and companies like it made the decision to
embrace their political visibility by fighting fire with fire. ARCO took a page from
the assertive and visually present tradition of Ivy Lee's PR strategy after the turn
of the twentieth century, when Lee's controversial clients included the Pennsylvania
Railroad and the oil monopolist John D. Rockefeller. ARCO's strategy was to create and fund multilevel, local and national programs of CSR and invest up to 5 percent
of their net profits in the spirit of the 5 percent standard for CSR, originated in the
mid-1940s by the Minneapolis-based Dayton retail companies.

For PR, the move toward CSR is not a "function" but a strategy whose politics
aim at tackling what may be the most important challenge for PR and for a company as visible as ARCO: legitimacy. In a sense, all roads lead back to the question
of legitimacy – for client, PR and citizen.

Entertaining the citizen

It may appear that regarding PR as political must be limited to the relatively exotic,
if highly visible, environment of the world's largest corporations. But the linkage
between PR and politics need not be limited to the functionalist perspective of corporate communications. PR's political nature need not be necessarily understood as
a function; nor is there a need for the political nature of PR to be limited to organizational entities according to size. In the broader sense, the political is not functional,
but constitutive; that is, it comprises relationships throughout the communication-
theory taxonomy of face-to-face, interpersonal, group and mass communication. However, even that taxonomy is, for our purposes, inadequate to account for
"what is really going on here," in Goffman's (1986) terms. (It is worth noting that
Goffman's interest in politics was virtually invisible.)

PR need not be understood as an innumerable collection of functions working
together by some willed and abstract force of "integration." Beyond (or alternative
to) the slices and dices of PR functionalism, there is another way of understanding
PR that does not portray it as a mechanistic collection of pieces and parts and functions. The alternative perspective borrows from the theatrical stage. On it, actors –
with relative degrees of power, standing and agency – come prepared with their
lines and their gestures. On this stage, or wherever the producers and directors

locate or build their stages, the actors speak, move and, when confronted with the unplanned and unexpected crisis, they improvise. In doing this, they perform with as much dramatic discipline as they can muster. At all points in their performance, are they at risk of falling out of character and thus losing their face claims to be who they say they are.

This, then, is a holistically and dramaturgic perspective of PR, an alternative to the conventional paradigm of functionalism. Linda Hutcheon (1989) noted the tendency in postmodernism toward collapsing and convergence. Opera raps; fiction appropriates e-mails; art museums mount graffiti. If there is a politics in such convergence, it found expression in the adage that "the personal is the political." The application of this theory, which was particularly favored by the feminist movement of the 1960s and 1970s, opened the opportunity for journalists like the American columnist Ellen Goodman to be moved "up" from the "low" (personal) space of the Women's Page to the "high" (political) space of the Op Ed Page. Having been repositioned from personal to political space, Goodman and other journalists adumbrated the postmodernist convergence of high and low culture, the ironic quotations around "high" and "low" falling further and further out of cultural relevance. On the Women's Page, childcare was both personal and gendered; on the Op Ed Page it became political, and its gender was transformed from the assumption of its femininity to a critical and cultural question of power and equity. Typically, if perhaps unfortunately for PR scholarship, its notions of negotiation, symmetry and "willingness to change" never entered into that conversation. Certainly, these theoretical perspectives would have been relevant, but rarely if ever has PR scholarship been admitted to the issues table populated by public officials, religious figures, educators, historians, sociologists, psychologists, political scientists, journalists, broadcasters, celebrities and, especially in the age of social media, just plain folks.

My speechwriting, op eds and other persuasively oriented ghostwriting in big corporate political environments involved complex issues such as state and federal regulatory policies, legislation affecting taxation, drilling, land-leasing, environment, conservation, synthetic and solar energy systems and international relations. But as arcane and technical as those issues were, they did not exist at the "high" level of government; they were of vital, daily concern to the lives of citizens. Here, then, is another angle of convergence, well described by the subtitle of Liesbet van Zoonen's (2005) *Entertaining the Citizen: When Politics and Popular Culture Converge.* She argued against the "essentialist" position of those critics of popular culture like Neil Postman, who theorized that we are "entertaining ourselves to death." For Postman and like-minded observers, popular culture and politics are as incapable of mixing as oil and water. To them, the media – and primarily TV – is so constructed in its rapacious economics and the oversimplifications of its time-driven format that it has become incapable of being a serious format for the complexities of politics. Van Zoonen believes otherwise. In her view, entertainment fosters political engagement.

Evidence of van Zoonen's thesis can be found in the U.S. broadcast media. Satirizing (or "sending up") the "official" mainstream news programs earns impressive ratings among that young demographic that long ago tuned out the major network evening news shows. Those shows, formerly the province of such highly credible journalists as Edward R. Murrow, Walter Cronkite and Howard K. Smith, are no longer watched by upwards of 50 million American families at their dinner hour; their audience has narrowed to the gerontocratic 60-plus demographic. Meanwhile, young (and presumably politically disaffected, if not alienated) viewers have flocked to such "fake news" American cable-television programs as *The Daily Show* and its close cousin, *The Colbert Report*. Politically, these shows attract viewers who are relatively progressive, if not partisan, Democrats. At the same time, politically conservative viewers have also switched channels from what former U.S. presidential candidate Sarah Palin called "the lamestream media." What politically engaged conservative youth, along with tens of millions of religious and cultural conservatives, are watching is another news format that sends up the "lamestream" media: FOX News, a politically and culturally conservative empire under the aegis of Rupert Murdoch. Fox News's ironic tag line is "fair and balanced," which mocks the perceived pretentiousness of what the right wing calls the "government media" (Pew Research Center, 2008).

This trend away from the straight, dignified and officially sanctioned can be understood in part as a manifestation of a postmodern turn. On the political right, America's persuasion and opinion culture has witnessed the rise of conservative ideology that reinvented and came to dominate the talk radio industry. Here, star performers are led by Rush Limbaugh, whose daily audience includes more than 20 million listeners.

Entertainment and engagement comprise the acting strategies in the theaters of both progressive and conservative performers. Starting out as an ideologically conservative talk show host, Limbaugh was given to sonic as well as verbal innovations. They included his curious, never-before-heard habit of crumbling paper close to his microphone, which produced an effect not unlike a teacher clapping his hands together to command the class's attention. Limbaugh's "bag" (an actor's term to describe reliable and effective stage techniques) has included such culture-war verbal coinages as *feminazis* and *reporterette,* terms meant to chide feminism; the meta-linguistic "anti" usage of *liberal* to connote moral weakness; dropping the *-ic* suffix from *Democratic Party* to critically delegitimize America's liberal institution; and a raft of ironic self-puffery such as calling his radio show the "institute for advanced conservative studies," which expresses the conservative trope that liberal colleges and universities are overstuffed with their own self-aggrandizing, Ivy League nomenclature. Limbaugh's hyperbolic, grandiose, manly–adventurous, larger than life, quasi-populist style is largely consistent with the American literary tradition of tall tales, lapel-grabbing, snake-oil hawking and mythicizing that flourished on the American frontier in the era of Barnum and Mark Twain. Limbaugh is a modern equivalent of what literary historian R.W.B. Lewis (1959) called "the American Adam," a manly, risk-taking, fearless, visionary adventurer on a brand-new continent whose vastness promised the fulfillment of the boldest dreams.

Like conservatives, liberals (or progressives) are enacting their own forms of politically engaging entertainment. Their arsenal of provocations includes what could fairly be called "liberal" use of profanity (pun intended) such as the notorious F-word and what cultural conservatives would call the vulgar terms for the procreative, erotic and defecatory habits of men and women. Put more plainly, the ironic, "fake news" correspondents deploy expletives with a comic brio that mocks the perceived prudery of political conservatives. Despite the bleep-censoring of the F-word by the cable-station broadcasting authorities, the word itself is abundantly clear in the context of its delivery. In a way this comically intended verbal aggressiveness resonates with the American tradition of rebelling against the manners, morals and customs of Europe, but especially of England. The comic-progressive vocabulary of theatrical gestures have included Jon Stewart grabbing his crotch, giving "the finger" and other similar provocations more familiar to actual theater and movie audiences.

Like the sonic and verbal provocations of ideologically conservative radio talk show entertainers, the liberal-progressive TV swearing and rude gestures carry a clear, forcefully rhetorical meaning. For some observers, these messages are so obviously *political* that they could not be considered as PR. But this is a distinction without a difference. These enacted comic–satiric entertainments are clearly intended to do exactly what PR insists it does: generate engagement and conversation. Or *buzz*. The burden of proof that these politically provocative entertainments are *not* PR is on those who argue for such a distinction.

Where cable-television "fake news" programs and their celebrity "hosts" may seek to achieve partisan political engagement from outside professional politics and journalism, elected officials with significant backgrounds as professional entertainers seek engagement from the inside. Al Franken, a progressive Democrat elected in 2009 by the citizens of the state of Minnesota to the U.S. Senate, emerged from a background that included writing and performing comedy sketches for *Saturday Night Live*.

But perhaps no professional entertainer has had a deeper, broader, and more paradigm-changing effect on American politics than Ronald Reagan, the fortieth president of the United States. Reagan, a Hollywood movie star before transitioning to become a corporate spokesperson for General Electric and then to the governorship of California before his election to the U.S. presidency in 1980, remains after 30 years the most revered ideological conservative Republican elected to American public office in the last half century. With a folksy style that downplayed the sharp edges of his politics, Reagan uncorked such warmth and charm up and down the American and world hierarchies that he came to be known as The Great Communicator.

Marshall McLuhan, who famously focused his attention on the first-ever televised debate between U.S. candidates for the presidency, offered the dictum that the medium is the message. The process of engaging citizens by entertaining them can be understood more as performance than communication.

That the citizen can be politically engaged via entertainment is a challenging argument on several levels: epistemological, cultural and historical. For starters, it is, as van Zoonen (2005) indicated, hedonistic, although not in the common or vulgar sense of mindless frivolity but in the Aristotelian sense that the purpose of human life is the pursuit of happiness. Millennia after Aristotle, and centuries before the invention of broadcast, that foundational document of American political philosophy – the Declaration of Independence – affirmed the right of citizens to "life, liberty, and the pursuit of happiness."

Another angle of objection to what has been called the "entertainment industrial complex" has been cultural, if not national or, less charitably, provincial. Debord (1967/1994) mounted a blisteringly Marxist assault on what he regarded as the evolution of a "spectacle economy" that has devolved humanity into becoming "Homo Spectators" of the corrupting, brutal bread-and-circus entertainment society that found its most egregious example in the alienating image machines of America's entertainment and advertising industries. Although Debord didn't specifically include PR in his sweeping, cultural critique, PR's place may be assumed. His critique was targeted at what he called the destructiveness of the American cultural, marketing, advertising and communication system itself, along with the decadence (in his view) of that system.

Broad as it is, Debord's furious approach resonates with arguments such as Herman and Chomsky's (1988), launched specifically against what could be called the American PR industrial complex. In his critique of PR, Boorstin's (1992) rejection of the "image" is in some respects similar to Debord's animus against the "spectacle." Both image and spectacle are regarded as categorically unreal, untrue, unethical and universally corrupting. Although Chomsky approached matters from the more apparently political angle that considered Bernays's "manufacturing of consent" as nothing more than propaganda, Chomsky's argument rested on Platonically dualistic assumptions about "reality": specifically, that there exists realms of "true" and "false" information and communication, or put as another dichotomy, "natural" and "manufactured." For Chomsky all of PR was the categorically false product of made-in-America propaganda to advance economic, social and political hegemony, with tragic results for the world. All three critics have advanced essentialist and dualistic arguments with varying degrees of apocalypticism.

Corporate bohemianism

The political nature of PR found a cultural expression in the anti-authoritarian countercultural ethos and movements of the 1960s and 1970s, with the appearance of long hair, love beads, bra burning, flag burning and marijuana smoking, not to mention the protests over the Vietnam War, racial segregation, environmental depredation and gender and sexual repression.

Corporations in America and Europe saw the writing on the wall and capitalized on the rise of counterculturalism to establish their political brand and credibility. In New England, Ben & Jerry's, an ice cream manufacturer and marketer, was among the thought leaders in the emerging corporate trend toward countercultural political branding. From the beginning, Ben & Jerry's marketing and advertising was inspired by the Deadhead hippie libertarianism and social–environmental activism of its founders, Ben Cohen and Jerry Greenfield. The company's brand is extremely well known and admired in the United States. Not content to color within the corporate lines, the company has never been content with a single mission statement. It has three, which it ranks on its website hierarchically. From first to last, these are social (i.e., corporate responsibility, the localism of buying milk from neighboring Vermont farmers); product (commitment to wholesome, natural sources and operating practices); and economic (operating sustainably and profitably with opportunities for employment). In keeping with the epistemology of "wholeness," a feature of modern corporations known in managerial terms as *integrated*, Ben & Jerry's website describes its missions as "interrelated" (www. benjerry.com/company). In 2000, the company was acquired by Unilever, a U.K.-based consumer brand company with a similarly social (and, in its founding, Socialistically) oriented culture. Unilever seeks brands with similar cultures. As of this writing – in summer 2013 – Ben & Jerry's is legally constituted as a B Corporation, which identifies a company with a track record of social and environmental responsibility (www.benjerry.com/company).

The limits of politics

Merleau-Ponty offered a phenomenology of our relationship to the world as an artistic creation. From the perspective of PRe, then, our lived experience is, in its way, like a Cezanne. If the nature of the human is artistic, it is no less political. That human nature has a political character is a theme found in in the tradition of Aristotle's *Politics,* which has had a far-reaching and long-standing influence in Western civilization, as Thomas Fleming (1988) observed in his book, aptly titled *The Politics of Human Nature,* Aristotle's influence, well observed on the rhetorical nature of PR, resonates, as well, in a religious and spiritual context. That religion has long "embraced" PR is a theme I explored in an article entitled "The Strategic Heart" (Brown, 2014). In *Augustine and the Limits of Politics,* the Christian feminist scholar Jean Bethke Elshtain (1998) crafted a reading of a thinker whose influence on Western civilization has been so great as to be beggared by the PR term for it: *thought leader.* In my previous sins against PR scholarship, I attempted to demonstrate how another Christian thought leader, Saint Paul, offered a confounding example to the theory of symmetry – one that would lead to the absurdity of dismissing the saint's persuasiveness as lacking in symmetry (Brown, 2003). What Elshtain (1998) identified in Augustine are those tensions and contradictions that animate and define not only politics but its source in Augustine's analysis of human nature. In a review of Elshtain's book, these oppositions are spelled out as

> sin and grace, cupiditas and caritas, freedom and predestination, power and humility, will and reason, memory and hope.
>
> (Stackhouse, 1997, p. 421)

Lest this seem impossibly far afield from PR, it should be said that any PR theory that fails to ground itself in human nature will also fail to account for the political nature of PR and the behavior of its practitioners. Augustine's vision turned on the tension between two cities, one earthly, the other heavenly. There could be no code of ethics to resolve their contradictions outside of faith.

That political (and implicitly secular) nature of PR is an abiding theme of Hiebert's (1966) biography of a modern PR pioneer Ivy Lee. One need look no further than the epigraphs of the biography to find two passages, the topmost from Abraham Lincoln that "public sentiment is everything" and the bottom from Lee:

> The people now rule. We have substituted for the divine right of kings, the divine right of the multitude. This new sovereign has his courtiers, who flatter and caress precisely as did those who surrounded medieval emperors.

It is not surprising that Lee's historically and politically minded biographer Ray Hiebert, would found the first research journal of PR, *Public Relations,* to be steeped in historical and political thinking. Hiebert (1966) offered a broadly political and historical defense of PR, holding that "the techniques which Lee helped develop did aid in the preservation of democracy in mass society" (p. x). The historical context of that preservation was what Hiebert called the "crisis of democracy in a mass society [that] reached its climax during Lee's life" (ix). The notion that modern PR has its origins in a crisis resonates with the argument in Chapter 3 of this book that proposes that CSR "erupted" from an environmental and political crisis brought on, in part, by a major oil spill.

The ambiguity that characterizes PR's ethics (discussed at length in Chapter 9) is also found in the PR's political nature. This should not strain PR's credibility. Both institutions – politics and PR – offer ample examples of reason and contradiction, inspiration and tedium. Both are problematic; each is necessary. Indeed, the necessity of PR suggests a reason to imagine it as something more basic and continuous to humanity and thus to doubt its conventional historiography as modern. PR textbooks often cite the rousingly inspirational writing of Tom Paine and, in sharp contrast, the meticulously judicious essays of Hamilton, Madison and Jay in *The Federalist Papers* (1961) as examples (Hamilton, et al., 1961) of "early" PR. Writing to persuade, publicize and engage, in the fashion of PR, all these authors recognized the tensions and contradictions in the expressive dramatics of their words. A half-century after, Thoreau would highlight – in words and deeds – the definitive opposition between the individual and society in the political framework of freedom.

Political communication and PR

At Emerson College in Boston, the study of political communication, abbreviated as *policom,* is integrated with the study of PR. Emerson's leading political communication scholar, J. Gregory Payne, makes sure that policom majors become well versed in theories and practices of PR, crisis communication and, in recent years, in public diplomacy and dramaturgy. For the undergraduate major, the program's requirements include communication theory, leadership, politics and social advocacy, argument and advocacy, and politics, advocacy and public opinion research. PR scholars (myself included) lecture each semester on public affairs, crisis communications, PR theory and public diplomacy. In recent years, the policom department has made explicit its interdisciplinary character by establishing a website called PD/PA/PR (public diplomacy, public affairs, PR). PR, at least at Emerson College, is thus as much in the sensibility of policom as vice versa. It should be noted that although it's a separate program within Emerson College, theater studies has been part of the college's identifying brand since the institution's founding in 1880 (www.emerson.edu).

As policom professor Payne has said in conversation, there has been a convergence of public affairs, PR and public diplomacy. Payne has been long sponsored by the U.S. State Department's Public Diplomacy Division to travel abroad as a public diplomat. On these travels, he has represented the public diplomatic strategies and interests of the United States with public and private individuals in Jordan, Saudi Arabia, Indonesia, Turkmenistan and Libya, where he was invited to meet with Muammar Gadhafi, the former ruler of Libya. Payne's conclusion: what was really going on in those interactions represented the political nature of PR and the convergence of PR, public affairs and public diplomacy.

That PR is politically conscious is not to equate it, as a discipline, with political communication. Still, this consciousness offers yet another illustration of disciplinary convergence. As the political communication scholar Dan F. Hahn (2003) observed:

> A better approach, I think, [than seeing politics as concerning power] is to see politics as a process that takes place through communication – from identifying a problem in society (perhaps through conversations with those suffering from it), through proposing a solution, debating the need for a solution (i.e., why this is a more "pressing" problem than a myriad of others), arguing the relative merits of this solution over others proposed, explaining the resulting law to the citizens and to those in the government whose job it is to enforce it, and so forth.
>
> (p. 2)

Political communication, like PR, is conventionally understood as "politics that takes place through communication" (Hahn, 2003, p. 3). That our argument in "the public relations of everything" frames the process of PR as taking place dramaturgically, that is, enacted in a variety of scenes by actors, is not intended to call into question PR's self-identification as a communication discipline. Rather, a dramaturgical perspective is intended throughout this book to rethink PR in other terms: sociological, phenomenological, aesthetic, religious and dramatic.

But it is not only as drama and performance that PR reveals its nature. It is also as politics.

References

Bachelard, G. (1965). *The poetics of space*. Trans., M. Jolas. London: Orion Press.
Bernays, E. L. (1923). *Crystallizing public opinion*. New York, NY: Boni & Liveright.
———. (1928). *Propaganda*. New York, NY: Horace Liveright.

———. (1965). *Biography of an idea: Memoirs of public relations counsel Edward L. Bernays*. New York, NY: Simon & Schuster.

Black, J. (2001). Semantics and ethics of propaganda. *Journal of Mass Media Ethics,* 16(2–3), 121–137.

Boorstin, D. (1992). *The image: A guide to pseudo events in America*. New York, NY: Vintage.

Brown, R. E. (2010). Symmetry and its critics: Antecedents, prospects, and implications for symmetry in a post-symmetry era. In R. L. Heath (Ed.), *Handbook of public relations II* (pp. 277–292). Thousand Oaks, CA: Sage.

———. (2012). Epistemological modesty: Ten reflections on public relations thought. *PR Inquiry,* 1(1), 89–105.

———. (2014). The strategic heart: The almost mutual embrace of religion and public relations. In B. Saint John & M. Lamme (Eds.), *Pathways to public relations* (pp. 11–27). New York, NY: Routledge.

Brown, R. E. & Rancer, A. S. (1993). Congruence of orientations toward public relations: A cross-cultural comparison of British and American practitioners. *World Communication Journal,* 22(1), pp. 1–6.

Connolly, W. (1987). *Politics and ambiguity*. Madison: University of Wisconsin Press.

Cornford, F. M. (1932). *Before and after Socrates*. Cambridge, England: Cambridge University Press.

Debord, G. (1994). *The society of the spectacle*. New York, NY: Zone Books.

Ellul, J. (1965). *Propaganda: The formation of men's attitudes*. New York, NY: Knopf.

Elshtain, J. B. (1998). *Augustine and the limits of politics*. Notre Dame, IN: Notre Dame Press.

Fleming, T. (1988). *The politics of human nature*. New Brunswick, NJ: Transaction.

Global 500 2014. (2014). Retrieved from http://money.cnn.com/magazines/fortune/global500/2012/snapshots/387.html

Goffman, E. (1986). *Frame analysis*. Boston, MA: Northeastern Press.

Hahn, D.F. (2003). *Political communication: Rhetoric, government, and citizens*. State College, PA: Strata.

Hamilton, A., Madison, J. & Jay, J. (1961). *The Federalist papers* (C. Rossiter, Ed.). New York, NY: New American Library.

Heath, R. L. (Ed.) (2001). *Handbook of public relations*. Thousand Oaks, CA: Sage.

———. (2010). *Sage handbook of public relations II*. Thousand Oaks, CA: Sage.

Herman, E. S. & Chomsky, N. (1988). *Manufacturing consent: The political economy of the mass media*. New York: Pantheon.

Hiebert, R. (1966). *Courtier to the crowd*. Ames: University of Iowa Press.

Hutcheon, L. (1989). *The politics of postmodernism*. London, England, and New York, NY: Routledge.

L'Etang, J. & Pieczka, M. (Eds.). (1996). *Critical perspectives in public relations*. London, England, and Boston, MA: International Thomson Business Press.

Lewis, R.W.B. (1959). *The American Adam*. Chicago, IL: University of Chicago Press.

Lippmann, W. (1922). *Public opinion*. New York: Harcourt, Brace.

Machiavelli, N. (2003). *The prince* (Q. Skinner & R. Price, Eds.). West Nyack, NY: Cambridge University Press.

McKie, D. (2010). Signs of the times: Economic sciences, futures, and public relations. In R. L. Heath (Ed.), *Sage handbook of public relations II* (pp. 85–98). Thousand Oaks, CA: Sage.

Newell, A. (2012). *Will corporate CSR positions grow or disappear as responsibility beco-mes a core function?* Retrieved from www.csrwire.com/blog/posts/636-will-corporate-csr-positions-grow-or-disappear-as-responsibility-becomes-a-core-

Pew Research Center. (2008). *What's on – and what's not on – The Daily Show*. Retrieved from www.journalism.org/node/10954

Pieckza, M. (1996). Public opinion and public relations. In J. L'Etang & M. Pieczka, (Eds.), *Critical perspectives in public relations* (pp. 54–64). London, England, and Boston, MA: International Thomson Business Press.

St. John, B. (2006). The case for ethical propaganda within a democracy: Ivy Lee's success-ful 1913–1914 railroad rate campaign. *Public Relations Review, 32*(3), 221–228.

Stackhouse, M. (1997). Living in God's city. *Christian Century, 114*(14), 421–425.

Taylor, C. (2010). Public relations in the enactment of civil society. In R. L. Heath (Ed.), *The Sage handbook of public relations II* (pp. 5–16). Thousand Oaks, CA: Sage.

van Zoonen, L. (2005). *Entertaining the citizen: When politics and popular culture con-verge*. Oxford, England: Rowman & Littlefield.

Vogel, D. (1980). Foreword. In T. Bradshaw & D. Vogel (Eds.), *Corporations and their critics* (pp. vii–xiii). New York, NY: McGraw-Hill.

9 Ambiguities (or ethics)

No man can serve two masters.

Matthew 6:24

"Ambiguity" itself means an indecision as to what you mean, an intention to mean several things, a probability that one or other of both of two things have been meant, and the fact that a statement has several meanings.

Empson (1931, p. 7)

This chapter is about the ethics of public relations (PR). PR is obsessed with ethics, and that is destined to continue. The obsession goes to the heart of PR's anxieties about its reputation, legitimacy and the foundation of PR's classic strength: the perception of its credibility. Absent this strength, PR would be strategically bankrupt.

The source of these problems appears to lie in PR's attempt to serve two, and sometimes more, masters. Put another way, the ethics of PR are structurally double. Not only must truth be served – so must the client. Whatever else it is, PR is a customer-service profession. The PR industry and PR scholars have labored passionately to rebrand PR with campaigns for licensure, the creation and tweaking of ethical codes and the aspirational cleansing of symmetry theory. But all the corporate social responsibility (CSR), cause branding and symmetrical theorizing have failed and are destined to fail because none of these strategies addresses the structural doubleness of PR. This is perceived as a problem that frustrates theorists and puzzles scientists. But it is just the sort of complexity best understood and accepted by the humanities, for the humanities are content with the existence of a paradox without trying to fix it.

PR's obsessions are inward facing, less concerned with facing the ethical complexities of PR than with the practice's anxiety about the world's perception of PR's legitimacy. The legitimacy of an organization has been called "central" to the practice of PR itself (L'Etang & Pieczka, 1996; Metzler, 2001). What's true of organizations holds as well for the institution and the idea of PR.

The paradox of PR is that its greatest strength – credibility – is its greatest weakness. Currently fashionable thinking within the PR galaxy is that effective

PR depends on process – the process of multiplatform messaging, digital story-telling, social media transmission and statistically compelling analytical measure-ment, as well as engagement, conversation, negotiation and the willingness to compromise.

But this process is an aggregation of tactics that are only supporting actors in the ongoing problems of PR with its credibility, reputation and legitimacy. What is not often remarked on is how well PR has done with a reputation that, if any-thing, is lacking is all those fundamentals.

A reasonable observer could hardly avoid concluding that there is a yawning gap between the aspirations of PR for credibility, reputation, and legitimacy. One can imagine that gap having a gravitational pull that has drawn numerous attempts by PR scholars and practitioners – quantitative, qualitative and miscellaneous – to publish research and opinion defining, defending or critiquing PR.

PR is the Narcissus of consultancies. Even more than other consulting practices such as law, accounting, management consulting, organizational development, financial planning, personal training and life coaching, PR continues to be obsessed with its own reputation. Despite PR's heralded distinctiveness – its credibility based on getting "others" to do the work of promotion – PR's obsession is far less with others than with itself. More than other consulting practices, PR stares into a mirror to gaze and admire but also to worry about its reflection.

Chapters on ethics are obligatory in PR textbooks. Scholarly PR journals devote special issues to it. In the index to *Essentials of Public Relations* (Wilcox, Ault, Agee & Cameron, 2001), there are more than 50 references to ethics. The ninth edition of Cutlip, et al.'s (2006) textbook, *Effective Public Relations* – con-sidered by many the industry standard – gives ethics 10 pages; *PR Today*, by the British authors Morris and Goldsworthy (2012), 30 pages. Guth and Marsh (2000) plunked ethics right in the middle of things by entitling their book *Public Rela-tions: A Values-Driven Approach*. At what may be the furthest end of the ethical spectrum is L'Etang (2008), whose *Public Relations: Concepts, Practice and Critique* is a critical exploration of the PR's ethical problems in the guise of a textbook. McKie and Munshie (2009) and other critical thinkers operate from what could be called a postethical PR perspective, where ethics are defined by advocacy, "action PR" and a socially driven philosophy of "good works" for community underdogs.

What can account for PR's obsession with ethics? For starters, it isn't surprising, given PR's reputation among the world outside of PR practitioners, teachers, and scholars. Scholarly concerns about PR ethics appear not to be quite so troubling to the industry's practitioners. At least not on the surface. Weber, the successful entrepreneur of several PR firms, may well be the most ethical of practitioners, but his book about PR, *Sticks and Stones,* lacks a single indexed reference to ethics and all of two pages to legal issues (Weber, 2009).

Nor is this to suggest that practitioners are not intensely concerned about ethics. Weber's (2009) theme was the sea change of PR caused by the Internet. One only has to observe – as this chapter does – the practitioner industry's strategic embrace of CSR and cause marketing to see where the industry's interest lies.

PR's ethical doubleness

PR's obsession with ethics may lie in its ethically complex situation. A doubleness composes PR. Unlike academic philosophy, which claims to serve truth, PR must serve two masters: truth and clientele. For this reason, PR occupies the ethical middle, an ethical space requiring strategic decisions that weigh costs and benefits.

The organizational theorist Eric Eisenberg (2007) identified the ways in which organizational management must be concerned about communicating a variety of delicate and complex information with, as it were, two ethical minds: one responsible to employees and the other responsive to the viability of the organization itself. This ethical doubleness is what Eisenberg called "strategic ambiguities," the title of his study.

Although this sort of ethical doubling is not the equivalent of duplicity, nor is it lying, it may well have the appearance of both. Ethically doubled communication can range from the subtle and undetectable to the transparent, self-serving, clumsy and embarrassing. Nevertheless, the mastery of this skill is one of the requirements for the kind of delicate diplomatic negotiations with two or more parties. The structure of such situations is itself a matter of doubleness, with communication that is direct and indirect, through back channels and front channels.

Epistemologically, this communicative doubleness resonates with the anthropologist Gregory Bateson's (1972) theory of the "double bind," which holds that the attempt to handle contradictory messages can produce stress that can be debilitating to the point of madness. More famously to Americans, perhaps, is the F. Scott Fitzgerald quote from "The Crack Up," his article in a 1936 issue of *Esquire* magazine, that "the test of a first-rate intelligence is the ability to hold two opposed ideas in mind at the same time and still retain the ability to function" (Fitzgerald, F. S. 1936; 2008).

It is this old and continuing duality that as much as anything is at the root of the ethics of the public relations of everything (PRe), every practitioner and, indeed, everybody. In particular, PR's structural, historical doubleness is palpable in the industry's problematic situation and in the continuing attempts by the PR industry to seek ethically rebranding strategies and PR scholarship to posit normative theories of ethics. Bowen (2010) provided a rationale supporting the case for a normative ethics. But what lingers, what will not be uncomposed, is a pervasive and ultimately inescapable sense of ethical ambiguity. Whether this ambiguity is prior to or follows from PR's doubleness will have to remain moot for now.

Ambiguity is baked into PR, as it is into everyday life. Eisenberg (2007) referenced Burke's (1945) idea that organizing involves the application of "one's resources of ambiguity" (p. xix). PR's ethical nature is the inevitable product of its cultural situation, which, in turn, determines the definitively strategic ambiguity of its response along with its invisibility and role-taking theatricality. Indeed, to the extent that our judgment of the ethics of an act depends upon our judgment of the actor's motives, ambiguity is inevitable in the impossibility of completely knowing the motives of another, or of oneself. What would tragedy be without such unknowing?

Ambiguity is baked into language, into the very words, and into the poetry from which rhetoric was born. William Empson (1931), a literary critic prominent among the "new criticism" that arose to explicate the ambiguity and opacity of modernist poetry, identified seven types of ambiguity in English poetry, the first of which was metaphor. In "Four Quartets," his homage to Beethoven, T. S. Eliot (1969) made memorable poetry of the incapacity of language itself to capture the music of lived experience:

> Words strain,
> Crack and sometimes break, under the burden
> Under the tension, slip, slide, perish,
> Decay with imprecision,
> Will not stay in place,
> Will not stay still

(p. 175)

A dream of clarity

From its ancient origins in the indirectness and complexities of poetry and rhetoric, PR has dreamed a dream of clarity, while all the time continuing its rhetorical practices. Chided by the modern institution of journalism, which is guided by a strict ethic of truth and the rejection and dismissal of communication that smacks of rhetoric ("spin"), PR has struggled in vain to legitimize itself. It is this struggle that has generated programs and theories like CSR, cause marketing and, in the academy, symmetry theory.

Perhaps nothing in human experience more perfectly than music brings home to the heart what is, at once, emotional clarity and the ambiguity of meaning. Even in the digital–social media era of PR, it remains primarily a medium of words posted, tweeted, attached, linked and spoken. PR understands well the limitations of words, and like advertising, underscores its messages with melodies. With ballets, photos and cathedrals. Sometimes simply with elision, evasion and silence. The PR practitioner, no less than the poet, is equally the victim and the beneficiary of the sliding imprecision of words. The ambiguity of PR provides it with both the "resources of ambiguity," in Burke's (1945, p. xix) phrase, for an ethically obfuscating indirectness, and in Hamlet's truth-seeking apothegm, "by indirections find directions out" (Hamlet: Act II, Scene 1). In the language of communication scholarship, "Explicit communication is a cultural assumption; it is not a linguistic imperative" (Eisenberg, 2007, p. 5). Put another way, PR's indirectness and ambiguity do not preclude its ethics any more than a simplification and directness amount to an ethical guarantee.

PR works, to some extent, under the impress of certain situations, to put ambiguity to good use. In PR there's a perpetual alternation between what's said and unsaid, seen and unseen, front stage and back stage, clear and ambiguous. PR lives liminally, in the space between light and dark, and sometimes simply in the twilight. Clarity has its profoundly redemptive values, of course. But it can be precisely the wrong thing at the wrong time, which every practitioner knows just as it is known by everyone else in everyday life. In *Propaganda,* 5 years after describing the process of "crystallizing public opinion," Bernays (1923, p. 178) hit on another metaphor that defines the conception of the PR practitioner, himself: "invisible wire puller" (Bernays, 1928, p. 5). PR is damned equally as a spectacle (Debord, 1970) and a mole. Eisenberg (2007) quoted Goffman's observation that "there is much to be gained by venturing nothing" (Goffman, 1967/2005).

From the perspective that the concept of PR should be expanded beyond the confines of organizational community, ambiguity describes what Goffman (1967/2005) called "strategic interaction," the title of his study. Goffman said of his microsociological focus, that

> one must come to terms with the fact that the central concepts in the area [of communication] are ambiguous, and the bordering fields marked off badly.
>
> (p. ix)

Rather than dismiss ambiguity as an eccentric way of thinking about PR, it would be helpful to recognize that ambiguity is the uncertain ground on which roles are performed in PR, as they are in everyday life. That such a perspective fails to accord with the prevailing organizational conceptualization of PR does not constitute a persuasive rebuttal. As Goffman insightfully demonstrated in a panoply of contexts, the social condition of human beings is fundamentally uncertain and ambiguous, leading directly to the comedy and pathos of strategic performances that has been well described as Kafkaesque. Consider Goffman's (1963) insight into the uncertainty that challenges stigmatized individuals in face-to-face interactions:

> Thus in the stigmatized arises the sense of not knowing what the others present are "really" thinking of him.
>
> (p. 14)

Surely, then, the corporate CEO of a company blamed for a preventable crisis is similarly stigmatized in face-to-face, small group, large group and mass communication contexts. So, too, are the supervisor, account executive and entry-level PR practitioner and so on down the corporate hierarchy.

Role is what the practice of PR pivots around, not the binary, made-for-quantitative analysis role conception of theorizing strategists and managers (Dozier, 1992). Rather, it is a very different idea of role: complex, curious, shifting, uncertain, ambivalent, strategic, improvisatory and multiple. Which is the nature of staged, enacted roles played in "everyday life," in Goffman's ethnography, as well as by individuals in adversarial professions (Applbaum, 1999). With respect to PR's issue-management, op-ed and crisis-management activities, PR is itself an adversarial profession.

Conscious, unconscious, planned and unrehearsed, the practitioner at the human center of PR cannot escape role-driven, ethical shape shifting to fit the duties owed to clients. Nor can PR escape its own structural ambiguities. Ethical ambiguity should not be surprising for a profession (or practice) that operates on the principle that perception is reality.

Acting in a PR fashion is not limited to organizations, as we have seen in previous chapters. As the authors of a PR textbook explained, "PR is a condition common to every individual and organization in the human environment – whether or not they recognize or act upon the fact – that refers to their reputation and relationship with all other members of the environment" (Center, Jackson, Smith & Stansberry, 2007, p. 9).

Clarity, since ancient times, has remained the gold standard of communication. However, if communication is characterized by anything, it isn't clarity. It's ambiguity. Clarity is, like symmetry theory, normative. An ideal. An aspiration. It is rarely, if ever, achieved. It very achievement is to a certain extent quixotic. Ambiguity leading to misunderstanding is coin of the realm not only for negotiations of organizations and stakeholders, but between nations, regions, religions, teams, tribes, married couples and friends. Such is the status of things even within the self – intrapersonally as Lev Vygotsky (2006) and other sociologists and linguists observed at the beginning of the twentieth century. The psychological tensions within the self constitute the plot of Herzog, the novelist Saul Bellow's (1964) eponymous, epistolary philosopher whose letters to Nietzsche and God, among other projected correspondents, are further evidence of the structural division of the self.

PR exists despite, and because of, the universality of ambiguity. Although the commonly stated objective of PR practice is the sunlight of clarity, it is a fundamental strength of PR to prefer shade to sunlight. Not always, of course. There are occasions to prefer the éclat of a "special" event, or even a spectacle. But although the declarative pitch (now obediently cross-platform) remains a PR practice staple, PR's great and definitive strength is its ability to orchestrate raids on public opinion invisibly and obliquely. PR practice combines this well-planned backstage minimalism with what the organization theorist Eric Eisenberg (2007) called "strategic ambiguity" (p. 10).

It is from this subtle combination that PR wields its influence. Its preference for shade has been seen by its critics as evidence of PR's lack of ethics, particularly in the current Internet-influenced zeitgeist of transparency, engagement and sharing. But if PR continues to be viewed widely (if misleadingly) as a-ethical or cynically unethical, it has always understood the political values of doubleness – of diplomatic "back channels" and prudent avoidance of candid or, what is worse, confessional speech. The charm of PR practice has been to achieve legitimacy for its clients – be they individuals, organizations or nations – at the cost of the facile, harsh and relentless battering by its many critics.

The notion of doubleness – a feature of the art of novelists Joseph Conrad and Saul Bellow, among many others – is important because it challenges PR strategy to be accountable to ethics. Can the practice of PR operate without its constitutive dualities? This is not a rhetorical question, but a cost–benefit calculation. If, as most ethical codes of PR express or imply, communication competency is a requisite ethical value for the industry's obligation to clients, then the discarding of that ace in the hole of doubleness would weaken PR and loosen the bonds of its ethical loyalties to clients.

There is a parallel to this ethics–competency problem in diplomacy. It is axiomatic in the practice of diplomacy to preserve, protect, grow, develop, maintain and repair front and back channels. Doubleness is that healthy communicative status that permits diplomats to utter obliquely in public what can be said candidly in private. What some would call *duplicity*, diplomacy understands as an ethical strategy with the singular capacity to bring resolutions to complex and seemingly irresolvable impasses. Contradictions, equivocations, silences, denials, ambiguities: these are the tools of diplomacy, which, like PR, is thoroughly theatrical and performative.

Were PR to cross the boundary from partial shade into the "disinfectant" sunlight of journalism's deontological ethic, it would not only court institutional failure for itself and the clients to whom it owes its professional allegiance – it would simply cease to be. And although PR ought to avoid claiming to be an art itself, when PR operates in the partial shade it resonates with some of art's most compelling qualities – subtlety, nuance, obliqueness, opacity and the resolve to avoid the obvious, flat, open and simplistic. These qualities comprise a respect for complexity and a horror of fatuity. As the poet Emily Dickinson (1999), celebrated universally for minimalist profundity, advised: "Tell the whole truth but tell it slant" (p. 494). Dickinson's poetic advice suggests the possibility that the doubleness of PR can be understood, after all, because the truth of complex issues is so infrequently simple or flat.

What is at work here is not that the truth is too ambiguous to be told. Rather, it is that truth's complexities require the approach of the artist, the craftsman, the poet. It is an argument that recalls the embedding of the truths in the parables of Jesus. It is an argument that reminds us that PR is not only the dissemination of information but a shaping, rhetorical, storytelling art.

Official ethics

The idea that ambiguity is utterly and shamefully contrary to the ethics of PR will be fairly objected to by followers of symmetry, cause branding and CSR. The industry's ethical code (Public Relations Society of America [PRSA], 2009–2014) flatly contradicts shady assertions of doubleness, back channeling, opacity and ambiguity, advising professionals to follow these guidelines:

- Be honest and accurate in all communications.
- Reveal sponsors for represented causes and interests.
- Act in the best interest of clients or employers.
- Disclose financial interests in a client's organization.
- Safeguard the confidences and privacy rights of clients and employees.
- Follow ethical hiring practices to respect free and open competition.
- Avoid conflicts between personal and professional interests.
- Decline representation of clients requiring actions contrary to the Code.

- Accurately define what PR activities can accomplish.
- Report all ethical violations to the appropriate authority.

This official statement of ethics was placed into a scholarly context for managers by the economist Susanne Holmström (2010), who called for "reflective management" (p. 274), which seeks to imbue PR at the management role level with an ethical legitimacy whose source is symmetry's normative or aspirational prescription: that managers adopt a balanced and negotiated approach amid the contemporary era's increased complexity, uncertainty, globalization and diversity. The sticks that complement those carrots are the array of countervailing powers arrayed against organizational autonomy: demands of activists, governments and flash-mobbed heterogeneous individuals in the public square for transparency and accountability – all supported by the withering risk of aggressive surveillance.

"Fluid modernity." This imagistic phrase appears near the end of Holmström's (2010) essay on "reflective management" (p. 274). Fluid modernity is fifth on Holmström's list of six "social trends, issues, and contexts for decision making to consider"; the others being a symmetrical "balance" of the profit motive with the "considerations of life and nature" proving the organization is worthy of trust in "diverse, complex, fluid, uncertain, and unpredictable" times; respect for and cooperation with multiple and diverse stakeholders; understanding the organization lives within "a larger independent societal context"; and globalization's effect that "activates latent legitimacy conflicts between previously independent cultures and societal forms" (all quotations from p. 274).

The ideology of clarity

Speaking specifically of organizational communication, Eisenberg (2007) asserted that "*clarity is only a measure of communicative competence if the individual has as his or goal to be clear*" (p. 7, italics his). But, as Eisenberg contended, in issues of complexity requiring nuanced explanations, an ideology of clarity often turns out to be more of a problem than a solution. Yet this ideology of clarity extends to "our ideas about human development and specifically on the development of identity" (p. 242). He cited Arthur Bochner (1984), who questioned "whether our beliefs about effective communication reflected actual practice or felt ideology." Other scholars who "championed the virtues of equivocality and randomness in decision making" include the Austrian organizational theorist Karl Weick (1979), who showed "how such practices both inspired creativity and confused the competition" (Eisenberg, pp. 241–242).

It is of course not difficult to realize that championing ambiguity can become a proverbial slippery slope. What Eisenberg is proposing is not some sort of categorical imperative for communicative equivocation, but that equivocation – ambiguity and its cognates – represents a sophisticated level of communication competence, which is a duty consultants owe their clients. It is, thus, an obligation rooted firmly in ethics.

The sanctioned, official voices of PR are anything but equivocal about clarity. The PR industry's American trade organization, PRSA, offers bulleted pointers on its website (2009–2014). Its "ethical guidance for PR practitioners" makes no specific mention of clarity, but its emphasis is implied by ethically oriented terminology. Two types of metaphors are used to make the case that clarity is necessary for PR ethics – positive and negative. There's the metaphor of freedom ("free flow of information"); of good–bad, right–wrong kinds of space ("open" vs. "closed" communication), and there's the familiar insistence on PR's distinctiveness ("defining what public relations can accomplish").

The positive sanctions include the affirmative obligation of disclosure and revelation (e.g., of paid sponsorships). At a spiritual level, if you will, salvation is available only in the instance of the self's willing disclosure and revelation, as in the famous passage in Corinthians (I:13, New Revised Standard Version) in which Paul's metaphor for salvation opposed the ambiguous murkiness of seeing through a glass darkly (i.e., looking into a murky mirror) to the transparent clarity of seeing God and the self "face to face" (1: Corinthians: 13). Lest a skeptic dispute about relevance of religion in the context of PR ethics, a good source is Tilson (2011) who, in *The Promotion of Devotion,* asserted the existence of a "covenantal" relationship that can be identified in the PR of "saints, celebrities and shrines," the subtitle of his book.

Of the negatively sanctioned behaviors, the ethical obligation to avoid anonymity and unfair billing reflects Biblical law in Deuteronomy. Significantly, notwithstanding the detailed list of ethical guidelines founded on clarity, the PRSA (2009–2014) website pays tribute to ambiguity: "Have an ethical dilemma? PR members seeking counsel on ethical matters are invited to confer with PRSA's Board of Ethics and Professional Standards" (See www.prsa.org).

Performing transparency

The consensus for clarity – of message and mission – is particularly emphatic in the United States in an age of "accountability" that followed on the heels of scandals that brought down the giant energy trader, Enron, in 2001; sent America's beloved home-baking recipe maker and CEO, Martha Stewart, to jail after her indictment for stock-trading fraud in 2003; and led to the impeachment of President Bill Clinton in 1998 for lying about sexual improprieties. Although these falls from high places preceded the age of social media, the ethic and ethos of transparency has only expanded in the age of "net neutrality" and social media.

Whether transparency ethics are consistent with organizational (or personal) strategy is not a simple matter. Following L'Etang's (2008) call for a sociological movement for PR scholarship, it is useful to turn once again to Goffman's (1986) *Frame Analysis,* which demonstrates that the organization of experience is anything but transparent, but involves "social rules" (p. 24) that are compared with rules governing games.

Among the tactics that appear to be logically and ethically consistent with transparency is CSR, or what came to be bumper stickered as "doing well by doing good." Vogel (2006) turned a critical eye on CSR by insisting it be viewed in the larger context of economics where there exists, in the title of his treatise, "a market for virtue." In a 2008 article (Brown, 2008), I theorized that CSR "erupted" when a Union Oil pipe burst in the pristine waters off Santa Barbara, California in 1969, threatening the coast of Los Angeles so profoundly that within a year, the U.S. Congress created a new regulatory body to monitor such threats: the Environmental Protection Agency. L'Etang and Pieczka (1996) dated the origins of CSR to the philanthropic wave of nineteenth century capitalists (p. 84).

When subjected to critical and rhetorical analysis, CSR is an economic decision framed and disseminated as an ethical one.

A case of purity

Nevertheless, in classrooms where PR is taught – in my own classrooms – students are exposed to innumerable examples of what appear to be entirely unambiguous PR objectives, strategies and tactics. It would be difficult, for example, if not churlish, to find ethical shade in a press release issued by the Perrier Group of Greenwich, Connecticut, an American division of the French-headquartered maker of "pure" sparkling water. The press release – in the by now old, traditional era of the "press" – was Perrier's response to a crisis: the poisonous chemical, benzene, had been discovered in its pure sparkling water. The Perrier brand shivered at risk. Perrier's self-defense press release was a model of rhetorical *logos:*

PERRIER
The Perrier Group
777 WEST PUTNAM AVENUE BOX 2313 GREENWICH, CT 06836

FOR IMMEDIATE RELEASE   CONTACT Jane Lazgin
(203) 531–4100
(203) 863–6240

GREENWICH, CT., February 10, 1990 – The Perrier Group of America, Inc., is voluntarily recalling all Perrier Sparkling Water (regular and flavored) in the United States. Testing by the federal Food and Drug Administration and the State of North Carolina showed the presence of the chemical benzene at levels above proposed federal standards in isolated samples of product produced between June 1989 and January 1990.

"While the federal Food & Drug Administration advises us that the levels reported do not pose a significant health risk, we're acting aggressively and responsively in the interests of the public," said Ronald V. Davis, President of the Perrier Group of America.

Perrier sparkling water is drawn from a natural mineral spring in Vergeze, France, and is bottled only at the source. No benzene has been discovered in the source in regular testing by Perrier and by the French government.

The search for a possible cause of the chemical intrusion is focusing on the packaging and distribution process. In the meantime, the company has stopped all shipment of Perrier into the United States.

FDA officials have told the company that the levels of benzene found in 13 product samples (12 to 19 parts per billions) does not pose a significant short-term health risk.

An FDA spokesperson was quoted today as saying that even if one drank 16 fluid ounces of Perrier per day containing the levels of benzene found in the isolated samples over the course of their lifetime, the probable cause of health risk would be only one in one million.

Perrier is cooperating fully with the FDA and the state of North Carolina, and has set up a toll-free 800 number beginning Sunday, February 11, 12:00 noon EST to handle consumer questions: 800–937–2002. (Barton, 1993, pp. 130–131)

Rhetorically

On the surface, Perrier's was nothing more or less than a textbook-perfect crisis response. From another perspective, the company offered a rhetorical performance of CSR.

Primarily deploying the rhetoric of *logos,* it offers evidence of the ethic of CSR in language that frames its case narrowly and specifically with both descriptive and inferential statistics: enumerating "isolated" batches of "product" between two dates that are fairly close to each other; and using a credible third-party source (an FDA spokesperson) to offer the remote possibility of risk (one in one million).

Adverbs

Although the editorial strategy to diminish opacity and increase transparency is to cut and tighten sentences and eliminate such verbal dross as adjectives and adverbs, Perrier avoided that simplistic strategy. In the all-important (for media relations and publicity) lede (i.e., initial) paragraph, the voice of Perrier (ghosted, anonymous, corporate), made strategic use of the adverb *voluntarily*, a word whose PR message is that of transparency, immediacy and openness to the classic PR metaphor of the two-way street and all stakeholders. In the ghostwritten quoted second paragraph, the adverbs *aggressively* and *responsibly* are used to send the crisis-response message of transparency and immediacy. Because CSR is understood to require a "buy-in" from top management, the tonal color of the company president is clear, firm and direct, a reflection of the classic triad of effective management: planning, organizing and controlling.

Adjectives

In the paragraph quoting the putatively source-credible (and necessarily visible) leader, the American group's president, the voice of the release ghostwrote (we assume) the adjective *significant* in framing the health risk as minimal: "the levels reported do not pose a significant health risk."

Verbs

President Davis was quoted as saying that aggressively and responsibly is the way "we're *acting*"; the final paragraph sends the textbook message of transparency by saying that the company is "cooperating fully" (a participle strengthened by an adverb) with the FDA and the state of North Carolina, a performance that indicates corporate humility in the public interest. This a CSR staple that is meant to demonstrate effective management that stakeholders can trust.

Succinctness

As the six-word adage observes, brevity is the soul of wit. Perrier's press release is concise. It packs a great deal of salient information into a rhetorically sophisticated performance. For the most part, its sentences are short. Subjected to a Flesch analysis, the reading level of the release would be well within a comfortable range for mass communication.

Jargon scrub

Press releases do well to avoid jargon-laden prose – a red flag to the skeptical journalistic gatekeepers, particularly a generation since the rise of the blogosphere, the attrition of copyeditors and the rise of "citizen journalists" and Twitter. Perrier's release is free of jargon, the company's strategic recognition that jargon is the enemy of transparency.

Voice

Of the release's 10 sentences, six are passive and four are active. That is, six lack a clear "actor" doing the action at the beginning of the sentence; four identify the actor as the subject doing the action at or toward the beginning of the sentence. For example, consider the sentence: "The search for a possible cause of the chemical intrusion is focusing on the packaging and distribution process." The technical vocal passivity of the sentence occurs in the absence of an actor at its beginning: who, in fact, is doing the "search" (noun) for that "possible cause" (minimizing, shading, and reducing the offensiveness) of the "chemical intrusion"?

The technically active voice occurs both in the opening (or lede) beginning "The Perrier Group of America is voluntarily recalling" and the final sentence beginning "Perrier is cooperating fully." Put another way, the active voice – preferred by gatekeepers and considered a vocally transparent strategy – is wrapped around the strategic use of six passive-voiced sentences. Passive voice is a common strategy for avoiding blame for, say, the bombing of a village by American B-52s during the Vietnam War. America's official Defense Department and State Department communiqués used the grammatical device of the passive voice. They would use language like "the village was pacified," instead of "American planes bombed a village." Their goal was to try and positively reframe the U.S. bombing runs that destroyed villages. In this fashion, the Perrier press release employs the passive-voice construction to deflect stakeholder perception that the company was to blame for causing the contamination of Perrier. The press release explained that Perrier was taking responsible action to investigate the cause: "The search for a possible cause . . ."

Wordsmithing

Perrier's use of the euphemistic phrase "chemical intrusion" is an example of agenda-setting reframing. Put another way, it is what crisis theorists William Benoit (1992) and Tim Coombs (2012) identified as "blame-shifting," which can be an effective crisis-response strategy. Wordsmithing can be a creative and compelling way of reducing a potentially negative and blamable perception to what crisis theorist Tim Coombs termed a less-blamable "victimage" frame (Perrier reframed as the victim of an "intrusion"). The shift relocates the locus of blame from inside to outside, an example of the kind of rhetorically centrifugal force of which wordsmithing is capable.

Clearly, then, Perrier can be credited with crafting a brilliantly rhetorical press release, regardless of whether any press release alone can fairly be held accountable for managing Perrier's crisis.

Movements in ethical space

The perception of PR ethics outside the industry itself has been a source of continuing dismay for the PR industry. PR's dubiously ethical reputation contrasts sharply with the general and widespread perception of its effectiveness. None of the modern era PR pioneers identified this problem more clearly than Bernays (1923/2011) who launched a decades-long campaign to reposition the status of fledgling practice to a profession.

Nominal ethics

Words matter, which is why changing them permits PR not merely wiggle room but rebranding and reputational transforming. By changing the name of his firm from Propaganda Bureau to Public Relations Counsel in the 1920s, Bernays set in motion a number of changes, not only in his business model but in the model of the industry. The deletion of *propaganda* sought to cleanse the taint that had begun to sully the word.

Contradictions and reversals

In his long-popular PR textbook, the former American bank PR executive Fraser Seitel (2012) identified the six core values of the ethical code of PR. They are, in no particular order of significance, advocacy, honesty, expertise, independence, loyalty and fairness. Although a chapter could be devoted to exploring each of these, there is only sufficient space here to observe that when subjected to critical inquiry and case histories, these intuitively ethical values betray a host of contradictions and complexities. Ethics is no philosophical pushover; the really interesting ethical questions tend to involve intellectually and legally challenging arguments between the more compelling of two rights; not the obvious outcome of right versus wrong.

L'Etang (1996) identified the structural connections existing between issues management and programs of CSR to be less about a demonstration of ethics than the deployment of strategic ambiguity. Strategic in that for PR, CSR is "instrumental to its own status" (p. 95); ambiguous in the sense that CSR is an example of the doubleness of PR ethics – or rather, the organizational performance of ethics. Performances by their very nature always involve the duality – linked and separate – of actor and enactment, actor and "character."

Crossing boundaries

As a boundary-spanning practice, PR should be careful not to cross certain ethical boundaries, although like legal practitioners, PR operatives occasionally violate their own codes of ethics. The PR industry continues to aspire toward professionalism. But therein lies the problem in the crossing of boundaries that ought not to be crossed. If the movement upward from mere practice to esteemed profession promised reputational benefits for the PR industry, it also brought the complications associated with the expectations that attend an elevated status. The propagandist could afford to be relatively untroubled with ethical niceties; not so the PR counsel.

In *Lying,* her insightful study of ethics, Sisela Bok (1989) raised one such complication resulting from intimacy, whether fiduciary or familial. In her chapter entitled "Lies Protecting Peers and Clients," she quoted a published statement by one Charles Curtis whom she identified as "a well-known Boston lawyer" (p. 158):

> The relationship between a lawyer and his client is one of intimate relations. You would lie for your wife. You would lie for your child. There are others with whom you are intimate enough, close enough, to lie for them when you would not lie for yourself. At what point do you stop lying for them? I don't know and you are not sure.
>
> (p. 158)

Understandably, the ethical relativism of that statement provoked controversy. Bok (1989) observed that "Curtis himself drew the line at lying in court" (p. 158). Bok cited another provocative observation about the professional obligations of lawyers to their client – a statement by the dean of Hofstra Law School who was also "the author of a well-known book on legal ethics" (p. 158):

> The criminal defense attorney, however unwillingly in terms of personal morality, has a professional responsibility as an advocate in an adversary

system to examine the perjurious client in the ordinary way and to argue to the jury, as evidence in the case, the testimony presented by the defendant.

(p. 159)

It poses a challenge to any simple right or wrong view of lying to understand that in the case of the client who lies, the lying is not only acceptable under certain circumstances. It is also a circumstance that an attorney, in the context of his profession, is ethically obligated to protect and defend. The state of affairs enables and even affirmatively sanctions lying. This is contrary to any commonsensical notion of ethics. Bok (1989) explained it, in part, as an example of the "tribal ethic of avoiding harm to oneself and one's own" (p. 159). The socially and legally justified status of client privilege and communication confidentiality, Bok explained, derives from "shadier privileges claimed through the ages, ranging from the feudal sexual privilege to the excesses of 'executive privilege,' as to require no defense" (p. 159).

Clearly, Bok was identifying how, in certain cases of ethical doubleness, the consultant (be she lawyer or PR consultant), under the pressure of a tribal allegiance, is unfortunately moved to cross the line from telling the truth "slant" to outright lying.

From a PR ethical perspective, tribalism represents a complexity and contradiction. Although adherence to the client corresponds to the coded ethical value of loyalty, it also undermines the value of honesty. This positions ethics – PR and legal both – as a cost–benefit analysis, at a far remove on the ethical continuum from the rigors of a classically deontological position that rejects lying under any circumstance. Clearly, neither PR nor law is able to operate consistently under the stricture of a categorical imperative. For both PR and law, what surfaces are the coded values of expertise and competence, which are commonly associated with professionalism. To the extent that PR practitioners and lawyers owe not only loyalty and advocacy to their clients but a professionalism that comprises expertise and competence and occasionally a fiduciary duty as well, the core value of honesty must be sacrificed, along with the broader meaning of fairness that extends beyond fairness to a client. Clearly, then, tension and contradiction are the de facto state of affairs in the performances that occur in the court of public opinion and the court of law.

Although the status of lawyers differs in important ways from that of PR practitioners (licensure via passage of a required examination being perhaps the most definitive one), the comparison of the court of law and the court of public opinion is commonplace. In an important way, however, the weight of the comparison proceeds no further than metaphorically; the courts of law are grounded in a physical and spatial actuality unlike the court of public opinion. This is not, of course, to deny the power of public opinion, or that in some ways individual and aggregated opinion is not "adjudicated." But as Bernays understood, PR would only be perceived as a profession if and when its entry required the web of accredited education, examinations and ceremonial induction of the legal, medical and other professions whose entry was rigorously institutionalized.

If and until that sea change, PR would remain both legally and perceptually an industry and a practice whose professionalism could be no more than a matter of aspirational comparisons, job titles, monetary compensation and professional recognition limited to the communities of practitioners. In this sense, the socioeconomic sector that PR most resembles is neither law nor medicine. Instead, it is for-profit private-sector businesses.

As a result, PR exists in a perceptual, professional and ethical gap, a liminal space of codes and metaphors. It is a liminality that explains, in part, PR scholarship's persistent engagement not so much with its ethics in practice, as with its *normative* ethics, to borrow Grunig's term. The liminal space of PR's professionalism and ethics also explains why PRSA has regularly devoted its September newsletter to ethics in the effort to inculcate normative ethical principles in the education of undergraduate majors.

Independence

In addressing the PR coded ethical values, nothing has been said about the sixth, independence. Presumably, ethical independence implies that in its quasi-professional, quasi-industrial condition, the agencies and departments practicing PR must, in their strategies, programs and decision making, be free of any undue influence by outside parties and the weight of their interests. What this means in practice is that PR agents must eliminate or severely minimize the influence of journalists, citizen journalists, tweeters, bloggers, lobbyists, elected officials and the sway of money – particularly undisclosed compensation.

Whether and to what extent PR practice is in fact independent would be a fitting research project for a content analysis. Anecdotally, agencies, departments, practitioners and their managers can hardly be expected to avoid occasional situations that involve an undue dependence on that array of outside influencers at whose pleasure PR serves.

The Grace case

When a PR agency wishes to sever its relationship with a client, the term for its disengagement is *resignation.* Years before the case of W.R. Grace & Co. joined the ranks of the Love Canal, Three Mile Island and U.S. high-profile toxic waste environmental cases, the PR firm of Newsome & Co., which had been hired by Grace as crisis communications counsel, resigned the account.

The concept of a PR agency "resigning" from an account was new to me when I joined Newsome & Company in 1984, the same year they resigned from the Grace account. The fact that I was a speechwriter for W.R. Grace & Co. from 1981 to 1983 may have played a part in Newsome offering me a job as a senior account executive. I had tendered my own resignation from Grace in 1983 for entirely other reasons, which bear on matters of ethics. (I have published an article about those reasons in the magazine known as *Sextant* [Brown 2006], itself a standard PR "tool" common to universities. A reflection on the ethics of my personal resignation concludes this chapter.)

The facts of *Anne Anderson et al. vs. W.R. Grace & Co. et al.* would become one of the best-known environmental contamination and legal liability cases of the

1980s. It was the subject of Jonathan Harr's 1996 book *A Civil Action,* a finalist for a National Book Award, and eventually a movie starring John Travolta. The suit was filed in 1982 by plaintiffs in the Massachusetts town of Woburn, alleging that the deaths of five children of leukemia, along with the contraction of that disease and other severe health problems by other residents, was directly traceable to the toxic chemicals in Woburn town wells. The suit alleged that these were chemicals that had been negligently disposed of by W.R. Grace & Co. and two other defendant companies. Not long after the filing of the suit, the two other defendant companies were permitted to be removed from the case, leaving Grace as the sole defendant. The suit sought more than $300 million in damages (Carlton College, 2008).

The trial, framed by intense media coverage in the press and on television, began in March 1986. The immense technical and legal complexities eventually made it impossible to assign epidemiological and legal responsibility for the deaths to Grace. An out-of-court settlement was reached in September 1986 for $8 million – far less than the hundreds of millions of dollars requested.

In 1991, following appeals and public outcry, the U.S. Environmental Protection Agency developed a settlement of $69.5 million in a finding of guilt for Grace and four other offending companies (Carlton College, 2008).

Newsome & Co.'s resignation from the Grace account suggests, at the very least, ethical complexity, if not ambiguity. The reason for the resignation, according to the office grapevine, was that Grace's representatives had lied to or withheld crucial information from Newsome (presumably including information bearing on the company's toxic chemical waste removal actions by its putatively offending Woburn division, known as Cryovac; Grace & Co. headquarters were, at that time, in New York City).

The Atlantic Richfield case

Although CSR in America did not begin in 1970s, it did become a growing trend at that time. This was particularly true for high-profile companies whose products, which citizens depended on, represented a serious environmental threat. In particular, these included oil, chemical, coal mining and nuclear energy companies whose operations seemed poised on the edge of environmental disaster.

In January 1969, a Union Oil company undersea pipe burst in the pristine waters of the Santa Barbara Channel off the treasured beach coastline of the small city of Santa Barbara and the metropolis of Los Angeles to the south. The environmental threat raised such a furor that within 6 months then-President Richard Nixon signed an executive order establishing the Environmental Protection Agency, which began its regulatory life in 1970.

The public, not only in California, clamored for government intervention while unleashing a furious attack on the oil industry. As oil company reputations fell to record lows, the lesson wasn't lost on their senior managements. In the era of heightened anxieties about oil spills and other environmental disasters, traditional damage control would be woefully inadequate as a crisis management strategy. It was weak and reactive. The new approach had to be proactive, highly visible, widespread and continuous. What emerged were the beginnings of mid-century CSR. High-impact companies would adopt a doing-well-by-doing-good policy, seeking to balance their responsibility to their investors with their obligations to society (Brown, 2008).

A rhetorical doubleness marked the framing of the oil company's CSR. The company proposed that it could serve not merely one but two bottom lines, one above and one below. Both the traditional bottom line of profits and what the company called "below the bottom line," or CSR.

In the late twentieth century, American corporations and others around the world adopted CSR and justified its doubleness. Vaaland and Heide (2008) observed that CSR "is rapidly gaining importance for businesses all over the world" (p. 215). Brown and Rancer (1993) surveyed PR practitioners in the United States and United Kingdom and found, however unsurprisingly, a statistically significant preference for Grunig's (1992) two-way symmetry (DeBussy, 2013). Ethically speaking, among the most common rationales for the ethics of CSR is enlightened self-interest, which Gower (2003) defined as "self-interest, or egoism [that] contents that an act is morally right if, and only if, it best promotes the individual's long-term interests" (p. 7). This was the express rationale for the Atlantic Richfield Company's (ARCO's) multimillion-dollar investment in undertaking a wide-ranging program of CSR. Today, CSR is both prevalent and virtually obligatory for highly visible public companies. However, when ARCO was launched in the 1970s, CSR was considered controversial and vigorously criticized by business thought leaders like Milton Friedman. The Nobel Prize–winning economist dismissed CSR as an irresponsible waste of corporate resources that were foolishly diverted from performing the fiduciary and economic mission of business (Friedman, 1970). For Friedman, the corporation could not and ought not attempt to serve two bottom lines.

It is a much different scenario today. Unsurprisingly CSR programs are numerous among the largest publicly held corporations in America and the rest of the world. Among the largest of these players are oil, chemical and other companies whose operations exert an impact on society, including often controversial effects on the environment. Indeed, the case has been made (Brown, 2008; Vogel, 2006) that the root of the late-twentieth-century CSR needs to be understood in historical, political and economic terms, rather than uncritically accepted as the cliché "doing well by doing good."

A decade later, amid the oil-price spikes by OPEC and the painful rationing of gasoline that further sullied the reputation of oil companies, I was recruited by ARCO, then the twelfth-largest publicly traded corporation in the United States. Dozens of other professional communicators were hired along with me, with specialties ranging from television reporter to graphic designer. More than 250 souls worked in the PR and public affairs departments at ARCO headquarters in Los Angeles.

Public outrage made oil companies among the most disliked businesses in the United States. According to J. G. Geer (2004), "At the height of the oil crisis, in

1979, only 13 percent of the U.S. public blamed OPEC for the high oil prices; 65 percent of Americans blamed the oil companies and the U.S. government for the oil crisis" (p. 290).

With the help of its PR and public affairs staffs, ARCO launched a reputational counteroffensive. Its rhetorical strategy was to craft a message that addressed its perceptual double trouble: the public perception of a company making "obscene" profits with a policy of what CSR theorist Duane Windsor (2013) termed "corporate social irresponsibility" (pp. 1937–1944). To briefly summarize a complex theory, CSR and another construct – corporate social citizenship – are framed as "positive" in that they prescribe socially and economically beneficial corporate behaviors from philanthropy to regulatory compliance.

ARCO's strategy was to perform and publicize its service to both investors and the public, as a profit-making corporation and a responsible public citizen. The evidence of this doubleness is abundant, including in the statement by Lodwrick M. Cook, the CEO of ARCO, that is the introduction to the corporate publication called *To Make A Difference: Arco and Society* (ARCO, 1987), the company's CSR report. Ghostwritten by the PR staff, the language sought to integrate the company's financial and operational competency with its mission of corporate social citizenship. It was, of course, an example of persuasive communication, notwithstanding the way in which the theory of symmetry would be likely to frame it as an example of two-way symmetric communication.

Strictly speaking, the decades-old model of two-way symmetry could not include CSR because of the clash of the normative status of symmetry and the positive pragmatics of the practice of CSR. What this further suggests is that the normative frame of two-way symmetry renders it an idealistic but empty box. As such, it lacks the actuality of practices. That theoretical deficit may account in part for the theory's "evolution" (or devolution) from rigorously measured to the vastly lesser desiderata of a "willingness to change." The word *change* and its variants, indicating the ethics of organizational malleability, appeared six times in Grunig's (2013) theoretical redescription. "The willingness to change" itself is in a discussion of Grunig's retrenchment or defense, depending on one's point of view, in De Bussy (2013, p. 84).

In the era following the spike in environmental awareness and advocacy of the 1960s and 1970s, the popularity of CSR expanded beyond oil and chemical companies. Along with ARCO, brand-name corporations in banking (Bank of America and Citi Group), retail (Dayton-Hudson) and food manufacturing and distribution (Borden) adopted CSR. Dayton-Hudson established a policy of allocating 5 percent of the company's pretax income to what were, in its judgment, community needs, a policy the company called "the five-percent solution" (Dayton, 1979). However, the rising tide of environmental activism fell most heavily on the shoulders of the largest U.S. oil companies, which suggests the reason for their prominence in the reputational counteroffensive grouped under the broad rubric of CSR.

In the wake of the negative public (and government) opinion of oil companies that followed on the heels of oil spills, supply deficits and price hikes in the 1970s, the management of ARCO embraced and helped to define CSR for the late twentieth century.

Company grants went, interestingly, to ARCO's natural adversaries, including Greenpeace ($2,100) and the Sierra Club Foundation ($1,570). The $10 million for CSR was, of course, a small fraction of the company's profits, which were upwards of $1 billion. Even the company's strategic CSR largesse was far below the ideal level of 5 percent of net earnings posited by Dayton-Hudson (Dayton, 1979).

The doubleness of issues management

From the perspective of the public relations of everything (PRe), a compelling illustration of the doubleness of PR can be found in the practice of issues management. In the world of corporate public affairs, an issue needs to be managed because it can expand into a problem and explode into a crisis with seriously negative consequences for the organization. An issue, moreover, is quite often perceived as a question with two mutually exclusive solutions, a story with two sides, a he-said/she-said affair.

In 1980, ARCO, one of America's largest producers and marketers of fossil fuels, identified the rising negative perception of fossil fuels as a priority issue to be managed. Energy was (and continues to be) an issue around which arguments and advocacies face off in direct contradistinction, offering an example of how issues management is framed by a doubleness. In 1980, as today, a set of dramatically opposed frames, assumptions, facts and predictions are at the burning heart of the energy issue.

The "clean solar energy" argument against fossil fuels concentrated on the grounds of environmental depredation, health effects and resource unsustainability. ARCO's rebuttal was based on economic and technological unfeasibility. Doubtless, energy policy is extraordinarily complex. ARCO grasped this communication challenge and recognized an opportunity. The company crafted an advertising campaign that played on the rhetorical doubleness of the complex issue. The campaign's message was that there were two energy-policy choices: one fallacious, the other realistic. To the advocates of solar energy, power from the sun is free, unlike power from oil and gas. But ARCO's argument was that although sunshine is free, the technology required to store and transmit it is anything but.

In a sense, then, the ARCO issues-management case reveals that PR's doubleness can suggest a strategy of ambiguity that can play to the advantage of an organization in the court of public opinion. Certainly, in the case of ARCO's No Easy Answers campaign, the company's strategy was to highlight the two-sidedness of a highly complex issue by critiquing the assumptions of the activist forces arrayed against it. The campaign pointed away from passion and simplicity and focused on economic rationalism and ambiguity.

PRe rethinks PR as being caught between a rock and a hard place, where the best answer is not necessarily the clearest. Having launched into such deep, open and uncertain seas, it is fitting to give the final word in this chapter to a poet famed for charting them:

> Tell all the truth but tell it slant,
> Success in circuit lies,

Too bright for our infirm delight
The truth's superb surprise;
As lightning to the children eased
With explanation kind,
The truth must dazzle gradually
Or every man be blind.
(Dickinson, 1999, p. 494)

References

Applbaum, A. I. (1999). *Ethics for adversaries: The morality of roles in public and professional life.* Princeton, NJ: Princeton University Press.

ARCO—Atlantic Richfield Company. (1987). *To make a difference.* Los Angeles, CA.

Barton, L. (1993). *Crisis in organizations: Managing and communicating in the heat of crisis.* Cincinnati, OH: South-Western.

———. (1993). *Crisis in organizations.* Cincinnati, OH: South-western.

Bateson, G. (1972). *Steps to an ecology of mind: Collected essays in anthropology, psychology, and epistemology.* Chicago, IL: University of Chicago Press.

Bellow, S. (1964). *Herzog.* New York: Viking.

Benoit, W. (1992). *Accounts, excuses, and apologies: A theory of image restoration strategies.* Albany: State University of New York Press.

Bernays, E. L. (1923; 2011). *Propaganda.* New York, NY: Horace Liveright.

———. (1923/2011). *Crystalizing public opinion.* New York, NY: IG.

Bochner, A. (1984). The functions of human communication in interpersonal bonding. In C. Arnold & J. Bowers (Eds.), *Handbook of rhetoric and communication theory* (pp. 544–621). Newton, MA: Allyn & Bacon.

Bok, S. (1989). *Lying: Moral choice in public and private life.* New York, NY: Vintage.

Bowen, S. (2010). The nature of good in public relations: What should be its normative ethic? In R. L. Heath (Ed.), *Sage handbook of public relations II* (pp. 569–583). Thousand Oaks, CA: Sage.

Brown, R. E. (2006). Memoirs of a ghostwriter. *Sextant.* XIV(1), 34–42.

———. (2008). Sea change: Santa Barbara and the eruption of corporate social responsibility. *Public Relations Review, 34*(1), 1–8.

Brown, R. E. & Rancer, A. (1993). Congruence of orientations toward public relations: A cross-cultural comparison. *New York State Speech Journal, 7*(1), 25–31.

Burke, K. (1945) *A grammar of motives.* New York, NY: Prentice-Hall.

Carlton College. (2008). *Science in the courtroom: The Woburn toxic trial.* Retrieved from http://serc.carleton.edu/woburn/woburntrialchrono.html

Center, A. H, Jackson, P, Smith, S. & Stansberry, F. R. (Eds.). (2007), *Public relations practices: Managerial case studies and problems.* Upper Saddle River, NY: Pearson.

Coombs. W. T. (2012). *Ongoing crisis communication.* Thousand Oaks, CA: Sage.

Cutlip, S. M., Center, A. H. & Broom, G. M. (2006). *Effective public relations.* Upper Saddle River, NJ: Pearson.

Dayton, K. N. (1979). *The case for corporate philanthropy.* Retrieved from www.umkc.edu/whmckc/PUBLICATIONS/MCP/MCPPDF/Dayton-12–13–79.pdf

Debord, G. (1970). *Society of the spectacle* (F. Perlman & J. Supak, Trans.). St. Petersburg, FL: Black & Red.

De Bussy, N. M. (2013). Refurnishing the Grunig edifice: Strategic public relations management, strategic communication and organizational leadership. In K. Sriramesh,

168   *The humanities of public relations*

A. Zerfass & J.-N. Kim (Eds.), *Public relations and communication management: Trends and emerging topics* (pp. 79–92). New York, NY: Routledge.

Dickinson, E. (1999). *The poems of Emily Dickinson* (R.W. Franklin, Ed.). Cambridge, MA: Belknap Press.

Dozier, D. (1992). The organizational roles of communications and public relations practitioners. In J. E. Grunig (Ed.), *Excellence in public relations and communication management* (pp. 327–355). Mahwah, NJ: Erlbaum.

Eisenberg, E. (2007). *Strategic ambiguities: Essays on communication, organization and identity.* Thousand Oaks, CA: Sage.

Eliot, T. S. (1969). Burnt Norton. In V. Eliot (Ed.), *The complete poems and plays of T. S. Eliot* (p. 175). London, England: Faber & Faber.

Empson, W. (1931). *Seven types of ambiguity.* New York, NY: Harcourt, Brace and Company.

Fitzgerald, F. S. (1936; 2008, February 26). The crack-up. *Esquire.*

Friedman, M. (1970, September 13). The social responsibility of business is to increase its profits. *New York Times.* Retrieved from www.colorado.edu/studentgroups/libertarians/issues/friedman-soc-resp-business.html

Geer, J. G. (2004). *Public opinion and polling: A historical encyclopedia.* Santa Barbara, CA: ABC-Clio.

Goffman, E. (1963). *Stigma: Notes on the management of spoiled identity.* Englewood Cliffs, NJ: Prentice-Hall.

———. (1967/2005). *Strategic interaction.* Philadelphia: University of Pennsylvania Press.

———. (1986). *Frame analysis: An essay on the organization of experience.* Boston, MA: Northeastern University Press.

———. (1967; 2005). *Interaction ritual: Essays on face-to-face behavior.* New Brunswick, NJ: AldineTransaction.

Gower, K. (2003). *Legal and ethical restraints on public relations.* Prospect Heights, IL: Waveland Press.

Grunig, J. E. (Ed.) (1992). *Excellence in public relations and communications management.* New York: Lawrence Erlbaum

———. (2013) Furnishing the edifice: Ongoing research on public relations as a strategic management function. In *Public relations and communications management: Current trends and emerging topics*, pp. 1–26. (Eds.) K. Sriamesh, A. Zerfass & J. N. Kim. London: Routledge.

Guth, D. W. & Marsh, C. (2000). *Public relations: A value-driven approach.* Boston, MA: Allyn & Bacon.

Harr, J. (1996). *A civil action.* New York, NY: Random House.

Holmström, S. (2010). Reflective management: Seeing the organization as if from outside. In R. L. Heath (Ed.), *Sage handbook of public relations* (pp. 261–276). Thousand Oaks, CA: Sage.

L'Etang, J. (2008). *Public relations: Concepts, practice and critique.* London: Sage.

L'Etang, J. & Pieczka, M. (1996). *Critical perspectives in public relations.* London, England: International Thomson Business Press.

Metzler, M. S. (2001). The centrality of organizational legitimacy to public relations practice. In R. L. Heath (Ed.), *Handbook of public relations* (pp. 321–334). Thousand Oaks, CA: Sage.

McKie, D. & Munshie (2009). Theoretical black holes: A partial A–Z of missing critical thought in public relations. In R. L. Heath, E. L. Toth & D. Waymer (Eds.), *Rhetorical and critical approaches to public relations II* (pp. 61–75). New York, NY: Routledge.

Morris, T. & Goldsworthy, S. (2012). *PR today: The authoritative guide to public relations.* New York, NY: Palgrave.

Public Relations Society of America. (2009–2014). *Ethics: Ethical guidance for public relations practitioners.* Retrieved from www.prsa.org/aboutprsa/ethics/#.UnlM3ySxMzU

Seitel, F. P. (2012). *The practice of public relations.* Upper Saddle River, NJ: Pearson.

Tilson, D. (2011). *The promotion of devotion: Saints, celebrities and shrines.* Champaign, IL: Common Ground.

Vaaland, T. I. & Heide, M. (2008). Corporate social responsibility: Investigating theory and research in the marketing context. *Corporate Communications: An International Journal* 13(2), 212–225.

Vogel, D. (2006). *A market for virtue: The potential and limits of corporate social responsibility.* Washington, D.C.: Brookings Institution Press.

Vygotsky, L. (2006). *Thought and language.* Cambridge, MA: MIT Press.

Weber, L. (2009). *Sticks and stones: How digital business reputations are created over time and lost in a click.* New York: Wiley.

Weick, K. (1979). *The social psychology of organizing.* (2nd ed.) Reading, MA: Addison-Wesley.

Wilcox, D. L., Ault, P. H., Agee, W. K. & Cameron, G. T. (2001). *Essentials of public relations.* New York, NY: Addison-Wesley.

Windsor, D. (2013). Corporate social responsibility and irresponsibility: A positive theory. *Journal of Business Research,* 66(10), 1937–1944.

10 Humanities

I mean Negative Capability, that is when man is capable of being in uncertainties,
Mysteries, doubts, without any irritable reaching after fact and reason.
John Keats (from a letter to his brothers)

The argument of this chapter, which includes a literary archetypical model of
public relations (PR), is that PR belongs with the humanities. A humanities classification is not limited to the traditional disciplines of literature, history, philosophy, art and religion but also includes the social sciences. To rethink PR in this
way is to understand it as protean rather than distinctive.

What is further offered in this chapter is a literary model of PR.

For a generation, PR scholarship has understood that its mission is to build its
own house on a foundation of theory. The premise of this project imagined that
theory building would not only provide PR with a more substantial degree of
academic legitimacy but also that it would expand PR. More than that, the theory-
building project imagined it would provide PR with an entrée to the conversations
carried on by the broader scholarly and ideological communities – historians,
artists, political scientists, journalists and social scientists.

Studia Humanitatis

Historically, the usage of the words *humanities* and *humanism* were traced by Paul
Kristeller, a scholar of the Renaissance, to the fifteenth century (Kristeller, 1990):

> For although the word "humanism" as applied to the Renaissance emphasis
> on classical scholarship and on classical education originated among German
> scholars and educators in the nineteenth century, it developed from the term
> "humanist," which had been used ever since the fifteenth century in a specific
> sense and which originated probably in the slang of the Italian university
> students of that time: a humanist was a professor or student of the *studia
> humanitatis* – as distinct from a jurist, for example.
>
> (p. 3)

During the Italian Renaissance, whose influence spread throughout Europe, the two branches of the humanities are curiously consistent with the modern practices of PR. The humanities were based in Classical rhetoric and comprised the art of writing, including the composition of letters according to medieval principles of *ars dictaminis*, which were treatises on the art of letter writing. A second source of the Renaissance humanities was the medieval *artes dictandi*, which comprised certain formal aspects of letter writing such as the theory of punctuation and the parts and organization of letters (Kristeller, 1990, pp. 237–238). The second of the two branches, or genres, of the prose-driven humanities was the speech – "deliberative, judiciary and epidectic" (Kristeller, 1990, p. 238).

To a PR scholarly community tunnel focused on the present and future and largely uninterested in history – much less ancient, medieval and Renaissance history – it may seem the height of irrelevance to bracket tech-driven contemporary PR with *studia humanitatis*. But scholars who embrace the enlightening potential of intellectual history might find such connections worth considering. Following the adage of communication theory that context gives meaning, surely history does no less.

What is it that PR practitioners practice if not the composition of letters, memos, speeches, Facebook posts and tweets? It certainly was the bulk of my practice in the departments and agencies of PR that employed me and to which I would serve as a consultant, editor and teacher.

The great convergence

Despite or because of all the theory building, PR scholarship has yet to receive an invitation to the broader cultural conversation. In the second decade of the twenty-first century, there is no evidence that PR scholarship has achieved these goals. PR's dubious reputation persists in the wider world, regardless of PR's theory building. It may be that a generation of PR scholars who hooked their wagon to the star of science imagined they were building out the boundary of PR when in fact they were pushing it in.

The physics of theory building may have turned out to be more centripetal than centrifugal – an intramural discourse. Yet this is far from the whole story of the previous generation of PR scholarship or of the industry itself. In many ways, what has marked the past generation of PR has been a great convergence. An international group of scholars who could not be seriously described as a school have generated shelves of research and theory from the margins. At the same time, the PR industry itself has rushed to capitalize on the innovations of the digital–social era, which has had the transformative effect of doing what technology does: it erases boundaries. Despite the strenuous efforts of PR scholars and of PR's official trade-industry voice to define away the heretical intrusions of marketing, integrated marketing, branding, and other invaders, the convergence of these practices has been taking place – largely with the avid cooperation of PR itself.

Today, the traditional claims of PR to be "distinctive" have become obsolete – a relic of the ideas of PR conceived during the first decades of the twentieth-century. What characterizes today's PR, if not the majority of its scholarship, is inclusiveness. Not of one thing, but of everything. It is from this broader perspective that the idea of PR is being rethought. It is a rethinking that has lagged behind the great convergence. PR entrepreneurs like Larry Weber (2009) envisioned a significant convergence event a decade before the rapid rise of the World Wide Web.

As William Carlos Williams (1963) wrote in the epic poem *Paterson,* his radical mission for American poetry was to dismantle the old house in order to build a new American *ars poetica.* For the poet (and, to some extent, for the public relations of everything [PRe]), the animating idea is to struggle beyond the limits of conventional thinking:

> Blocked.
> (Make a song out of that: concretely)

(p. 78)

The house of PR ought to be reimagined as inclusive and capacious, more than exacting and distinctive. Its historical and theoretical space must have room for Isocrates, Aristotle, Paul, Pascal, Shakespeare and the Reformation popes, as well as for the four-step process, the two-way street and a single methodology.

From history to theory

A social theory begins with history. Such is the lesson of historical sociology – that all social theory is rooted in history. Because PR theory is social theory, PR theory must base its theory in a compelling idea of its history. This is also the argument of rethinking PR as the PRe.

"In my end," wrote the poet T. S. Eliot (1943), "is my beginning." And so, this book's final chapter returns to its first. Chapter 1 posed the epistemological questions, "What is really going on here? What is PR, really?"

The answer is that, contrary to the weight of conventional thinking, research and scholarship, PR is about everything. Everything, that is, in the sense that what PR *really* is simply cannot be adequately accounted for by squeezing it into the boxes of a "distinctive management function," a nineteenth-century American origin myth, an evolutionary theory masking a teleological defense of PR ethics and one single and exclusive quantitative methodology.

Those boxes will not do because PR is too intellectually omnivorous, ancient, multidisciplinary, social and human to be boxed in. Indeed, the scholars for whom the boxes are virtually axiomatic include among PR's axioms that of its adaptability – another way of saying, in the language of symmetry – a "willingness to change."

As with the attempt to arrive at the meaning of anything, the meaning of PR may properly begin with its history. In their monograph that demonstrated the intellectual weakness of PR's conventional historiography, Lamme and Russell (2010) wrote, "We propose that a new theory of the history of public relations begin with the public relations function itself" (p. 355). Whatever its limitations, functionalism opens the portals of PR to reveal that what is really going on must include not only Edward Bernays and Ivy Lee but Saint Paul and Pope Gregory XV.

To come face to face with PR as it is must be to recognize what it was and has been. Bernays's distinction between the ancient history of PR and the PR firms of the twentieth century is that modern PR is a "vocation" (Bernays, 1965, p. **xx**). But, as Lamme and Russell (2010) argued in their monograph, PR history ought not to exclude its religious history. Indeed, the meaning of *vocation* was clearly at the heart of Saint Paul's editorial tours of the primitive Christian churches in his perilous journeys on the Internet of the Roman roads. The meaning of *mission* was inarguably in the plans of Pope Gregory XV for the founding of the PR agency known as the *Propagandio.* These leaders were as mission driven as the CEOs of modern corporations. Paul (2 billion Christians) and Gregory (whose organization continues to the present day) were as professional, ethical or excellent as modern corporations that invest in corporate social responsibility.

PR: The humanity

The term *humanities* is meant here to include the social sciences because they share with the humanities a critical focus on the interaction of the relationship of self and society. It is in this sense that PR can be understood as a humanity whose nature is sociological as well political. This is an expression of the principle of inclusiveness, which underlies PRe. The recent scholarly interest in the methodology and conception of the digital humanities testifies to the reason for PR scholarship to prefer the ethic of inclusiveness to alternative exclusionary and unitary approaches.

However, significantly, the usage of *humanities* is not meant to be conflated with *humanistic* or *humanism,* terms whose contemporary usage present the humanities in a generous, kind, rational and altogether sunny and ethical light that is inconsistent with the fierceness, ambiguity and irrationality that are inseparable from a study of the humanities. The idea of PR as a humanity – *humanity* in its most inclusive sense – is consistent with the framing of PR as advanced by L'Etang and Pieczka (1996). Or, as in the words of William James,

> The recesses of feeling, the darker, blinder strata of character, are the only places in the world in which we catch real fact in the making.
> (quoted in Dodds, 1951/2004, epigraph)

What, then, ought to comprise a new theory of PR that, to paraphrase Lamme and Russell (2010), is unspun?

The answer proposed in this chapter is that PR theory be approached in way that is consistent not only with a reconstituted and broader theory of history that now prevails but also with a new theory framed from the perspective of the humanities. Although a multitude of options present themselves, the one proposed here is structural. More specifically, the theory rethinks PR as Northrop Frye rethought literary theory a half century ago: generically and archetypically.

Northrop Frye is credited with being among the most influential literary theorists of the twentieth century. At midcentury, his *Anatomy of Criticism* (1957) offered an alternative to the prevailing theories of literature based on the "close reading" of the New Criticism spawned in the 1930s and an alternative to the perceived arbitrariness of critical theory based solely on taste. What Frye proposed was an approach that resonates with the critical thinking and humanistic vision that animates PRe. The *Anatomy of Criticism* offered a whole new way of understanding English literature, a vision that is systematic without pretending to be scientific.

Disclaimers, defenses and rationales

Before modeling PR according to the structural archetypes of literary theory, four objections can be anticipated and answered: One, that the application of such a theory is irrelevant; two, that it is outdated; three, that it is arbitrary; four, that it is unscientific.

Objection 1: Irrelevant. That objection may be answered by indicating the theory's consistency with the fundamental thesis of PRe: that because PR is far broader, deeper and older than the prevailing thinking, it requires a theory that approaches it from a broader, deeper and older perspective.

Objection 2: Outdated. The prevailing thinking in PR scholarship relies on the flawed assumptions that PR is evolutionary and progressive. True, structuralism is no longer as popular as poststructuralism, which, in turn, is less popular than cultural theory, postcolonialism, feminism, and action theory. All of this could lead to the idea that linking PR with the humanities is outdated. However, popularity has less to do with the establishment of validity than the variations of sensibility.

Objection 3: Arbitrary. On the contrary, what is particularly striking about the prevailing historiography of PR theory is the arbitrary and ethnocentric assumptions of situating its origins in nineteenth-century America as well as in a too-narrow idea of the vocation of PR.

Objection 4: Unscientific. PR scholarship appears to have overreached because in its ambition to rebrand itself as a science, it has been plagued with the curse of scientism. Among PR's problem with its identity has been its aspirational but intellectually questionable relationship to science. PR scholars L'Etang and Pieczka (1996, 2006) have long been critical of PR's scientistic overreach. In their attempts to frame PR as a science – soft or hard – PR scholars must acknowledge that scientific language, like all language, is metaphorical. They should not argue that scientific metaphors common to systems theory confer scientific objectivity on PR.

The assumption that a theory of history or any social theory must be, or even can be, scientific is problematic at best. From the perspective of medical science, it is true that the germ theory of disease rendered outdated the ancient theories of humours and spirits. But the same thinking can only be arbitrarily forced on PR theory by conflating the science of medicine with the scientism of the general symmetrical quantitative theories of PR. PR's problem of scientism is likely to have its source in Edward Bernays's famous metaphors from the sciences. Imbued with the opinion-shaping influence of science, engineering and technology, Bernays (1952, p. 157) made the case that public opinion could be "crystallized," and consent "engineered."

In a polemical article in the *New Republic* magazine, Leon Wieseltier (2013) offered a succinct and reasonably balanced definition scientism's "central objective" as the "translation of nonscientific discourse into scientific discourse."

> It is also the source of its intellectual perfunctoriness. Imagine a scientific explanation of a painting – a breakdown of Chardin's cherries into the pigments that comprise them, and a chemical analysis of how their admixtures produce the subtle and plangent tonalities for which they are celebrated. Such an analysis will explain everything except what most needs explaining: the quality of beauty that is the reason for our contemplation of the painting.
>
> (Wieseltier, 2013)

Prudence dictates, especially in the age of Big Data and algorithmic measurement, that scholars plying such a social, aesthetic and subjective discipline as PR would do well to pay closer attention not only to what can be quantified but also to what cannot.

The seasons of PR

The ahistoricism that underlies O'Malley's theory of cultural styles was applied to the PR of everything in this book's chapter on history (Chapter 5). Similarly, Northrop Frye's structural–archetypal perspective of literature replaces historical periodicity with the simultaneity of structure and archetype. Among the culminating features of his multileveled theory of literature, he anatomized literature according to the natural cycle of the seasons. Central to this anatomy is Frye's idea of literary history itself – that it emerges from ancient and classical *mythoi* that, in turn, express human desire.

Unlike conventional historical PR's time, which is linear and progressive, literature's time is cyclical. Literature does not improve with time, nor is it saved by a deified apocalypse. Unlike the conventional conceit of PR, literature does not progress from primitive to excellent or from morally deficient to ethical. This is a conception of time that parallels the rethinking of mid- to late-twentieth-century anthropologists such as Claude Levi-Strauss and Clifford Geertz. They were among the anthropologists who proposed a nonprogressive view of culture rather than accept the prevailing bias of "primitive" cultures as simple and "modern" ones as complex. In the arts, such temporal rethinking was seen on the canvasses of Picasso and in philosophy, in the aesthetically oriented phenomenology of Merleau-Ponty.

PR as literature: A model of PR genres

PR is an institution that speaks. It wants to be heard, to frame, to educate. To encounter PR is to become aware of its voice, or more precisely, its voices.

The literary theorist Northrop Frye's structural theory anatomizes literature into four *mythoi* (which, for PR purposes, we will call *voices*): comedy, romance, tragedy and irony. In Frye's cyclical model of literary history, the four voices emerge from the natural world's four seasons: spring, summer, fall and winter, as follows:

Spring (romance). Comprising romantic and adventurous fairy tales from King Arthur to Cinderella to *Star Wars*.

Summer (comedy). Seen in the mistaken-identity buffoonery of Shakespeare's *A Midsummer Night's Dream* and certain films of Laurel and Hardy and the Marx Brothers.

Fall (tragedy). Found in *Macbeth*, Keats's ode "To Autumn" and F. Scott Fitzgerald's *The Great Gatsby*.

Winter (Irony). As in *A Winter's Tale*, *Gulliver's Travels* and David Lodge's farcical academic novels that parody the pretensions of literary theorists. The ironic voice ranges from light, verging on comedy, as in E. M. Forster's *A Passage to India,* to dark, verging on tragedy, as in Swift's *Travels.*

The voices of PR

PR may be literature, but it too has its seasons and its voices. These voices of PR may be understood, as well, to be examples of cultural styles, a schema of history explored in the chapter on history. To speak of the voices of PR is no more than to recognize PR's story-telling nature. It is a reference that embraces not only the long history of PR's verbal storytelling, but the equally or even longer history of its visual storytelling. Today, this also includes digital storytelling. Effective PR tells stories. Like literary stories, they have plots. And while the official (trade industry) conception of PR corresponds to comedy (PR resolves issues, problems and crises), comedy is not PR's only voice. From a cyclically theoretical perspective, its voices are heard as follows:

Spring (romance) is PR's erotic voice

PR's eros is aspiration. If a story's engine is fueled by the protagonist's discontent with her situation, PR begins with that sort of problem, which it seeks to resolve. The erotics of PR (to appropriate Susan Sontag's memorable aspiration for the literary text) signifies a voice that ranges from keening love and sexuality to the conspicuous consumption decoded by the sociologist Thorstein Veblen, and upward and inward to religion and spirituality (Brown, 2014). Aspirational PR is a common trope in the PR of fashion, beauty, entertainment and celebrity culture. It is lipstick, lingerie and masculine body spray. It is PR in the mode of Beaudrillardian seduction. Here, PR's voice ranges from the ecstasy of Saint Teresa's promotion of devotion (in Tilson's [2011] phrase) to the hormonal, hypermasculine growl of Budweiser beer-sponsored rock concerts pitched to undergraduates. In the spectacular outpourings of popular love for Princess Di, Tilson (2011) saw a counterintuitively spiritual model of PR as a covenant. In a postmodernist fashion,

Tilson flattened history by elucidating the spiritually compelling similarities between the sixteenth-century saint and the twentieth-century princess. Teresa and Di not only became famous, but the nature of their fame could be understood as a spiritual covenant between them and the worshippers and mourners who came to mourn and worship both saint and celebrity. It is in this sense that Tilson has noticed that the relationships in PR can have the spiritual qualities of a covenant.

PR campaigns that tell stories of transformation and liberation are vocal inflections of PR's spring. One of the PR case studies in Swann (2010) told the tale of how the American colonial town of Salem, Massachusetts, known for its witch-burning past, transformed itself into a modern, gentrified city (pp. 197–199). The fashion PR agency NYPR Diva (Siena Media Group, n.d.) reported that it "generates buzz" for its fashion role-model clients including The Black Girl Project, The Queen's Corner and Super Hussy. Schwartz PR (2013) created push polls for the dating site OK Cupid that promote the transformation of loneliness to love.

Summer (comedy) is PR's playful voice

Summer is silly season: Monty Python and Groucho Marx, but not Franz Kafka. The game can be zero sum, as in competitive sports and Heath's "wrangle in the marketplace." Or the game can be win–win, in the common refrain of the negotiation model of PR. The games can verge on spring's romance, as in spin the bottle (you get to kiss whomever the spun bottle points to). Or the game can verge on fall's tragedy, as in the violence of rugby and American concussion-inducing football.

In *Homo Ludens,* Johan Huizinga (1938; 1971) theorized that humans are game players and that play is a crucial element of culture. PR's insightful game theorists, including Murphy (1991), have explored PR as *homo ludens:* the practitioner as a competitive player. The game can be zero sum, although PR officially brands its strategy as win–win – the general theory of negotiation.

The literary theorist C. L. Barber 1959/1972) analyzed Shakespeare's "festive comedies" as hilarious and anarchic timeless environments of deception, mistaken identity and misrule, which channel Roman Saturnalia festivals. The summer voice is an expression of release from the constraints of social norms understood, a release that is ultimately seen to be harmless, if disorienting. Contemporary youth culture furnishes examples, such as undergraduate frat parties and so-called "raves" where the frenzied or frozen dancing is fueled by the recreational drug called Ecstasy.

In the history of PR, it is in PR's summer that we hear the voice of P.T. Barnum, PR's Falstaffian Lord of Misrule. Under Barnum's circus tent, and in the dark and alluring spaces of his museums, audiences were treated to the marvelous sight of "freaks" of nature – dwarfs, giants, bearded ladies, mermaids and "jumbo" elephants. Poor Barnum! His place in PR is as the whipping boy of the industry's reformist and progressive aspirations and mythical historiography. Yet there is a fabulous poetic about Barnum that brilliantly illustrates the profundity of the experience that the phenomenologist Gaston Bachelard (1965) called "intimate immensity" (p. 193).

There is artfulness in the gigantic and the infinitesimal. It can be found in the incongruous conceptual art of Cristo's immense fountains, trees, and 8 miles of umbrellas. Barnum was the seminal conceptual artist of PR. However, PR – seeking to divorce itself from flimflam and humbuggery and channeling the magic-bullet idea of the target audience as passive "suckers" – has completely misunderstood the magical summer voice of Phineas T. Barnum.

When Bernays clothed silent movie stars and society folk all in green to stage what Boorstin (1992) derided as a "pseudo event," Bernays was singing a summer tune. It is in the voice of summer that PR dispenses with its strenuously maintained ethics and seriousness and gives itself to the anarchy of play. To watch Barca's football juggernaut battle Real Madrid is to experience the joyous liberation of *homo ludens* PR.

Today's PR industry has discovered the persuasive power of the dramatic voice in its appropriation of YouTube, digital storytelling and guerilla marketing. In Harvard Square some years ago, I was stopped in my tracks by the sight of young women done up in wolf costumes, tumbling and dancing on the streets of Cambridge. Attracting media coverage, the lady wolves were promoting *Wild Animus* (Shaperd & Coyote, 2005), an audio book read by the wolfishly named actor, Peter Coyote.

Anarchy can, of course, misfire with unpleasant consequences. Comedy entails risk. The pratfalling actor breaks a leg – literally. The tiger onstage mauls the magician. The standup comic unintentionally offends his audience. When the radio "shock jock" duo, Opie and Anthony, staged a contest in New York City to discover which couple could have sex in the most outrageously public place, the "winners" were arrested for doing it in St. Patrick's Cathedral. The CEO of the Sam Adams Brewing Company went quickly into the mode of mortified apologia for having sponsored the contest (CBS, 2002).

Fall (tragedy) is PR's political voice

Although PR, unlike dramatic literature, is averse to tragedy, the practice and theory of PR are keenly aware of the contingencies that are the seedlings of crisis. As the chapters on crisis and convergence have detailed, late-twentieth and twenty-first-century PR has moved crisis communication from the margins of a PR specialty to the very center of PR, where it shares prominence with marketing PR in the social–digital–algorithmic mode. In that center, PR is less about winning games than anticipating catastrophes. PR's political voice is less concerned with play than fear and more with diplomacy than desire. This voice is that of public affairs and public diplomacy.

As this book's chapter on politics (Chapter 8) indicates, PR may not *be* politics, but it has a political nature. PR is political in the ways it studies and makes use of the levers of influence and power not only in strictly political environments but in the commercial marketplace and between persons. The personal, as feminist theory has asserted, is the political.

It may be necessary for the PR industry and scholarly researchers to frame public affairs and government relations as a specialized application of PR (Cutlip, et al., 2006, p. 15). The nomenclature was intended to avoid confusion. Public affairs is commonly conceived as "relations with citizens" (Cutlip et al., 2006, p. 15). Today, in a globalized world, public affairs is quite clearly also about relations among nations. In the mode of public diplomacy, public affairs becomes about relationships between private citizens of one nation and private citizens or public officials of another. The cultural diplomacy sponsored by the U.S. State Department, which exported musicians like Duke Ellington to the former Soviet Union and the American ping-pong team to China to play their Chinese counterparts, were well-publicized diplomatic strategies. On a political stage, these were examples of the adamantly nonpolitical sociologist Erving Goffman's (1970) strategic interaction.

Significantly for the dramaturgic concept of PRe, from Goffman's socio–anthropological–qualitative perspective, "the broadening of the concept of communication . . . has been a doubtful service; communication systems have been neglected and the field of face-to-face *interaction* embraced by arms too small for it" (Goffman, 1970, p. ix). The idea that communication theory may be insufficient to account for PR may well be the most controversial of all the controversial speculations in the critical reframing of PR.

Although fall is the season of tragedy in Frye's (1957) literary theory, PR is clearly averse to the tragic. But it is in the tragic fall season that the observer encounters the natural disasters, terrorist attacks, school shootings and celebrity scandals that comprise crisis communication. More dramatically than any other season, fall's essence is risk. Summer's comedy may give offense or fall flat, but fall's risks are frequently about bankruptcy, devastation, injury, fatality and, internationally, war. During one of the battles between Israel and its nonstate antagonist, Hamas, the Israeli defense minister sought to promote and defend Israel's cause in the 140-character language of Twitter. The Israeli Defense Ministry tweets @IDFSpokesperson. During the Israeli–Hamas war of 2008, Emily Greenhouse (2012) wrote in the *New Yorker* that the Israeli Defense Force had used Twitter, then in its infancy, to announce ongoing bombing of Hamas targets: "The IDF has begun a widespread campaign in the #Gaza Strip, chief among them #Hamas and Jihad targets."

On a personal note, as a speechwriter for a giant oil company that assessed the risk of operating in nations hostile to U.S. interests, the voice of my ghostwritten speeches for the company's C suite was political: worldly, diplomatic, prudent. My speeches on the economics of synthetic fuels and my brochure copy on the significance of price elasticity for energy conservation was delivered in a political voice: meticulously quantified. Its tone was the middle diction of the modern executive, not the high diction of the prophet.

Lobbying is another place for PR's political voice. As Theaker and Yaxley (2013, pp. 240–243) illustrated, the political voice of PR was channeled from the bully pulpit of government relations in 2011 when the U.K. government established the Public Health Responsibility Deal "to tap into the potential for businesses and other organizations to improve public health and tackle health inequalities through their influence over food, alcohol, physical activity and health in the workplace" (p. 240).

Along with the activity of lobbying, issues management requires PR's political voice. One of the convergences so characteristic of PR is found in the experience of corporate employees whom the organization seeks to enlist to burnish or repair its reputation for corporate citizenship and charitable giving. Here, the voice of politics resonates with what the nineteenth century knew as political economy.

Winter (irony) is PR's angular voice

It is most clearly heard (and seen) in the snarky tone of many widely admired, cutting Twitter and Facebook postings, immersive infographics, viral YouTubes and TED Talks. The angular tone ranges from clever and witty to cynical and dark. Still, the voice avoids rant, pomposity and overt moralizing at all costs. Its message is generally indirect, even as it is succinct, as in the poetry of Emily Dickinson, which is at once cryptic and devastating ("tell the truth but tell it slant"; Dickinson, 1999).

Snark rules social media. The digital–social world hears virtually every sort of voice, but new media lavishes thousands of Pinterest, Twitter and Instagram followers and Facebook friendships on the ironists. Because brevity is the soul of wit, Twitter's 140-character limit rewards succinctness. If a picture is worth the proverbial thousand words, a witty and enlightening infographic or 30-second YouTube channels the power of the Internet, which is, in turn, appropriated as the wintry voice of PR.

A decade before this writing, Ries and Ries (2004) wrote that "advertising is funny, public relations is serious" (p. 259). Having established his reputation as a theorist of positioning strategy in advertising, Al Ries pivoted toward PR as the more influential mass communication strategy. Even before the rise of Facebook and other social media, the effect of free or dirt-cheap publicity on the Internet had given PR more power than advertising when it came to building brands. Here, we have another convergence affecting the nature of PR in the Internet age: one where advertising crosses over, and virtually disappears into, PR.

PR's angular voice finds its inspiration not only in the brevity of Twitter and the perpetual conversational banter of instant messaging. The ironic voice is an oft-remarked feature of the postmodern cultural zeitgeist. It was the pervasiveness of irony in American society that the 24-year-old author, Jedediah Purdy (1999) found not only grating but a threat to civic culture. The intensity of Purdy's antipathy to the ironic voice, which situated his sensibility at apparent odds with that of his ironic generation, can be placed at one extreme of a continuum with the cultural theorist Lisbet van Zoonen (2005). Purdy argued that the ironic culture's endless unseriousness was alienating the citizen from "trust and commitment in America," in the words of his book's subtitle. At the opposite extreme, van Zoonen argued that the typically ironic voice of pop culture does precisely the opposite: it speaks in a voice that engages the citizen. (A detailed examination of van Zoonen's thesis is found in this book's chapter on the political nature of PR.)

The contrasting perspectives on irony deserve a closer look. Politics is no laughing matter. The substance of the affairs of organizations and nations is serious business. Purdy (1999) sensed that in pop culture, laughter and irony had crossed the boundary from entertainment to civic anesthesia. But van Zoonen (2005) perceived the ironic entertainment culture to have a positive, civically stimulative effect on a generation of young people whose interest in politics had been numbed by the hypocrisy, betrayals and scandals of public officials.

PR as comic genre

If politics – apart from the irony and satire that comment on it – is generally understood as a sobering endeavor culminating in uncertainty, PR is widely regarded outside the PR industry itself as unserious. PR speaks of itself to its constituencies in serious terms. The industry pitches itself as strategic, performance-oriented, results-driven, managerial and ethical. At the same time, the genre of PR is comedy. The case histories of PR are constructed as stories in which a protagonist faces a problem and with the counsel of PR overcomes it. All's well that ends well.

What, after all, would be the point of PR if the problem facing the organization, nation or individual devolved into tragedy? Surely, it sometimes does. Indeed, what motivates clients to seek PR counsel is their belief that their problem can be solved.

The problems of organizations and individuals may be no laughing matter to them. However, all too often they become a laughingstock. In business, as in life, where credibility and reputation are precious, to appear the fool may be the greatest crisis of all. The sting of humiliation – being laughed *at* rather than *with* – is a cruel death on the debate stage, Twitter feed, YouTube, and American TV programs like *The Daily Show*.

When PR practitioners speak of PR, much is made of its seriousness – its strategies, its planning, its tactics, its return on investment. All these emerge from the trope of control. The insistence on control comes from the insider's rhetorical framing of PR as the practice able to overcome challenges and exert control. But the reality of PR has more to do with the lack of control and the art of improvisation.

This, too, is management's idea of itself. It is, in its colloquially metaphorical self-conception, *buttoned-up*. It keeps confidential information *close to the vest.* It gets its *ducks in a row.* After all, management imagines and promotes itself in the familiar motto of *planning, organizing and control.*

Control is the essential idea of PR in the classroom and on the whiteboard. It is a *four-step process.* It is *objectives, strategies and tactics.* It is a *system* that produces *results.*

Were it not these things, what possible face claim could be made by PR? What could be the perceptual basis of its credibility? Surely, according to conventional wisdom, the answer could never be that PR is improvisation. Or poetry. Or art. Or that the source of PR is found in the imagination. In ideas. In drama. Or, more absurdly – in comedy.

Yet, if we look more closely, we find a very different situation. We see that PR *is* more about imagination and improvisation and less about systems and control. We see that PR has far more in common with the humanities, as well as with the arts.

What, then, are PR ideas? They are not empirically based hypotheses to be tested and replicated. Instead, they are inspirations that spring from the imagination.

Take the Mullen PR–Social agency idea known unofficially as *celebrity baggage.* The Boston-based PR agency's client, JetBlue Airlines, faced a business problem: in the competition to fill airplane seats with paying customers in the Los Angeles market, JetBlue was losing badly to its rival, Southwest Airlines. Southwest had created a buzz with its advertising campaign that took off, so to speak, on its marketing-driven policy, "Bags Fly Free." How, then, could Mullen make things turn out well for JetBlue?

Mullen's answer was an idea that sprung from a celebrity-culture catch phrase: *celebrity baggage.*

The tabloid news media is famously fond of stories about celebrities acting out – caught cheating on spouses, getting married and quickly divorced, trashing hotel rooms, getting drunk, getting arrested. All of which creates what is known as *baggage.*

It was the modernist (some say postmodernist) poet William Carlos Williams who celebrated the ugly as the beautiful. He was not alone in the modern–postmodern literary tradition. Sade, Poe, Baudelaire, Rimbaud and William Burroughs come to mind. But none of Sade's ugliness, Poe's horror, Rimbaud's drunken boat or Burrough's heroin dens could be described as comic. Not that one person's comedy is another person's affront, as in this epigraph in W. H. Auden's (1948/1962) "Notes on the Comic":

> If a man wants to set up as an innkeeper and he does not succeed, it is not comic. If, on the contrary, a girl asks to be set up as a prostitute and she fails, as sometimes happens, it is comic.
>
> (p. 371)

Mullen's solution was to persuade celebrities to donate their suitcases to be auctioned off for a charitable cause. Thus, their baggage became stories in the generic comic mode. Under a glass case in the Los Angeles International Airport terminal of JetBlue, the motley assortment of celebrity valises, briefcases and rolling baggage generated plenty of buzz on social media as well as coverage in the traditional print press and witty little spots on cable and network broadcasts. The well-known reputational baggage of actress Lindsay Lohan (arrested), mogul Donald Trump (nasty lawsuits) and reality TV star Jessica Simpson (noisy breakups) were transformed from the gossipy lead to corporate social responsibility gold. Here's how JetBlue's Corporate Social Responsibility executive framed it:

> Celebrity baggage is some of the most intriguing, highly-coveted and photographed accessories to ever fly in and out of LAX and across our network," said Icema Gibbs, Director of Corporate Social Responsibility. "Thanks to the generosity of these celebrities, we are excited to give everyone the opportunity

to take home a piece of that magic while supporting a great cause. JetBlue remains committed to supporting youth groups in L.A. and across the country with our long-standing partner, DoSomething.org, while generating fun and friendly competition over America's most-sought after baggage."

(PR Newswire, 2011)

Comedy is the literary form and plot of the story that PR practitioners tell. In the case of celebrity baggage, the tone of the laughter provoked by the reputational baggage of celebrities was transformed from mocking satire to something approaching reputational redemption because the celebrities invested their risible public flaws in a socially responsible cause: motivating young people to volunteer through DoSomething.org.

Housing the multidiscipline

The comedy of PR's plot, its several voices and its continual absorption of ideas from other disciplines continue to pose the question of its proper placement in the academy. The short answer to that question has been approximately everywhere, which is consistent with the idea of PRe.

Twenty years ago, I organized a panel of distinguished PR scholars for the annual convention of the Eastern Communication Association. They were tasked with a question familiar to PR in academia: "Where in a university does the discipline of PR belong? In which 'house?' "

Unsurprisingly, the panelists offered various rationales, all of them plausible. The PR department could be housed in a department of speech or mass communication or communication studies or business. Or, as in Professor Grunig's preference, as a stand-alone. In its own stand-alone space, PR could thus live up to the discipline's self-conception as "a distinctive management function."

If these alternatives were the options of a multiple-choice question, the answer doesn't appear. From the perspective of PRe, the answer is: "all of the above."

PR is like the weedy flower in the William Carlos Williams poem. Once rooted, it sprouts everywhere, from soil or concrete.

It is perhaps this tendency to crop up everywhere that was behind L'Etang and Pieczka's (1996) argument to situate PR as interdisciplinary.

To recognize the generic comedy of PR is to situate it in the humanities.

The evidence for such a minority opinion –PR has been long taxonomized as an "applied social science" – has accrued from the prior chapters.

What could possibly be the reason for positioning PR as a humanity? Mere contrarianism? Not so. Nor does such an idea of PR conflict with its academic position within interdisciplinary studies, as L'Etang and Pieczka (1996) proposed.

Rethinking PR as a humanity follows logically from the understanding of PR as a staged but improvisatory performance – one that can not be limited to organizational communication but can be more broadly understood as the reputational branded face claims of people in social settings.

Rethinking PR follows from discarding the conventional historiography of PR as exclusively American and modernist. What needs to be accepted is that, in the deepest sense, the history of public relations must no longer exclude its ancient and classical past, or fail to see its historical continuity from ancient roots to its postmodern expressive forms. Of equal importance to a thorough rethinking is to reject the simplistic notion that public relations is the child of technologies.

For PR to be understood as a child of the humanities, it is also necessary to recognize that the humanities are not the exclusive province of the rationality and the goodness of the symmetrists but the irrationality and evil found in the arts from Euripedes to Al Qaeda. Which is another way of saying that there is a difference between the breadth and depth of the vision of the humanities and the more limited idea of the humanistic.

For PR to be understood in the family of the humanities is to opt for multiple methodologies rather than a single quantitative one. The humanities may be understood to borrow from the social sciences without becoming one of them.

For PR to be framed as a humanity is to see it from the perspective of the poet Keats's "negative capability," a capability to live in uncertainty and even mystery rather than rush headlong after correctness or "truth."

In the textbook ambitiously entitled *The Essentials of Public Relations* (Wilcox, et al., 2000), what's "essential" is the conventional idea PR has had of itself as distinctive. However, it would appear that the idea of the distinctiveness of PR is – if not a solecism or a vanity – more honored in the breach than the observance.

Still, the textbooks persist in making a case that manages to be, at once, obvious and empty: that PR isn't advertising or marketing. Of course, there are differences between PR and advertising or marketing. Yet, such an insistence on separating PR flies in the face of our daily experience of PR and contradicts PR organizations' historic and continuingly profitable use of the ideas and tools of advertising and marketing. But rather than risk recognizing the sort of marriages that characterize the advertorial and the concept of market segmentation, PR has continued to insist on its distinctiveness at the cost of confusing its constituencies.

Particularly now – in the era of digital–social media, when information and communication fly about at warp speed on innumerable platforms and apps – there is simply no future in holding for PR as a "distinctive management function." The physics of the PR universe is a multiverse of objects drawn into a phenomenal space, moving together rather than flying apart. Such is the physics of the Information Age.

PR exists in a world of convergences; of multiplicities, multitasking and multiplatforms. The practitioners of "distinctive" advertising, marketing, politics and PR are having to learn a common set of skills, tools, tactics and technologies. This reality is among the greatest challenges to teachers, managers, students and employees new and old. It is this challenge that animates the goals of PR academia as well as its competitors and partners in massive open online course education.

What follows are further reflections of the place of PR in the humanities.

The practitioner as poet

Making you see

Even in the lateral thinking of PRe, certain distinctions are critical. That PR is a humanity does not lead to the conclusion that PR is humanistic or humanitarian. The same applies to literature, history, philosophy and the other humanities.

What the humanities offer has not generally been, nor should it be, a kind and charitable view of the world and the self. As the novelist Joseph Conrad (1978/2007) wrote:

> My task which I am trying to achieve is, by the power of the written word, to make you hear, to make you feel – it is, before all, to make you see. That – and no more, and it is everything. If I succeed, you shall find there according to your desserts: encouragement, consolation, fear, charm – all that you demand; and, perhaps, also that glimpse of truth for which you have forgotten to ask.
>
> (Preface, p. 708)

What PRe shares with Conrad is the capaciousness of its space, its moral ambiguity, its pride in its communicative powers and its passionate goal: to reach us, to move us, to make us see and, perhaps above all, to make us hear its voice.

The essential value of PR is neither corporate responsibility nor cause branding nor philanthropy. Well intended and moral, for PR these are, at best, a footnote to the contributions PR makes to the world. Nor does the programmatic imposition of cause branding and corporate social responsibility amount to a genuine rebranding of PR or even help answer the question we ask about PR: what is really going on?

Remaining invisible

Having been asked recently to write an article on PR and the humanities for a PR journal, I recalled the poet Keats's (1959) famous letter to his brothers. In it, in the quotation that appears as an epigraph to this chapter, he makes a distinction that has generated two centuries of interpretation and for me, a connection to pursue:

> I mean Negative Capability, that is when man is capable of being in uncertainties, Mysteries, doubts, without any irritable reaching after fact and reason.
>
> (p. 261)

Writing in 1817, amid the fierce Romantic rejection of eighteenth-century Enlightenment's epistemological standardization of empiricism, rationalism and science, Keats declared what for him distinguished the sensibility of the humanities from that of the sciences. In Keats's vision, fact and reason were inferior not only to truth and beauty but to that condition the scientist could never abide: acceptance.

On one level, PR is hardly content with accepting perceptions. The adage that perception is reality is both the beginning and the end of PR. PR's task – well rehearsed in the textbooks – is to investigate perception, determine the size of the gap between it and a more desirable perception and work to close the gap. In this process, PR is less about science than imagination, less about reaching after facts than creating a collage from alternate facts, less about negotiation than persuasion. The practitioner is an artist, a poet, a performer – this she must be to succeed. Strictly speaking, training in the sciences is not a prerequisite for PR.

The practitioner's aspect recalls the title of a cult movie, *The Invisible Man*. In this, practitioners assume the negative capability of Keatsian man. If the practitioner stages a spectacle – such as a press conference, editorial tour or rock concert – she remains backstage. It is not her spectacle. It is out of her hands. What her clients want is for her to back away and take no credit, which will liberate them to be generous or not.

The ideal practitioner has the voice of an angel and the body of a ghost, as in the title of the poet Wallace Stevens's "The Good Man Has No Shape."

Rationalizing irrationality

A Google search for "crowdsourcing" turned up 6,580,000 hits and 12,980,000 for "crowdfunding." In an era when the emerging paradigm of twenty-first-century PR is engagement and conversation, the crowd is king. Crowdsourcing purports to generate rationality – indeed, wisdom – from the conventional idea of the crowd's irrationality. It has become fashionable for communication theorists to celebrate what James Surowiecki (2005) called "the wisdom of crowds," his book's title. The trope of crowd wisdom, as I wrote in a book review, is that crowds are smarter than individuals:

> The mechanics of the stock market furnishes another example of crowd-wisdom. Soon after the space shuttle Challenger exploded, in January 1986, the market correctly blamed – and punished – the company that eventually turned out to be most responsible for the fatal accident: Morton Thiokol, the manufacturer of the notoriously defective O rings. It would take six months before a commission, by painstaking induction, confirmed the market's instantaneous judgment. Twenty-one minutes after the explosion, the stocks of the major NASA contractors – Lockheed, Martin Marietta, and Morton Thiokol – were all taking a hit. But in its crowd-wisdom, the stock market hit Morton Thiokol the hardest of all: At the end of the black day, Thiokol's stock had sunk 12%, while the other two companies' shares had recovered to within 3% of their pre-crash levels.
>
> (Brown, 2004)

PR historian Ray Hiebert (1966) wrote of modern pioneer Ivy Lee that he was a "courtier to the crowd," the title of Hiebert's biography. It was the courtier role, Hiebert theorized, that formed the basis for Hiebert's thesis that as a result of its respect for the power of public opinion, PR has become an engine of democracy, flourishing in existing and emerging democratic societies.

To court public opinion is to look into the toothy mouth of what Alexander Hamilton is alleged to have said of "the people" – that "your people are a great beast." What can be understood of public opinion, among its other attributes, is its beastly instability, irrationality, and unpredictability. Dutch history offers a famous example of the insanity of the crowd in the bizarre period when tulip bulbs sold for thousands of dollars, a financial bubble reminiscent of the global financial meltdown of 2008.

To court the crowd must be to court the irrational. In its long history, PR has been ever keen to observe and not to turn away from the opinion of the crowd as well as that of individuals. To practice PR is to turn one's attention to the crowd, whether in the aggregate as "the people," in the insight of marketing as "segments," that of PR as "publics," or that of the theater as "audiences." Actors may speak their lines and get silence in the matinee, but laughter in the evening.

The high-profile modern theorists of public opinion and PR – Lippmann and Bernays (1923) – believed they had discovered something new and scientific. But their ideas of the crowd as a herd echoed the nineteenth-century sociological theorists Le Bon and Mackay, who portrayed the crowd as irrational – even delusional – and, therefore, easily led. It is a perspective that resonates with Plato in whose *Republic* poets were not welcome, owing to their seductive power to enslave the minds of free men.

Poetry, according to poet Wallace Stevens (1959), is dangerous, as he wrote in "Poetry is a Destructive Force":

> That's what misery is,
> Nothing to have at heart.
> It is to have or nothing.
>
> It is a thing to have,
> A lion, an ox in his breast,
> To feel it breathing there.
>
> Corazon, stout dog,
> Young ox, bow-legged bear,
> He tastes its blood, not spit.
>
> He is like a man
> In the body of a violent beast.
> Its muscles are his own . . .
>
> The lion sleeps in the sun.
> Its nose is on its paws.
> It can kill a man.
> (pp. 92–93)

To understand PR as a humanity goes against the grain of the scholarship of the past generation and of the ambitions of the modern pioneers. To venture this way is to rethink the history of PR with respect to its ancient poetic and rhetorical sources. PRe encounters PR as theater, institution and idea. What such a perspective makes possible is not only a literary model of PR but the creation of postsymmetric models that belong in the family of the humanities. Acknowledging PR's membership in that family may even enable PR scholars to join more fully than ever their peers in the humanities and social sciences in the crucial conversations that take place in the public sphere.

Finally, it is not the "literature" of PR (memos, press releases, pitch letters, slide copy, advertorials, brochures, newsletters, writing for the web) that makes PR literary. What makes PR literary and defines it as a humanity is its ancient and continuing legacy of encouragement, consolation, fear and charm, as well as its glimpse of reality.

In truth, what more can we ask of PR?

References

Auden, W. H. (1948/1968). *The dyer's hand and other essays*. New York: Vintage.

Bachelard, G. (1965). *The poetics of space* (M. Jolas, Trans.). New York, NY: Orion.

Barber, C. L. (1972). *Shakespeare's festive comedy*. Princeton, NJ: Princeton University Press.

Bernays, E. L. (1952). *Public relations*. Norman, OK: University of Oklahoma Press.

———. (1965). *Biography of an idea: Memoirs of public relations counsel E. L. Bernays*. New York, NY: Simon & Schuster.

Boorstin, D. (1992). *The image: A guide to pseudo-events in America*. New York: Vintage.

Brown, R. E. (2004). Is PR irrational? *Public Relations Review, 30*(4), 513–517.

———. (2014). The strategic heart: The nearly mutual embrace of religion and public relations. In B. St John III, M. O. Lamme & J. L'Etang (Eds.), *Pathways to public relations: Histories of practice and profession* (pp. 11–27). New York, NY: Routledge.

CBS (2002). www.cbsnews.com/news/djs-dumped-over-church-sex-stunt/, Retrieved July 29, 2014.

Conrad, J. (1978/2007). Preface. *The nigger of the Narcissus and other stories*. New York, NY: Penguin.

———. (1978). The condition of art (Preface to *The nigger of the Narcissus*), in M. D Zabel, ed., *The portable Conrad* (pp. 705–710). New York: Penguin.

Cutlip, S. M., Center, A. H. & Broom, G. T. (2006). *Effective public relations*. Upper Saddle River, NJ: Prentice-Hall.

Dickinson, E. (1999). *The poems of Emily Dickinson* (R.W. Franklin, Ed.). Cambridge, MA: Belknap Press.

Dodds, E. R. (2004). *The Greeks and the irrational*. Berkeley: University of California Press.

Eliot, T. S. (1943). *East Coker: In four quartets*. New York: Harvest Books.

Frye, N. (1957). *The anatomy of criticism*. Princeton, NJ: Princeton University Press.

Goffman, E. (1970). *Strategic interaction: Conduct and communication*. Philadelphia: University of Pennsylvania Press.

Greenhouse, E. (2012). www.newyorker.com/news/news-desk/the-tweets-of-war, retrieved July 29, 2014.

Hiebert, R. E. (1966). *Courtier to the crowd: The story of Ivy Lee and the development of public relations*. Ames: Iowa State University Press.

Huizinga, J. (1938; 1971). *Homo ludens: A study of the play element in culture.* Boston, MA: Beacon Press.

Keats, J. (1959). *Selected poems and letters: John Keats.* (D. Bush, Ed.). Cambridge, MA: Riverside.

Kristeller, P. O. (1990). *Renaissance thought and the arts.* Princeton, NJ: Princeton University Press.

Lamme, M. O. & Russell, K. (2010). Removing the spin: Toward a new theory of public relations history. *Journalism Communication Monographs,* 11(4), 280–362.

L'Etang, J. & Pieczka, M. (1996). *Critical perspectives in public relations.* London, England: International Thomson Business Press.

Moloney, K. (2014). Personal correspondence.

Murphy, P. (1991). Game theory models for organizational/public conflict. *Canadian Journal of Communication,* 16(2). Retrieved from http://cjc-online.ca/index.php/journal/article/view/606/512

PR Newswire. (2011, May 24). *JetBlue airways asks celebrities to let go of baggage for a good cause.* Retrieved from http://investor.jetblue.com/phoenix.zhtml?c=131045&p=irol-newsArticle_print&ID=1567042&highlight=

Purdy, J. (1999). *For common things: Irony, trust, and commitment in America today.* New York: Vintage.

Ries, A. & Ries, L. (2004). *The fall of advertising and the rise of PR.* New York, NY: Harper Business.

Schwartz PR. (2013). OK Cupid. www.businesswire.com/news/home/20070402005220/en/OkCupid.com-Poll-Reveals-Kinkiest-Loneliest-Religious-States#.U9hdSEivzu0, Retrieved July 29, 2014.

Shaperd, R. & Coyote, P. (2005). *Wild animus.* San Francisco, CA: Too Far Books.

Siena Media Group. (n.d.). *Siena Media Group case studies* [Blog post]. Retrieved from http://nyprdiva.wordpress.com/ny-pr-diva-case-studies/

Stevens, W. (1959). *Collected poems.* (S.F. Morse, Ed.). New York, NY: Vintage.

Surowiecki, J. (2005). *The wisdom of crowds.* New York, NY: Anchor.

Swann, P. (2010). *Cases in public relations management.* New York, NY: Routledge.

Theaker, A. & Yaxley, H. (2013). *The public relations strategic toolkit.* London, England: Routledge.

Tilson, D. (2011). *The promotion of devotion: Saints, celebrities and shrines.* Champaign, IL: Common Ground.

Van Zoonen, L. (2005). *Entertaining the citizen: When politics and popular culture converge.* Lanham, MD: Rowman & Littlefield.

Wieseltier, L. (2013, September 3). Crimes against humanities: Now science wants to invade the liberal arts. Don't let it happen. *New Republic.* Retrieved from www.newrepublic.com/article/114548/leon-wieseltier-responds-steven-pinkers-scientism

Wilcox, D. L., Ault, P. H., Agee, W. K. & Cameron, G. T. (2000). *The essential of public relations.* Boston, MA: Allyn & Bacon.

Williams, W. C. (1963). *Paterson.* New York, NY: New Directions.

Epilogue
The gist of everything

The Public Relations of Everything challenges the theory of symmetry, which has been the dominant paradigm of the field for almost half a century. The public relations of everything (Pre) rethinks public relations (PR) as a humanity. In the digital–social media era when practitioners are advised to focus their efforts on fomenting engagement, sharing and conversation, these can be understood as the very hallmark of the humanities.

Like permanence, change is a constant. But that PR has changed is a far cry from what amounts to the general theory of PR, symmetry–excellence. Indeed, the theory itself has changed in the 30 years since its publication.

Pre offers a close, detailed, critical examination of symmetry–excellence theory and its direct and indirect influences on PR. The book's 10 chapters critique the theory's assumptions about PR, identify the theory's confounding flaws and raise serious concerns about the effects of the uncritical acceptance of symmetry–excellence on PR.

Among the assumptions challenged by the book of "everything" are these:

- That PR is exclusively a product of modernity, specifically nineteenth-century American history.
- That PR "evolved" in a single century from the deceptions and manipulations of P.T. Barnum to the "symmetric" ethics of a "two-way" mechanical balance as witnessed in programs of corporate social responsibility.
- That PR can be best understood as the product of technological innovations.
- That persuasion can be neither "excellent" nor "ethical."
- That PR is communication management.
- That PR is a science.
- That primary consideration must be given to PR research conducted quantitatively.

My experience over many decades as a PR practitioner, consultant, teacher and publishing scholar has stirred my skepticism of those and other assumptions and propositions of the dominant paradigm of symmetry–excellence and its legacy of influence.

Kevin Moloney, the PR scholar (*Rethinking Public Relations*, 2006) who serves as the editor of the Routledge series on PR, which includes my book, offered a fair summary of PRe in a personal email to me (2014):

> Brown is rejecting symmetry as the master measure of PR and wants to replace it with more earthy measures of human expression. He's opening up PR to include all forms of expression (architecture to ads; painting to pitches) which narrate public meaning past and present. He describes and analyses these forms in terms associated with the literary theory of Northrop Frye who framed literary works into the categories of romance, comedy, tragedy and irony. Brown replaces symmetry of communications amongst organisations with emotive modes of making and receiving meaning in public communications, whether they be press releases, paintings, palaces or propaganda.

In the final analysis of public relations, there really is no finality. While PR may not be "evolving" in the sense of the eons intended by Darwin, there is little doubt that both the techniques and the influence of public relations have come to be accepted, if not entirely respected, worldwide.

It is because of PR's power today, when the flurry of new technologies and the reliance on data analysis have created a false expectation of fast and simple answers, that it is vital that we not lose touch with the emotional, performative, aesthetic and social core of public relations. Neither must we permit the theorists and practitioners to forget or exclude PR's long and continuing history.

References

Moloney, K. (2006). *Rethinking Public Relations: PR, Propaganda and Democracy* (2nd ed.). New York, NY: Routledge.
Moloney, K. (2014). Personal correspondence.

Index

humanities 108, 113, 123; persuasion
125; politics 137; practitioner 62, 63,
65, 68, 136, 190
Exxon BP 9
Exxon-Mobil 132
Exxon Valdez oil spill 27

face 37–54; besieged 42–3; branded
44–6; disruption 48–9; dramaturgical
discipline 48; dramaturgy 43–4; faceoff
40–1; metaphor 40; prudence 49–50;
saving 47; silence 50–2; sociology 41–2;
symbolism 47–8; terminology 39–40;
vulnerability 46
Facebook 7, 12, 45, 46, 48, 55, 63, 64, 65,
93, 105, 107, 120, 171, 180
faceoff 40–1
Falco, S. 46
Ferlinghetti, L. 38, 57
Filler, M. 11
Fitzgerald, F. S.: "The Crack Up" 149; *The
Great Gatsby* 176
Fleming, I. 61
Fleming, T.: *The Politics of Human Nature*
142
FOX News 139
Franken, A. 140
Freud, S. 48, 80, 97, 123, 124
Frye, N. 43, 175, 176, 179, 191; *Anatomy
of Criticism* 174
Frymier, A. B. 103, 104

Gasset, O. 38
Gates, J. 20
Geertz, C. 175
General Mills 123
Global Crossing 22
Goffman, E. 7, 33; acting's emotional cost
62; actors 67; ambiguities 151; civil
inattention 44; dramaturgical theory 58,
60, 64, 116; face 37, 38, 39–40, 43–4,
46, 47, 48, 49; *Frame Analysis* 62, 155;
interaction 41; *Interaction Ritual* 40;
politics 137, 179; *The Presentation of
Self in Everyday Life*, 49–50, 98–9;
self-presentation 6; stigma 32; symbolic
interactionism 14
Goldman, E. F. 47, 106
Goldsworthy, S.: *PR Today* 76, 148
Gorgias 121
Grace, J. P. 16
Grandley, A. 57
Greenfield, J. 141–2
Grove, A. S. 43

Grunig, J. E. 72, 74, 94, 96; ambiguities
165; communication management 9, 16,
37; crisis 26, 29; excellence theory 81;
housing the discipline 183; ideology 82–3;
Managing Public Relations 82; normative
ethics 162; persuasion 41, 107, 114, 118,
119; situational theory 135; symmetry
theory 95; two-way symmetry 106, 164
Guth, D. W. 7, 46, 114; *Public Relations:
A Value-Driven Approach* 64, 148

Hains, R. 11, 12
Harlow, R. 118
Hart, J. 75
Hawthorne, N. 13
Hayward, T. 48
Hazelton, V., Jr. 71, 80; *Public Relations
Theory II* 79
Heath, R. L. 7, 14, 15, 22, 27, 74, 119;
ambiguity 80; Culture 2 94–5; Culture
3 96; fully functioning society 116, 132;
persuasion 104, 115; postsymmetry era
128; "wrangle in the market place" 29,
108, 113, 114, 130, 177
Heiman, S. T. 43, 75
Hiebert, R. E. 77, 80, 82, 107–8, 114, 132,
143, 186–7
Hill, W. 47
Hill & Knowlton-UK 93, 111
history 71–88; ambiguity 80–1; Bernays
72–4; definitions 76; evolution 85;
ideology 82–7; implications 80;
legitimacy 77–8; management 81;
metatheory 74–6; problematics 78–80;
progressivism 81–2; rethinking
functionalism 86–7; and theory 72–82
Hitler, Adolf 13, 100
Hochschild, A. 43, 49, 55, 56–7, 62, 63
Holmström, S. 154
Homer 4, 96, 97, 109, 122, 123; *Iliad* 103
Huizinga, J.: *Homo Ludens* 177
humanities 170–89; disclaimers, defenses,
and rationales 174–5; great convergence
171–2; history to theory 172–3; housing
the multidiscipline 183–4; practitioner
as poet 185–8; PR as comic genre
181–3; PR as literature 175–6; PR: the
humanity 173–5; seasons of PR 175;
Studia Humanitatis 170–1; *see also*
ethics; literature, PR as; persuasion;
politics; voices
Hunt, T. 106, 114, 118, 119, 135;
Managing Public Relations 82, 83
Hutcheon, L. 138

For Product Safety Concerns and Information please contact our EU
representative GPSR@taylorandfrancis.com
Taylor & Francis Verlag GmbH, Kaufingerstraße 24, 80331 München, Germany

www.ingramcontent.com/pod-product-compliance
Ingram Content Group UK Ltd.
Pitfield, Milton Keynes, MK11 3LW, UK
UKHW020955180425
457613UK00019B/698